THE SOVIET UNION SINCE THE FALL OF KHRUSHCHEV

THE SOVIET UNION SINCE THE FALL OF KHRUSHCHEV

Edited by

ARCHIE BROWN
AND
MICHAEL KASER

THE FREE PRESS
A Division of Macmillan Publishing Co., Inc.
NEW YORK

Introduction and editorial matter © Archie Brown and Michael Kaser 1975
Chapter 1 © Alec Nove 1975
Chapter 2 © Philip Hanson 1975
Chapter 3 © David Holloway 1975
Chapter 4 © J. A. Newth 1975
Chapter 5 © Peter Frank 1975
Chapter 6 © Peter Reddaway 1975
Chapter 7 © Michael Bourdeaux 1975
Chapter 8 © Martin Dewhirst 1975
Chapter 9 © Michael Kaser 1975
Chapter 10 © Archie Brown 1975

The Free Press
A Division of Macmillan Publishing Co., Inc.
866 Third Avenue, New York, N.Y. 10022

First published 1975 by The Macmillan Press Ltd.

Library of Congress Catalog Card Number: 75–39856

Printed in Great Britain

printing number
1 2 3 4 5 6 7 8 9 10

Contents

Contributors

MICHAEL BOURDEAUX was born in Praze, Cornwall, in
1934. He graduated from Oxford University with degrees in
Russian and French (1957) and Theology (1959) and studied
as a postgraduate student on a British Council exchange
scholarship at Moscow University during 1959-60. His most
recent visit to the Soviet Union was in February 1975. He has
held a variety of university posts and visiting lectureships and
is currently Director of the Centre for the Study of Religion
and Communism, Keston College, Kent, and editor of the
journal, *Religion in Communist Lands*. His many publications
include: *Religious Ferment in Russia* (1968), *Patriarch and
Prophets* (1970) and *Faith on Trial in Russia* (1971).

ARCHIE BROWN, born in Annan, Scotland, in 1938, is a
Fellow of St Antony's College and Lecturer in Soviet Institu-
tions at the University of Oxford. After studying as an
undergraduate and graduate student at the London School of
Economics (University of London), he was a Lecturer in
Politics for seven years at Glasgow University before moving to
Oxford in 1971. He has also spent over a year at Moscow
University on cultural exchange scholarships. Mr Brown is the
author of *Soviet Politics and Political Science* (1974) and of
numerous contributions to academic journals and symposia.

MARTIN DEWHIRST, born in Leeds in 1937, is a Lecturer
in Russian Language and Literature at the University of
Glasgow. He took his degree in Russian at the University of
Oxford in 1962 and spent two years as a postgraduate
student at the London School of Economics before moving
to Glasgow University in 1964. His numerous visits to the
Soviet Union include the academic year, 1959-60, which he
spent at Moscow University. He is a regular contributor to
The Year's Work in Modern Language Studies and is co-editor
(with Robert Farrell) of *The Soviet Censorship* (1973).

PETER FRANK, who was born in Whitby, Yorkshire, in 1934, is a Lecturer and the Director of postgraduate studies in Soviet politics in the Department of Government at Essex University. After studying Russian as an undergraduate and Soviet history as a graduate student at the University of Leeds, he taught Soviet history for several years at Leeds before moving into political science at Essex University in 1968. Mr Frank has made a number of visits to the Soviet Union as an academic and also as a television commentator in several documentary films about contemporary Soviet life. He is the author of several articles in academic journals on the Communist Party of the Soviet Union.

PHILIP HANSON, born in London in 1936, is a Senior Lecturer at the Centre of Russian and East European Studies of Birmingham University. An economics graduate of Cambridge, he took his Ph.D. at Birmingham and was a Lecturer in Economics at Exeter University from 1961 to 1967. He worked for short spells in both the Treasury and the Foreign Office and has made several extended visits to the Soviet Union since 1964. He is the author of *The Consumer in the Soviet Economy* (1968), *The Development of Advertising in the USSR* (1971), *The Development of Advertising in Eastern Europe* (1972) and *Advertising and Socialism* (1974).

DAVID HOLLOWAY, who was born in Dublin in 1943, is a Lecturer in Politics at the University of Edinburgh. He previously studied or taught at the universities of Cambridge, Oslo, Manchester and Lancaster and he has made several study visits to the Soviet Union. Mr Holloway is the author of *Technology, Management and the Soviet Military Establishment* (1971) and a number of scholarly articles.

MICHAEL KASER, who was born in London in 1926, is a Fellow of St Antony's College and Reader in Economics at the University of Oxford. After taking the Economics Tripos as an Exhibitioner at King's College, Cambridge, he served in the British Foreign Service in London and Moscow from 1947 to 1951 and in the United Nations Secretariat (with the Economic Commission for Europe in Geneva) from 1951 to

1963 when he moved to Oxford to teach Soviet economics. He has made a number of visits to the Soviet Union, most recently in March 1975. Among his publications are *Comecon: Integration Problems of the Planned Economies* (1965; 2nd ed., 1967), *Economic Development for Eastern Europe* (ed., 1968), *Planning in East Europe* (with J. Zielinski, 1970), *Soviet Economics* (1970), *Planning and Market Relations* (ed. with R. Portes, 1971) and *The New Economic Systems of East Europe* (ed. with H. Höhmann and K. Thalheim, 1975).

J. A. NEWTH was born in London in 1921 and studied as an undergraduate at Oxford where he took his degree in Arabic and Persian. Since 1957 he has been a Lecturer in the Institute of Soviet and East European Studies at the University of Glasgow. On a study visit to the Soviet Union in 1965, he spent several months in Uzbekistan. He is the joint author (with Alec Nove) of *The Soviet Middle East* (1965) and he has contributed many articles on Soviet nationality problems and on demographic topics to academic journals.

ALEC NOVE was born in Petrograd in 1915 but educated in England, graduating from the London School of Economics in 1936. Since 1963 he has been Professor of Economics and Director of the Institute of Soviet and East European Studies at the University of Glasgow. From 1947 to 1958 he was in the Civil Service (mainly at the Board of Trade) and from 1958 to 1963 he was Reader in Russian Social and Economic Studies at the University of London. Among his many well-known publications are the following books: *The Soviet Economy* (1961; 3rd ed., 1969), *Was Stalin Really Necessary?* (1964), *The Soviet Middle East* (with J. A. Newth, 1965), *An Economic History of the USSR* (1969), *Socialist Economics* (ed. with D. M. Nuti, 1972), *Efficiency Criteria for Nationalised Industries* (1973) and *Stalinism and After* (1975).

PETER REDDAWAY, who was born in Cambridge in 1939, is a Senior Lecturer in Political Science at the London School of Economics. After studying as an undergraduate at Cambridge University, he pursued graduate studies at Harvard and Moscow Universities and the LSE before taking up a teaching appointment at LSE in 1965. He is the editor or author of the following books: *Lenin: the Man, the Theorist, the Leader: a Reappraisal* (ed. with Leonard Schapiro, 1967), *Soviet Short Stories*, vol. 2 (ed., 1968) and *Uncensored Russia: the Human Rights Movement in the Soviet Union* (1972).

Introduction

The chapters which compose this book were delivered in
their initial form as papers in a series of seminars held at St
Antony's College, Oxford, during the summer and autumn of
1974, the year of the tenth anniversary of the fall of Nikita
Sergeyevich Khrushchev. Their authors have subsequently
expanded and revised them so that they take account of
developments in the Soviet Union up to the end of January
1975 or (in a number of cases) of even more recent Soviet
events and publications.

The aim of the editors and authors has been to provide a
thoroughly informed, up-to-date survey of the changes which
have taken place in the USSR since Khrushchev's departure
(while paying due attention, where appropriate, to the continuities). Though they naturally hope that the book will be
not without interest to their fellow specialists, the authors
have written their contributions with a much broader reader-
ship in view. Little or no previous knowledge of the country
on the part of the reader has been assumed, and it is hoped
that the book will review recent and contemporary Soviet life
for anyone interested in the USSR as much as for undergraduate and graduate students of Soviet politics and society.
As an acknowledged authority on the particular aspect with
which his chapter is concerned, each contributor was asked
to concentrate on one of the crucial areas of Soviet social,
economic and political life during the decade since
Khrushchev was abruptly forced to give up his party first
secretaryship and the chairmanship of the Council of Ministers.

The first two chapters deal with important developments
in the Soviet economy since 1964. Alec Nove demonstrates
that Leonid Brezhnev's guarantees and subsidies for farming
had significantly more positive effect than Khrushchev's con-
catenation of agricultural campaigns, while Philip Hanson

contrasts the selective but growing acquisition of advanced western technology with the previous self-assurance in Soviet scientific prowess born of the success of the sputnik. His chapter complements that of David Holloway, who examines foreign relations within a broad perspective and suggests that there is a certain incongruity between the persistently high defence expenditures sanctioned by the political leadership and the active pursuit of *détente*.

Chapters 4 and 5 are also interrelated. J. A. Newth's demographic analysis draws attention to a number of potentially important developments, including the decline in the overall rate of growth of the Soviet population and the differential rates of growth between the western and the eastern parts of the USSR. In his discussion of the changing composition of the Communist Party, Peter Frank also draws upon demographic data and considers the possible political implications of the wide gulf in terms of age and length of party service between, on the one hand, the mass membership of the party and, on the other, the most highly placed party cadres.

The next three chapters chronicle areas of Soviet life where, to a greater or lesser degree, political and social conflict may be discerned. Peter Reddaway, in a comprehensive survey, distinguishes between different types of dissent and opposition to be found in the USSR, taking note of the variations in ideological content from one dissenting group to another and of the differences among various ethnic groups. Michael Bourdeaux likewise considers all the major religious groups in turn, showing how official policy towards them varies substantially from one to another. While documenting their present difficulties, he also draws attention to the fact — which is perhaps insufficiently known — that the last years of Khrushchev's administration were, for most religious groups, the period of the greatest religious oppression since the time of the purges in the late thirties. By contrast, as Martin Dewhirst notes, literary censorship has become stricter and more consistent than it was under Khrushchev and, as a result, far fewer new creative works of outstanding literary merit are finding their way into print.

The final two chapters evaluate economic and political developments as a whole. They touch upon some aspects of economic and political life not discussed by the other contributors, but also attempt to place a number of the points made in the specialist chapters within a broader context. Michael Kaser chooses as a key to economic organisational changes the role of the enterprise and its manager: Alexei Kosygin began by enhancing their functions in the 1965 economic reform, but his policy was for a time swamped by attempts to control them by computers and cartels. The incomes of managers and technicians declined relatively to those of the farmer and shop-floor worker, but the reduction in spread was within a faster average rise than under Khrushchev. Archie Brown, while pointing to a number of apparently divergent trends in Soviet policy-making, draws attention to a certain underlying consistency in the behaviour of the present political leadership and to their broad strategy. He concludes by considering both sources of tension and sources of stability within the Soviet polity.

To facilitate use of this collective work as a textbook, a 'Calendar of Political Events' is annexed, detailing the more significant happenings in the Soviet Union from 14 October 1964 until the time of going to press in 1975.

1 Agriculture

ALEC NOVE

For years we spoke of agriculture as the 'Achilles' heel' of the Soviet economy, and wry jokes were current in the Soviet Union itself about the apparent hopelessness of the agricultural situation. Very considerable advances have been made in the past ten years, since Khrushchev fell. Can we now say that a decisive upturn has occurred, with a real take-off into sustained growth (to borrow a phrase from another context)? Are the gains real, are the official claims greatly exaggerated, and has the cost of the achievements been excessive? To these questions I hope this chapter will provide some sort of answer.

Let us begin with a few basic statistics.

If this was being written a year previously, when the so-called disastrous harvest of 1972 was fresh in our memories, it would doubtless emphasise the disgrace of having to buy record quantities of grain in the United States and other capitalist countries (that this was felt to be a disgrace was reflected in the unique fact that grain imports were omitted from the Soviet foreign trade statistics for 1972). Yet Table 1.1b shows that 1972 was not as bad as all that. The weather was certainly very unfavourable, as all foreign observers noted. In these circumstances, to have reaped a harvest which was the fifth highest in Soviet history was by no means discreditable. On the contrary. Consequently, it was very unfair to have dismissed the Minister of Agriculture, Matskevich, instead of rewarding him. Unless, of course, the harvest data were falsified. Regional statistics showed that very good harvests were obtained in Kazakhstan and West Siberia, quite good weather prevailed also in most of the Ukraine. The disaster was in the centre, east and south of European Russia proper (RSFSR). There may well have been abnormal harvest losses east of the Urals, but the real explanation for the massive imports was surely the desire of the

TABLE 1.1a: Soviet agricultural output

	1956-60 (average)	1960-5 (average)	1966-70 (average)	1970	1971	1972	1973
Gross agricultural output (millions of 1965 roubles)	59.2	66.3	80.5	87.0	87.9	84.3	96.1
Grain (m. tons)	121.5	130.3	167.6	186.8	181.2	168.2	222.5
Cotton (m. tons)	4.36	4.90	6.10	6.89	7.10	7.30	7.66
Sugar-beet (m. tons)	45.6	59.2	81.1	78.9	72.2	76.4	86.8
Potatoes (m. tons)	88.3	81.6	94.8	96.8	92.7	78.3	107.7
Meat (deadweight, m. tons)	7.9	9.3	11.6	12.3	13.3	13.6	13.5
Milk (m. tons)	57.2	64.7	80.6	83.0	83.2	83.2	87.2

Sources: Nar. khoz. (1972) p. 285; *Pravda*, 26 Jan 1974.

TABLE 1.1b: Grain harvest variations

	1960	1961	1962	1963	1964	1965	1966	1967	1968	1969	1970	1971	1972	1973
m. tons	125.5	130.8	140.2	107.5	152.1	121.1	171.2	147.9	169.5	162.4	186.8	181.2	168.2	222.5
centners per ha.	10.9	10.7	10.9	8.3	11.4	9.5	13.7	12.1	14.0	13.2	15.6	15.4	14.0	17.6

Source: Ibid., pp. 285, 286.

authorities to avoid the political complications of food shortages and, more important still, to maintain livestock herds.
They must have recalled that previous bad year, 1963, when
the pig population fell from 70 million to 40.9 million head.
They were successful in avoiding such mass slaughter in 1972.

In fact, comparison with 1963 was made specifically by
Brezhnev. He declared that, with the methods and techniques
of that year, and the worse weather of 1972, the grain
harvest would have been only 95 million tons, against 107.5
claimed for 1963.[1] We must allow for poetic licence, but the
fact remains that the 1972 weather was at least as bad as that
of 1963, and that the harvest seems to have been about 60
per cent higher.

The 1972 harvest figure might be inflated, but to show
that the increase was less than 60 per cent we would have to
argue that the 1963 figure was *less* inflated, i.e. that there has
been an increase in the degree of falsification. Of this there is
no evidence.

Then we have the record year 1973. It is evident that the
weather was very favourable, and that this accounts for the
bulk of the difference from the previous year. It is also true,
since Brezhnev himself told us so, that the sheer magnitude
of the harvest overwhelmed the available storage space, so
that losses were unusually high. But these very facts do show
that the harvest was indeed very good, even if the amount
available for use was well below the claimed 222 million tons.

When all allowance is made for water in the grain or in the
statistics, and also for the slower rate of progress in other
crops and in the livestock sector, the advance in output is
beyond any doubt impressive, in marked contrast to
Khrushchev's last years. Some may well say that this apparent success is also in marked contrast to the supply
position in towns: there are still indeed many shortages, and
this is reflected in the *kolkhoz* market prices being 60 per
cent higher than state prices.[2] However, these shortages are
attributable partly to the deplorably inefficient and ill-
equipped food distribution system, and perhaps even more to
the refusal of the state to raise prices when demand outruns
supply; the best-known case of this is meat, of which more
will be said shortly.

What are the causes of the progress made?

One way of approaching this question is to consider the causes of lack of progress in Khrushchev's last years. It must be recalled that the period immediately following the death of Stalin, i.e. 1953-8, was one of rapid increase in farm production. The official index shows a rise by just about 50 per cent in five years. This was the result of higher prices, better incentives, more investments, and also the first years of the virgin lands campaign, following a generation of neglect. However, the following five years showed no perceptible improvement. The reasons were, in my view, the following:

(a) The possibilities of quick gains were used up. For example, one can increase milk yields substantially by feeding formerly hungry cows, but further increases require either better breeds or better quality fodder, or both.

(b) The impatient Khrushchev insisted on quick results by 'campaigning'. The campaigns related to favoured crops (notably maize, which had to be sown everywhere regardless of local circumstances), to meat ('catch up and overtake the United States in two to three years'), to crop rotations (hostility to fallow and sown grasses), to methods of cultivation (peat-compost pots, two-stage harvesting, or cattle-breeding recommended by the charlatan Lysenko). The effects were confusing and often damaging.

(c) Khrushchev also had a mania for reorganising agricultural planning and administration. He virtually eliminated the Ministry of Agriculture, set up a bewildering variety of production administrations, and confused the structures of state and party in rural areas.

(d) In the period 1958-61, in connection with a price reform and the abolition of the Machine Tractor Stations, the net incomes of *kolkhozy* and of peasants were somewhat reduced, as was the production of farm machinery. True, Khrushchev did in his last years devote much attention to investments in fertiliser production, but this too was overdone, in the sense that he pressed the industry to expand faster than was technically possible, and much fertiliser was wasted because the farms lacked the means to transport it and spread it.

(e) Peasant interests were adversely affected by restrictions on private livestock.

(f) Apart from the inadequacies of the general price level,

there were also incorrect price relativities. Thus livestock-raising was almost everywhere a source of loss for the farms.

Khrushchev suffered a severe blow when the bad weather of 1963 caused shortages and livestock slaughtering, despite large imports from the West. Reserves had been too low. The much better harvest of 1964 did not save him, if only because his comrades had a number of non-agricultural reasons for getting rid of him.

Brezhnev showed that he, as general secretary, had special responsibility for agriculture by making the keynote speech at the March 1965 plenum of the central committee, where a series of measures were announced or (if already implemented) approved. These were:

(a) An end to reorganisation. The restoration of the Ministry of Agriculture and of the customary state and party organs in rural areas.

(b) An end to 'campaigns', and therefore greater scope for local officials and farm management to adapt output to local conditions.

(c) A promise to cease varying compulsory procurement quotas arbitrarily (a promise made also by Khrushchev, and disregarded in practice).

(d) Abandonment of the pressure on private livestock.

(e) Considerable increases in procurement prices, especially of livestock products. Further increases were decreed in subsequent years, notably in 1970. As retail prices changed little, large subsidies developed to cover a widening gap between procurement and retail prices, especially for meat.

(f) Larger incomes for peasants, and also (from 1966) a change of principle in the nature of pay in *kolkhozy*. Instead of being 'residuary legatees' paid in workday units (*trudodni*) of unknown value, peasants would henceforth be paid at fixed rates, with an end-of-year bonus added if financial results warranted it. This meant an effective guaranteed minimum, supported if necessary by bank credits. Old age pensions for *kolkhoz* members had been announced by Khrushchev before his fall.

(g) A substantial increase in agricultural investments, with special attention promised to the hitherto neglected centre and north. Though Brezhnev did complain that plans were cut back, the fact remains that expenditure did rise rapidly, as did deliveries of industrial inputs (tractors, equipment, fertiliser) to agriculture. It was appreciated that further increases in sown area could not be a major source of extra output. What was needed was intensification, greater efficiency, higher productivity per peasant, per hectare, per cow. In 1974 there is much being written about investment in land improvement, especially in non-black-earth areas: drainage, clearance, reclamation, better pastures.

These measures can be placed into very different categories. Some relate to planning methods and are not in themselves costly: thus it costs nothing to refrain from ordering farms to grow maize if they have no suitable soil, machinery and labour. However, many of the key measures relate to factor rewards or to additional inputs and investment expenditures. Let us see what changes have in fact occurred.

PAYMENTS TO PEASANTS

In *kolkhozy,* payments per day worked have risen as follows (cash and produce):

	1960	1965	1970	1972
(Roubles)	1.40	2.68	3.90	4.11

Source: Nar.khoz. (1972) p.388.

The total incomes of *kolkhoz* families have risen by less than this, since one must take into account the sales and own consumption of produce of private plots,[3] but the very large increase in payment for collective work is real enough; the payments in 1960 were very low, of course, and actually lower than in 1958. Anyhow, this large rise explains the high cost of production, given that labour inputs have fallen rather slowly, as we shall see.

Many *kolkhozy* were turned into state farms (*sovkhozy*) in the past fifteen years. Pay on state farms was and is higher, though allowance must be made for the usually smaller private plots. Wages have risen as follows:

	1960	*1965*	*1970*	*1972*
Average for all state agriculture (roubles per month)	55.2	75.0	101.0	117.7
of which: workers on farms	51.9	72.4	98.5	109.3
Average for workers and employees in industry	91.6	104.2	133.3	142.1

Source: Nar. khoz. (1972) p.516.

These figures show, firstly, that *kolkhoz* pay rose much faster (from lower levels) than *sovkhoz* pay, and, secondly, that both rose much faster than industrial wages and salaries. In other words, there was a marked relative change between rural and urban incomes in favour of the former.

Indeed, if one adds income (in cash and kind) from private plots, there is now only a quite small difference between rural and urban incomes. From this a very important conclusion follows: that the long period of 'exploiting' agriculture for the benefit of industry is over. It is hard to identify the various channels by which the agricultural sector was 'milked' for the benefit of industry, but in the last analysis the process found its expression in the relatively much lower *incomes* of the peasantry. Now, as we see, things have changed.

THE PRIVATE SECTOR

Here there has been no expansion. On the contrary, the number of private livestock is still slowly declining.

Private animals (1 Jan, m. head)

	1961	*1966*	*1971*	*1973*
Cows	16.3	16.6	15.5	14.7
Pigs	15.4	18.2	16.6	13.3[a]
Sheep	28.1	27.6	28.8	27.7
Goats	6.0	4.7	4.4	4.5

[a] Abnormally large full due to consequences of 1972 harvest.

Source: Nar. khoz. (1972) p.366.

While shortages of fodder may be a continuing explanation of the decline, another cause may now be more important. This is a consequence of improved pay for collective work and some overdue improvement in food distribution in rural areas. This leads some peasants to prefer leisure and to give up private livestock to save themselves extra work. *Some* of the peasants have kept a cow, a pig and a sheep because of necessity — otherwise no milk and meat — rather than choice. It is likely, on this interpretation, that the private sector will decline slowly. The volume of its output in 1970 was 14 per cent above 1960, and it fell in the bad year 1972 to a level 7 per cent above 1960.[4] Sales in the *kolkhoz* market may decline when the state shops have more and better produce to sell at official prices. (At present, market prices are much the higher, which pushes up the value percentage well above the volume.)

Kolkhoz **market turnover**

	1960	1965	1970	1972
1000 m. roubles	3.7	3.58	4.14	4.34
Percentage of total value of retail food trade	7.4	5.3	4.4	4.0

Source: Nar. khoz. (1972) pp.576, 577. First line calculated.

AGRICULTURAL INVESTMENTS AND INPUTS

Total, including *kolkhozy*

	1960	1965	1970	1972
1000 m. roubles, all 'agriculture'	6.2[a]	11.5	17.4	21.6
1000 m. roubles, 'productive' only	5.1[a]	9.5	14.2	18.1
Per cent of total[b]	14.2	16.7	17.3	19.2

[a] At different prices: slight understatement *Nar. khoz.* (1962) p.478.
[b] Per cent of *productive*, of total which includes private housing investments.

Source: Nar. khoz. (1970) p.483; (1972) pp.479, 482.

Clearly, the level of investments has risen rapidly and is taking close to 20 per cent of total Soviet investments from all sources, more than this if so-called unproductive investments in agriculture are taken into account. These figures *omit* repair depots operated by *sel'khoztekhnika,* agricultural education, some investments in building materials for agriculture, etc. The total for 1972, including these, is stated to have been 23,900 millions.

To this must be added the sizeable investments in industries serving agriculture, reflected in increasing deliveries of inputs, as follows:

Deliveries to agriculture

	1960	*1965*	*1970*	*1972*
Tractors ('000)	157.0	239.5	300.3	312.8
Grain combines ('000)	57.0	79.4	97.1	92.8
Lorries ('000)	66.1	70.2	125.8	153.2
Fertiliser (m. gross tons)	11.4	27.1	45.6	54.8

Source: Nar. khoz. (1972) pp.305, 353.

The most important item on this list is fertiliser: an almost five-fold increase in twelve years is impressive, and explains more than any single factor the much higher yields now being achieved in the non-black-earth areas, where fertiliser is the *sine qua non* of progress.

An interesting and vitally important question is: has the additional output been achieved at excessive cost? This has several aspects:

(i) The share of agriculture in total investment is high and has been growing. This represents a burden on the rest of the economy. Taking the highest of the figures cited, i.e. 23,000 millions, this is over 25 per cent of the total investments throughout the economy. Agricultural investments are less than 4 per cent of the total investments in the United States.[5] This suggests relatively wasteful use of investment resources, given that US agriculture is so much better equipped. (There are problems of statistical comparison, which may make it better to use a figure of 20 per cent rather than 25 per cent for the Soviet Union, but the contrast remains extraordinary.)

(ii) Investments can benefit other sectors of the economy if they save labour. Of course labour inputs are declining, but rather slowly, as the following figures show:

Directly engaged in agriculture (state and *kolkhoz*) (m.)

1960	1965	1970	1972
26.1	25.6	23.8	23.5

Source: Nar. khoz. (1972) p.406.

Labour inputs on private plots could not have declined, and these need to be added. But even if one ignores this complication, the fact is that labour inputs remain high by the standard of any advanced country. Productivity is rising, but is still low. Even in the good year 1973, yields per hectare and per cow are well below those of Poland or Hungary. Many machines appear to be of indifferent quality, and supplies of electricity are unreliable. It may well be that mechanisation has added to cost, because the cost and depreciation of the machine is not sufficiently offset by the labour it saves.

(iii) All this is duly reflected in the undisputed fact that the capital-output ratio in agriculture is high and rising, that is to say one needs increasing quantities of additional investment per unit of additional output.

PRICES AND COSTS HAVE RISEN

Prices were raised, as already mentioned, in 1965 and in 1970, and 50 per cent bonus prices for overplan deliveries have been extended to more crops and to meat. The subsidy required to maintain retail prices of livestock products unchanged[6] in the face of repeated increases in procurement prices has now become astronomic. It was already 6,500 million roubles in 1968[7] with no appreciable revision of retail prices.[8] Since then procurement prices have been increased and quantities have significantly risen too. It is quite probable that the 1973 figure is up to about 16,000 million roubles, which is getting on for $20,000 million at the official exchange rate, the most gigantic agricultural subsidy known in human history — or is it best seen as a consumer subsidy? Anyhow, although the state derives net revenue from crops (grain and sugar beet, notably), this is unlikely to offset the outgoings on covering losses on livestock purchases.

On the organisational side, two remarks must be made. One relates to the long-postponed Kolkhoz Congress. It finally did meet in 1968 and adopted an amended statute, which reflected the existing situation. A *kolkhoz* council was set up, but this proved to be dominated by ministers and officials (the then minister, Matskevich, became its first chairman), and there is no sign of it having any noticeable influence on affairs.

The second is the declared intention to develop joint *sovkhoz-kolkhoz* activities, which, as Brezhnev and *Pravda* editorials[9] have declared, will be a step towards the ultimate merging of the *kolkhoz* and *sovkhoz* on the basis of public (and on larger co-operative) property. However, this looks like being a gradual process. Involved in it will be local industrial developments, to provide off-peak employment, to process farm products, to make various implements and building materials, and perhaps also to develop output of miscellaneous consumers' goods. There is talk of agro-industrial complexes, as well as of concentrating peasants in large urban-style villages with modern amenities.

Both depend to a considerable extent on improvement in transport. This brings one to the still-existing weaknesses of Soviet agriculture, which help to explain the low productivity of its labour force and the inadequate return on the very large capital investments. One of these weaknesses is *bezdorozhie* ['roadlessness'], the sea of mud which twice a year cuts farms off from towns, and villages in the same *sovkhoz* or *kolkhoz* from one another. The loss can scarcely be computed.

This adds a further element to another major source of difficulty, *the very large size of farms*. In 1972, the situation was as in the table on page 12.

Too big, surely! These are very complex and diverse activities, mixed farming with a large labour force. It is hard to manage, and hard to devise relevant and effective incentives. Sometimes good pay encourages wasteful actions, as for instance rewarding tractor drivers for ploughing a large

Average *kolkhoz*	
Households	443
Agricultural land	6,200 ha.
Arable land	3,200 ha.
Tractors	32
Cattle	1,388
Pigs	964
Sheep & goats	1,680

Source: Nar. khoz. (1972) p. 388.

Average *sovkhoz*	
Workers & employees	592
Agricultural land	20,000 ha.
Sown area	7,600 ha.
Cattle	1,996
Pigs	1,143
Sheep & goats	3,586

Source: Nar. khoz. (1972) pp. 399, 400.

area in hectares at minimum cost, which leads to shallow ploughing.

However, it is important to note the possibility of decentralised decision-making *within* large and apparently unwieldy units. One important experiment concerns the autonomous (*beznaryadnoe*) *zveno* or link. This is a small group of peasants, perhaps only six or seven, who are left to cultivate a crop or crops on land set aside for the purpose and make their own working arrangements, being paid by results. Experiments on these lines are proceeding, but have run into problems, some of them of a practical kind: thus what are the members of the *zveno* and their equipment to do when the crop is growing, and how to avoid conflicts with other *kolkhoz* peasants or *sovkhoz* workers who are not benefiting from these arrangements (not all the work is 'divisible' into small *zvenya*). It is interesting to note that flexible arrangements of this kind have existed for some time in Hungary and are being tried out in Rumania. All this needs careful study.

Inadequate machinery, especially for the livestock sector, is a perpetual headache, as is the problem of spare parts. For instance, electric milking machinery breaks down far too often, necessitating a reserve of milkmaids as a standby. Some crops and processes are little helped by mechanisation. The resultant labour peaks create serious problems, met annually by a large mobilisation of townspeople (factory workers, lorry-drivers, students, clerks) to help bring the harvest in. This causes losses elsewhere in the economy. Vigorous attempts are being made to overcome these defects. One problem is the inadequate link between the farms that use the machinery and the industry which works it. The link is supposed to be assured by *Sel'khoztekhnika,* the state organisation supplying equipment to agriculture, but many vigorous criticisms have been directed at this body.

Labour problems relate not only to peak demand but also to quality. Too many skilled young people try to get to town, and despite restrictions on movement many succeed. The result is a shortage of 'mechanisers' and maintenance personnel, and a relative abundance of unskilled older women. Hence the paradox of frequent shortages of the right kind of labour, when the percentage engaged in agriculture looks very high by the standards of developed countries. A further trouble is regional maldistribution: overpopulation in Central Asia and probably also the western Ukraine, shortage in Siberia, to cite a few examples. A more thorough regional analysis is desirable, since efficiency also greatly varies. Some of the best results have been achieved in the relatively infertile republic of Estonia.

One source of resentment in rural areas lay in the fact that most residents did not have an internal passport, and this restricted their possibilities of movement, especially to urban areas. In one published short story, the point was made that this gave the peasant a feeling of being a second-class citizen. Under a new regulation adopted in December 1974, passports are to be issued to all citizens over the next few years. Of course, this does not of itself ensure freedom of movement to town, since a police registration (*propiska*) is still required and the would-be migrant might still face the problem of obtaining such a *propiska* if he were not formally released from membership of his farm. None the less, the fact that he will have in his possession the necessary document is undoubtedly a step forward and will be felt as such.

Fodder remains a major bottleneck. The demand for livestock products is not being met, and the government is urging farms to expand meat production in particular. But much requires to be done to improve hayfields and other pasture, and to provide more concentrates. A recent study by the US Department of Agriculture estimates that the USSR will need to import fodder grains on a large scale if it is to sustain its ambitious livestock programme. I was told in 1970 by a Soviet official that the high cost of fodder is one reason for the high cost of livestock products, and that it is due to lack of mechanisation and neglect of pastures. It is recognised that it takes much greater weight of fodder in the USSR than in the USA to fatten an animal.

Finally, *prices and procurement plans* are interlinked problems. Though better, prices are still irrational. I must at once admit that agricultural prices tend to be irrational the world over. However, in most countries farmers are free to respond to them. In the USSR, prices are in constant conflict with the desired pattern of production and deliveries. It is therefore impossible to leave the farm management free to choose what to grow and what to sell. Compulsory procurements remain, and so does interference from above in the farms' sowings, livestock holdings, even the date at which harvesting is completed. As already mentioned, this interference is no longer linked to national campaigns (except the annual harvest and procurement campaign), so there is more latitude for provincial party and state authorities, with greater possibilities for specialisation, and also for farm management to make representations to the (local) planners. None the less, the evidence shows that various inflexibilities continue because of the degree of political interference.

This contrasts with the position in Hungary, where compulsory procurements have been abolished, and farms are much freer to grow whatever seems to them most profitable, while making informal arrangements within the farm to stimulate the members to produce more. While the plans which are laid down are now more sensible than they were under Khrushchev, it does still seem that Soviet agriculture suffers from insufficient decentralisation to local management, as well as from the excessive size of the farms. Many examples could be cited to illustrate this. There is a built-in reluctance on the part of the leadership to relax control, to allow what the Russians call *samotyok* [spontaneity]. Yet perhaps *samotyok* is just what is needed.

Brezhnev in 1965 promised that compulsory procurement plans would be fixed for years ahead, so that farms could plan confidently in the knowledge of what their obligations to the state would be. This is not what has occurred. Overplan deliveries have (as usual) been effectively compulsory, since the procurement organs have their plans to fulfil.

Losses are also caused at the procurement stage, by lack of facilities for handling, especially of perishables. Persistent reports of shortages of vegetables and fruit in the shops coexist with reports that farms cannot get state wholesalers to accept vegetables and fruit. This is apparently due not only to lack of means of transport, packaging materials and storage space, but also to the narrow trade and handling margins, which cause financial losses in the case of perishables. We have already referred to grain losses in 1973 due to the fact that the bountiful harvest of that year greatly exceeded the grain elevator and storage capacity. Remedial action has been reported.

CONCLUSION

So we have clear evidence of progress, in output, yields, productivity, fertiliser supplies, availability of equipment, peasant living standards. Yet this apparently favourable picture must be seen against its background: thus, the advance has been from very low levels, and it has been achieved at very heavy cost, not only in investment but also in the high costs of current production. While much higher than in 1960, the productivity indicators of Soviet agriculture remain low by world standards, and by the standards of other Communist countries. There is still very much to do. The question is: how much can be done without major institutional changes in the *kolkhoz-sovkhoz* system?

NOTES

1 L. I. Brezhnev, *Voprosy agrarnoi politiki KPSS i osvoenie tselinnykh zemel' Kazakhstana* (Moscow, 1974) p. 307.
2 Calculated from *Nar. khoz.* (1972) p. 577. Scattered reports speak of attempts to fix maximum 'free' prices, in which case the true position is understated by the figure quoted.
3 In 1960, peasant families derived more from the private plot than from work for the *kolkhoz* (*Nar. khoz.* (1972) p. 563). This is no longer the case.
4 *Nar. khoz.* (1972) p. 288.
5 The contrast was pointed out by R. W. Campbell in his *Soviet-type Economies* (London, 1974) p. 75, and it deserves closer analysis.
6 There has been some 'adjustment' of quality categories, though.
7 *Finansy SSSR*, no. 3 (1969) p. 16.
8 According to *Finansy SSSR*, no. 4 (1971) farms in the Moscow region are paid an average of 3000 roubles per ton for beef cattle, with a wholesale price of 1546 roubles, so the loss per ton is enormous.
9 *Pravda*, 16 Dec 1973.

2 The Import of Western Technology

PHILIP HANSON[1]

INTRODUCTION

The Soviet-American *détente* of the early 1970s has been perhaps the most striking development in Russia's dealings with the outside world since the fall of Khrushchev. It can be argued, however, that it is only part of a more general and more gradual improvement in East-West relations, first expressed in Soviet doctrine by Khrushchev's formula of peaceful coexistence.

Nobody can say with any certainty how extensive and how reversible this change may be. It is often said that a major element in it, on the Soviet side, is a desire for more substantial East-West economic exchanges for the purpose of improving Soviet access to western advanced technology. How compelling that desire may be, though, is a matter of dispute.

One view of recent Soviet policy is that the Soviet leaders have come to perceive Soviet economic progress as critically dependent on the import of advanced western machinery and know-how. They therefore seek 'massive assistance from the West'.[2] If this is so, a case can be made for 'tough' western policies such as a stricter embargo to reduce Soviet economic and military potential or the systematic extraction of a political price (e.g. freer emigration from the USSR) for any commercial policy concessions by the West that facilitate the transfer of technology. Alternatively, if one believes the Soviet leaders to be seeking massive western assistance, one might prefer to draw less combative conclusions and see this as a symptom of convergence. One might then argue that the Soviet Union, compelled by those familiar but elusive imperatives of advanced technology, is being integrated willy-nilly into a world economy in which national and ideological boundaries are becoming less and less respected and in which East-West conflict will be less likely than in the past.

A very different interpretation of the Soviet interest in greater West-East technology transfer is possible, however. This is that the current emphasis on buying western technology is no more than a medium-term tactical expedient that will prove as reversible as the Concessions policy of the 1920s. On this view the Soviet Union, or the Comecon group as a whole, are and will remain closer to economic and technical autonomy than to dependence; the commercial or political price that can be charged for western technology is strictly limited (the apparent initial success of the Jackson Amendment notwithstanding), and the vision of a single, closely interdependent international economy of advanced industrial states is illusory.

This essay is an attempt to clarify this discussion and to show at least that some versions of what has been happening are more plausible than others.

The first kind of evidence is the evolution of Soviet published discussion and policy statements since the late 1950s. This I shall sketch very superficially in the next section, as a background to what follows. The following two sections of this essay are an attempt to identify and put into perspective what I have called negotiable technology transfer from the West to the USSR since the mid-1950s. The aim here is to assess the contribution to Soviet economic progress of the direct transfer of western technology to the Soviet Union by means of substantial commercial transactions — the kind of technology transfer, in other words, which is most amenable to government control and therefore most relevant to the politics of *détente*. The final section brings together the conclusions of the preceding sections.

Throughout this essay it is taken for granted that the acquisition of western advanced technology is a matter of at least some importance in Soviet policy. This is clearly implied in much of the Soviet discussion reviewed in the next section. If this view really is held by many Soviet policy makers it must rest, of course, on a belief that Soviet technology in at least some important areas is in some significant degree 'behind' that of one or more western countries and can be improved by the acquisition of the western technology. Many westerners and many Russians believe this to be the case, though the scope and size of the lag is hard to specify. A number of studies show a substantial lag of Soviet behind West European and American technology in many civilian industries; instances of substantial areas of parity or Soviet lead seem to be relatively few.[3] In what follows, I shall take this lag for granted rather than review the evidence for it.

I do not assume, however, that East-West technology transfer is exclusively from the West to the Soviet Union, since there are some examples of Soviet technologies taken up in the West. Nor do I assume that there must always be an imbalance in the exchange of technology between the USSR and the West. The sources of invention are very varied and every country without exception acquires new ideas, techniques and machines from other countries and would lose one source of productivity gain if it was isolated from the rest of the world. The relative isolation of the USSR from the huge international traffic of people and machines embodying new technologies must be one reason for relative Soviet backwardness, quite apart from the weakness in indigenous innovation which Soviet civilian production also seems to exhibit.

One final point is necessary in order to put the discussion that follows into perspective. A full account of the economics of the US-Soviet *détente* would have to consider western as well as Soviet interests. The western side is neglected here. The interest of American businessmen in competing on at least an equal footing with West European and Japanese businessmen in the Soviet market, and of all western governments in improving their trade balances and their future energy supply positions, will be obvious. The western economic interest should not, however, be exaggerated. Barriers to trade, equity investment and labour migration between the West and the USSR show no sign of being much reduced in the near future and the prospects of the Soviet Union's becoming a major trading partner of any major western country remain small. In 1973, compared with 1972, the share of all socialist countries in US merchandise exports doubled, but only from 1.8 per cent to 3.6 per cent.

This means that out of every $1000 of US national income in 1973, less than $2 were derived from merchandise exports to socialist countries.[4] The share of East-West trade in total economic activity in West Europe and Japan- would be somewhat higher, but still small.

The possibility of large-scale Soviet energy supplies to the West is perhaps the only source of a really compelling western economic interest, at the level of national policy, in *détente*. The Soviet Union already supplies oil, natural gas and enriched uranium to various western countries. For some western countries and some energy sources, such supplies could become important. I shall only note here that strategic considerations may well inhibit the western pursuit of this possibility, while the situation in this respect on the Soviet side is not symmetrical. The ability to cut off important energy supplies in a crisis is a rather more powerful card than the ability to cut off supplies of machine tools for making bumpers for Russian cars. In general, I assume the Soviet economic interest in *détente* to be stronger and less qualified by the most obvious strategic considerations than the corresponding western interest.

SOVIET OFFICIAL THINKING ABOUT THE IMPORT OF
WESTERN TECHNOLOGY

Soviet official views, as publicly expressed, about the acquisition of technology from the West have changed considerably since the latter years of Khrushchev's leadership. Khrushchev's speeches around the time of the announcement of the twenty-year Programme of the CPSU in 1961 are both confident and relatively unconcerned about the progress of Soviet technology. This did not prevent a very substantial import of western machinery and equipment for certain sectors around this time, notably for the chemical industry and shipping. The official perspective, however, appears to have been that this was a burst of once-for-all 'catching-up' in certain previously neglected sectors, to be followed quite quickly by a general 'overtaking' of the West. This mood has since been replaced by a cannier perception of the difficulties involved, an appreciation of the relative weakness of Soviet indigenous innovation, and of the disadvantages of being a less than full participant in the processes which facilitate the pervasive technological borrowing between western countries.

It is not surprising that this change occurred. The boost that *Sputnik I* must have given to Soviet morale about Soviet technology wore off, presumably, as the Soviet lead over the United States in space exploration was eroded during the 1960s. The slowing down of Soviet economic growth in the early 1960s simultaneously weakened confidence about 'overtaking'. It also directed the attention of policy makers to the apparent need, if growth rates were to be maintained, to rely less on the growth of capital and labour inputs, which was tending to slacken, and more on improvements in technology and organisation, at least one of which would have to come to the rescue. The correct diagnosis of the slow-down in Soviet growth is a matter of controversy, and the slow-down of the early sixties has been followed by a recovery to higher rates, but there is no doubt that the call for more 'intensive' growth has become a cliché in Soviet official talk, usually associated with another cliché about the need for a faster rate of technical change in the Soviet economy. Agricultural shortfalls and problems of quality and assortment in the supply of manufactured consumer goods also drew attention to the need for sharp improvements in the consumer sector.

There was at the same time an evolution of Soviet thinking about science, science policy and the process of innovation. The recognition of a number of 'new', rapidly-growing, 'science-based' industries in the modern world was elaborated into a body of doctrine about the 'scientific-technical revolution', originating primarily in the late 1950s but attracting more widespread discussion in the early 1960s and in due course entering the vocabulary of leadership speeches. Practical concerns about faults in innovation and the diffusion of new technology in the Soviet economy led to debate and organisational changes in the structures linking R & D to production.[5] Thus technical progress in the Soviet economy ceased to be something to be referred to as splendid and not otherwise thought about; it became something which was officially regarded as problematic (though a tone of fundamental cheerfulness is, of course, still required) and about which one had policies.

A review of speeches by the most prominent leaders at the last four party congresses will show how this change of thinking is reflected at the highest political level. It also shows how, eventually, in the speeches of Brezhnev and Kosygin, the concern about improving Soviet technology has come to be linked with a concern to enlarge East-West trade. Speeches by Soviet leaders at party congresses are of course a small and special sample of Soviet policy statements, but they are intended to set main guidelines for policy. Changes of emphasis in them should provide a rough guide to the broader kind of developments in Soviet public policy.[6]

Khrushchev's speeches to the XXI (1959) and XXII (1961) Congresses devote very little space to questions of technology. What little he had to say on the subject in 1959 consisted largely of passing references of unrelieved optimism. The same is broadly true of his speeches to the XXII Congress except that in one short passage a note of caution and concern appears, with a complaint about 'technological conservatism' in some areas of the Soviet economy and the need to make fuller use of domestic R & D and of 'the best that foreign experience can give'. An awareness that there are problems — an awareness apparent in Kosygin's contribution to the previous Congress but not in Khrushchev's — is clear in this passage.[7]

Brezhnev's and Kosygin's speeches at the XXIII Congress (1966) and the XXIV Congress (1971) are quite different. They devote a much larger proportion of their time to the problems of assimilating new technology. In 1966, in his report on the Eighth Five-Year Plan directives, Kosygin linked technology and East-West trade at some length.

Until recently we have underestimated the importance of trade in patents and licences. Yet this trade is playing an ever more noticeable role in the world at large. . . . Our scientists and technicians can create . . . excellent new machinery and equipment. Therefore we can and must occupy a worthy place in the world market for licences. And in turn it is more profitable for us, too, to buy a licence than to concern ourselves with the solution of this or that problem. The purchase of patent rights from abroad will allow us in the new Five-Year Plan to save hundreds of millions of rubles in scientific-technical work.[8]

Less conspicuous Soviet discussions and decisions suggest that this evolution of leadership statements about East-West trade is based on a serious reconsideration of the role of international transactions in the improvement of Soviet technology. Thus, for example, the doctrine that 'no one country, however large or powerful it may be in an economic or scientific-technical sense, is able nowadays to ensure an equal advance across the whole front of scientific research . . .' and therefore all countries must seek the widest possible international technological exchange, is now a commonplace in Soviet published policy discussion.[9]

An example of unobtrusive institutional developments which embody this rationale can be seen in the field of know-how and licence trade. *Litsenzintorg,* a foreign trade organisation specialising in the purchase and sale of patents and licenses, primarily in the developed West, was set up in February 1962. In 1965 the Soviet Union acceded to the Paris Convention on the Protection of Industrial Property. The primary importance of this move was almost certainly as an attempt to reassure western patent holders that they would have some recourse in law if their patent rights were infringed in the USSR by unlicensed copying or, if a licensing arrangement were made, by infringement of its terms. The Soviet accession to the Paris Convention has been followed, it would seem, by substantial Soviet purchases of western licences. From 1970 onwards, according to a Soviet source, systematic annual and five-year planning of the acquisition and use of foreign licences was introduced as part of the regular state planning process.[10]

In short, one finds explicitly stated in Soviet public discussion and reflected in the development of Soviet institutions during the past decade a realisation that technological change is continuous, rapid and worldwide and that any country that participates less than fully in the process of international diffusion of new products and processes is in some degree imposing a handicap on its own economic growth. The implication is that Soviet policy should be adapted to this perception for an indefinitely long time to come. The size and growth of licence trade between western countries has been noted and the Institute of World Economics and International Relations has projected a continuing expansion of world licence trade (eight to ten-fold increase between 1970 and 1990). The role of western transnational companies as vehicles for international technology transfer has been recognised, and referred to in explaining the rationale of the new Comecon international associations such as *Intertekstil'mash*. Japanese experience in the systematic scrutiny and licensing of foreign technology is described approvingly as an example to be learnt from. References to an indefinitely continuing and expanding Soviet participation in international technology transfer abound.[11]

Against this background of Soviet policy change we have seen individual East-West business projects of spectacular size, such as the Fiat deal, the Soviet-US trade agreements of 1972, and the associated flood of eye-catching schemes from the huge proposed liquefied natural gas deliveries to the USA to Dr Hammer's offer to Mr Brezhnev of a eighteen-hole golf course. It is hardly surprising that the Soviet interest in acquiring western technology is now widely believed to be compelling.

Our review of Soviet policy discussion suggests that the change is real and that it has proceeded rapidly in the period since Khrushchev's fall. But it is also clear that it can be traced back at least to the latter years of Khrushchev's rule. Obviously, Soviet acquisition of western technology, in a general sense, goes back, as Sutton has shown in great detail, to the very beginning of the Soviet era. What has changed, I suggest, since about 1960, is that more and more Soviet officials, academics and politicians have come to believe — in many cases perhaps for the first time — that there was a continuous and extensive process of technical change going on in the Western world, that it was likely to go on for some time, that 'catching-up' meant aiming at a moving target, that catching-up was extremely difficult and would take time and that it could best be done by large-scale Soviet participation in many of the international commercial practices by which western countries normally acquire new technology from one another, rather than by other, more 'arm's-length' approaches.

THE NATURE OF EAST-WEST TECHNOLOGY TRANSFER

For the purposes of this essay I shall take international technology transfer (henceforth simply 'technology transfer') to mean any process by which innovations (new products and processes introduced into commercial as opposed to experimental or pilot-plant production for the first time anywhere in the world) made in one country are subsequently brought into use in another country, not by a totally independent sequence of research, development, design, testing and evaluation, but with some resort to the experience of the foreign innovator, either directly or through some intermediary such as another foreign producer who has followed the original innovator.

The ways in which the experience of the innovator may be used are very varied. It may be only the basic idea that is known (as in the prison scientists' work on the telephone scrambler device in *The First Circle*). At the other extreme it might consist of the outright purchase of a new machine.

Technology transfer in this sense need not entail that the recipient country can subsequently reproduce the new product or process without further recourse to foreign assistance. It may be able to do so, whether by unassisted copying or through the purchase (as in the Soviet production at Bryansk of Burmeister og Wain marine diesel engines under licence) of licences, know-how and perhaps training. In this case we could perhaps speak of technology assimilation. This will often require a transfer of foreign technology into the machine-building sector.

Alternatively, the recipient country may simply acquire, say, a new machine and the ability to operate it, with associated gains in productivity, but without the ability independently to replicate the machine. In this case we could speak of technology acquisition. Thus a foreign special-purpose machine tool may be installed, say, at the Tolyatti car complex and be efficiently utilised in the production of *Zhiguli's* and yet incorporate design features and tooling which the Soviet machine-tool industry lacked the know-how or materials to replicate. This situation is probably quite common as far as sales of western special-purpose machine tools and chemical plant are concerned. The acquisition and successful operation of a polyester fibre plant is a different matter from learning how to build another one of the same kind.

Technology transfer, whether acquisition or assimilation, is not the same as technological 'catching-up'. It may merely mean that the gap between leader and recipient does not widen. Nor, *a fortiori*, does it impart an ability to 'overtake'. Its usefulness to the recipient country is that it saves resources that would otherwise have to be spent on re-duplication of the innovator's whole R & D process, and reduces lead-times. This saving may on the other hand conceal a longer-run disadvantage; it means that the recipient country forgoes a learning process which independent R & D would give it, and which would in the longer run enhance its capacity to overtake. This is the meaning of Sakharov's well-known metaphor for Soviet technological borrowing from the West: the skis, and perhaps the mental attitudes, suitable for following the trail of another, trail-breaking skier, may be unsuited to breaking trail oneself.

Technology transfer itself, however, takes time and re-quires resources. Industrial processes, designs and prototypes may be patented, kept secret or contain an element of practical know-how communicable only by on-the-job train-ing. It may be necessary to pay for these things. Even if this is not the case, copying is not costless. It is misleading to think of copying, let alone adaptation to local requirements, as a simple matter. The Caterpillar Tractor Company's evaluation of a Soviet copy of the Caterpillar D-7 led them to praise the skill that had gone into design changes to the metric system and 'complete re-engineering' to conform to Soviet workshop practice, manufacturing standard and domestically available machines and materials.[12]

There are many different ways in which a country may acquire or assimilate foreign technology; the only pre-requisites for some technology transfer from abroad would seem to be that the recipient country should not be totally isolated from possible sources of more advanced technology, e.g. by total embargo on trade or the movement of persons, and that its population should have some skills and know-ledge enabling them to make use of foreign products and processes new to them.

In considering the subject of East-West technology transfer and *détente* one can take it for granted that these conditions are met in the Soviet Union and that the interesting distinction is between a situation of Cold War and arm's-length dealing on the one hand, and on the other hand a more relaxed political environment facilitating regular and substantial commercial exchanges extending to licence and know-how sales, turn-key projects, and technical and production co-operation projects.

Some channels of technology transfer are useable even in an era of arm's-length dealing as long as some commercial exchange and diplomatic representation is in being. The monitoring of foreign technical journals, the once-off purchase of individual products which are then used and perhaps copied,[13] and perhaps some industrial espionage would all seem to come into this category. These we can for present purposes classify as non-negotiable technology transfer.

Large-scale machinery and other purchases, including the buying of know-how, inter-enterprise co-operation agreements, and more than minimal direct contacts with foreign scientists and technologists, in contrast, would seem to be in a different category. These we can call negotiable technology transfer, on the grounds that they are likely to require a degree of political and commercial goodwill between the countries concerned — probably formalised in some inter-governmental agreements; a narrowly rather than broadly applied strategic embargo on sales to the recipient country, and probably the extension to that country of MFN tariff treatment for its exports and the backing of government-guaranteed credits for exports to it.

In other words, it seems useful to consider some channels for the transfer of western technology to the USSR as being open and used more or less regardless of the pursuit of Cold War or *détente* policies and others — negotiable technology transfer — as being sensitive to commercial and foreign policy decisions short of total blockade and therefore as constituting a Soviet economic interest in *détente*.

To keep this interest in perspective, it also seems useful, furthermore, to look at it in terms of 'sources of growth'. If it makes any sense at all to separate changes in capital, labour, technology and other factors in explaining changes in output, it follows that total Soviet output would be likely to grow, through increments in capital and labour inputs, even in the complete absence of technical change. We must allow, further, that even if we ignore Soviet military production and accept even the sternest critics' views of the weakness of Soviet indigenous civilian innovation, there is at any rate some indigenous technical change in the Soviet economy. Finally, as Sutton has argued, prototype copying and other forms of what I have classified as non-negotiable technology transfer have also been a significant source of technical change in the Soviet economy. Negotiable technology transfer from the West has therefore been and is capable of being only one of a number of sources of Soviet economic growth.[14]

How large its contribution has been in the recent past, nobody knows. Estimates of the share of influences other than capital and labour inputs in any country's economic growth are still controversial. Western estimates for the USSR vary considerably. To make matters worse, the residual, even if correctly estimated, is only the net outcome of a number of influences, some of which may be negative. The only honest conclusion we can reach about the recent past contribution to Soviet growth of the transfer by negotiable channels of western technology to the USSR is that it is unknown, probably not dominant, but perhaps appreciable.[15]

We can say, however, that if international commercial arrangements allowed, such transfer could probably make a larger contribution to Soviet growth. Within the western world negotiable technology transfer between countries on a very large scale is taken for granted. Direct investment abroad, as the study of multinational companies shows, is one important vehicle. Large numbers of scientists, technologists and managers spend large parts of their working lives in more than one country. Machinery and know-how trade is extremely large and has grown rapidly. So far as new technology is concerned, interdependence between western countries is considerable, with even the USA absorbing a good deal of new technology from abroad.[16]

The Soviet Union has so far been only a minor participant, somewhat on the periphery of this network of transactions — a point which recent Soviet discussion now emphasises (pp. 19-23 above). The various constraints on East-West trade are well known. In addition, the Soviet government excludes western equity investment and restricts the movements of its nationals abroad and of foreigners on its own territory. All this limits the amount of negotiable technology transfer directly from the West to the USSR. The systematic scrutiny of western technical publications and the import of advanced machinery and know-how from East Europe (some of it indirectly from the West, as in the case of ships supplied by Polish shipyards which have technical agreements with western firms) is likely to compensate only partially for this handicap.

Thus in 1964, for example, Soviet purchases of western machinery and transport equipment were equivalent in value to only about 2.5 per cent of such purchases by OECD countries from one another. The role of western machinery in Soviet investment has been small. It is shown (on pp. 30-5 below) that the share of imported western machinery in total Soviet domestic equipment investment has not been more than about 4 per cent in recent years. If that share could be raised, the growth of capital and labour productivity due to the new technology embodied in newly installed machines would probably be enhanced. The optimal share of imported western machinery for the purpose of maintaining a maximum long-run growth rate of productivity would probably be a great deal higher than 4 per cent. It is true that the USSR also imports about three times as much machinery from East Europe as from the West, but this is almost certainly much less effective per unit as a source of productivity increase. If it is worthwhile for firms in the USA, the most technically advanced country in the world, to import machinery and transport equipment equal to around 11 per cent of equipment investment, such imports could almost certainly play a larger role in Soviet growth.[17]

It is hard to believe, therefore, that the Soviet economy would not benefit from a substantial further increase in negotiable technology transfer from the West, or that Soviet policy makers think otherwise. At the same time, one corollary of this argument is that Soviet dependence on such transfer, so far as overall growth rates are concerned, has probably not been very great. (Or rather, it is unlikely to have been very great unless it had substantial indirect effects on Soviet productivity by means of assimilation rather than mere acquisition.) A failure sharply to accelerate this transfer, or even its deceleration or decline, might not therefore have dramatic consequences for Soviet growth. The case for believing that the Soviet economy urgently needs an acceleration of the inflow of new western technology in order to maintain recent past growth rates is not a self-evident one. It must presumably rest on a further belief that the contribution of other sources to Soviet growth is likely to decline. The grounds for this latter belief are not strong.

EAST–WEST TRADE AND SOVIET INVESTMENT, 1955-72

Sales of machinery and know-how are the main channels of negotiable technology transfer that have operated from the West to the USSR since the mid-1950s. Technical exchange arrangements and co-operation in R & D are channels that have only lately begun to open appreciably, and will be neglected here. Sales of goods other than those grouped under machinery and transport equipment in the Standard International Trade Classification or the Soviet ETN nomenclature can also transmit new technology: large-diameter pipes would be an example. They are much less important than machinery, however. This section will therefore be concerned primarily with machinery sales and secondarily with trade in licences and know-how. The latter is normally conducted in conjunction with machinery sales and is very much smaller in value terms.[18]

It can be assumed that Soviet purchases of western machinery are a source of embodied technical progress over and above what would accrue from new domestically-produced machines. Soviet foreign-trade planners are supposed to ensure that an item is not available from domestic production or CMEA sources before allocating hard currency for its purchase from the West.

In general, I shall assume that the overwhelming bulk of western machinery imported by the Soviet Union falls into one of two categories. The first is machinery embodying a fundamentally innovatory principle: an example would be the machinery supplied by Pilkington Bros to the USSR under a 1967 agreement which also included the sale of licences to operate the Pilkington float glass process. The second is machinery operating on general principles already assimilated into Soviet machine-building but embodying detailed design features which give it a greater operating efficiency than its Soviet counterpart: an example would be western multi-spindle automatic lathes installed at Tolyatti; the Russians also make such lathes but apparently without certain design and tooling features that make the western machines more effective in high-speed assembly-line work.

I assume that two other possible categories of machinery import are on the whole rare. These would be imports of western machines whose effectiveness in use was identical with that of equivalent CMEA machines in normal production but which are imported either because they are cheaper or because a rigid requirement for such machines has been decided which exceeds CMEA supply capacity. Conversations I have had with a number of western exporters suggest that imports on these grounds are the exception, not the rule.

I therefore take imported western machinery to be, in general, a vehicle for technical change in the Soviet economy. Its direct effect is to raise labour productivity by more than would result from an equivalent addition to the capital stock in the form of domestically produced capital goods.[19] If the import leads to technology assimilation as well as acquisition there will also be a spin-off in the form of enhanced productivity of Soviet machines, subsequently produced, which incorporate the improvements embodied in the original imported machines.

Estimates of the size, growth and composition of Soviet imports of western machinery should therefore tell us a good deal about the nature and importance of negotiable technology transfer from the West to the USSR in the recent past. Table 2.1 uses western trade-partner data of exports to the USSR in SITC section 7. The 'West' has been defined narrowly here and excludes countries like Spain, Greece and Australia whose machinery sales to the USSR have been negligible. The only country omitted that has been a significant exporter of machinery to the USSR and that might normally be thought of as 'Western' is Finland. It seemed reasonable to omit Finland here because of her 'special relationship' with the USSR, expressed *inter alia* by the fact that she is a soft-currency trading partner of the USSR. The relationship of Fenno-Soviet trade to *détente* seems tenuous.

TABLE 2.1 USSR: imports of machinery and transport equipment from the developed West (USA, Canada, EEC, EFTA, Japan) 1955-73

	Imports of machinery etc. (US $m., fob, current prices) (A)	(A) as % all imports (fob) from the 'West' (B)	(A) as % Soviet previous year exports to West less grain imports (C)	(A) as index 1956 = 100 (D)	Equipment investment, 1969 prices, 1956 = 100 (E)	Imports of western machinery as % Soviet domestic equipment investment of following year (F)
1955	104	38.0	—	75		1.0
1956	139	30.3	25.0	100	100	1.2
1957	128	27.0	21.9	92	108	0.9
1958	123	24.0	17.4	89	124	0.8
1959	177	33.8	26.0	128	134	1.1
1960	310	38.3	35.3	222	145	1.7
1961	390	32.2	38.4	280	163	1.8
1962	436	41.8	41.0	314	184	1.8
1963	402	37.2	35.4	289	204	1.4
1964	489	35.8	44.8	352	231	1.6
1965	366	33.4	44.2	264	246	1.1
1966	395	31.2	35.5	284	261	1.1
1967	457	33.7	35.5	329	280	1.2
1968	639	38.3	35.5	460	303	1.6
1969	889	39.0	44.7	640	317	1.9
1970	905	35.0	40.2	651	356	1.7
1971	840	32.5	37.2	605	375	1.4
1972	1113	30.0	43.8	801	406	1.5
1973	1566	27.1	75.7	1131	437	—

Notes and Sources:

Column (A)   The data are western trade-partner data throughout, except that for 1960-3 figures for machinery imports from Japan were obtained from Soviet trade returns.

Sources: US Department of Commerce, *Trade between Free World and Communist Countries, Country-by Commodity Series* (annual) for 1955 through 1959. OECD, *Trade by Commodities*, Series C (annual) for 1960 through 1971. *Vneshnyaya Torgovlya SSSR za 1961g.* and *ditto*, 1963 (see above).

Column (B)   Using a compilation of western countries' total exports to USSR. These were for the same countries as in (A) except that Iceland's total exports were included throughout and total exports of Finland were included for 1970 and later. The percentage figures for 1970-3 are therefore not exactly comparable to those for earlier years.

Sources:	As for (A) plus MITI (Japan), *Foreign Trade of Japan, 1964* and OECD, *Overall Trade by Countries* (Series A).
Column (C)	Using Soviet, not western trade-partner data for (a) total Soviet exports to all 'industrially developed capitalist countries', (b) apparent grain imports from the same countries, derived as total reported grain exports less reported exports from soft-currency sources. The percentage values for $MK_t/(X_{t-1} - MG_{t-1})$ where MG is the column (A) Series and X and MG are Soviet exports to and grain imports from the West as defined above. Conversion to dollars is at official rates.
Sources:	For X and MG: *Vneshnyaya torgovlya SSSR, statisticheskii sbornik, 1918-1966* (Moscow, 1967) and annual *VT SSSR* for subsequent years.
Column (E)	Derived from Soviet official 'constant price' equipment investment data. 1956-60 data, originally given in 1955 prices, were converted to 1969 prices by chain-linking at 1961.
Sources:	*Nar. Khoz* (1961) pp. 538, 539; (1922-72) p. 322.
Column (F)	These are minimum estimates of the share of imported western machinery, based on Boretsky's estimated rouble-dollar conversion rates for all engineering products, which do not allow for certain quality defects in Soviet machinery.

Broadly, the procedure used here is to take Boretsky's geometric mean purchasing power parity for US 1964 engineering products prices in terms of Soviet 1955 prices, and adjust for (a) differences between Soviet 1955 and 1969 prices, (b) differences between US, West European and Japanese machinery prices in 1964 (giving an 'OECD' machinery ppp of $1.74 (1964) = 1 rouble (1969 estimated prices). This conversion rate to Soviet 1969 prices is adjusted, for years other than 1964, by applying to it a price index for OECD machinery exports to the USSR derived from West European wholesale price indexes. A price index for western machinery suppliers to the USSR was calculated from (a) wholesale machinery price indexes for major European countries, 1955-64, (b) wholesale price indexes for 'manufactures' for all the fourteen countries considered here, 1964-73 (in the absence of machinery price indexes for this period). National price indexes were aggregated into an overall index of machinery prices to the USSR using shares in western machinery sales to the USSR as weights, as follows: for 1955-9, shares in 1955-6; for 1960-4, average shares 1960-3; for 1965-70 (where the index covered all suppliers but was based on a broad 'manufactured' goods wholesale price index for each country), shares in 1964-5; for 1971-3, shares in 1971-2. Individual national whole-

sale price indexes were also adjusted to take account of
parity changes with the US dollar. Detailed worksheets
available on request from the author.

Columns (A) and (D) of Table 2.1 show that western
machinery sales to the USSR have grown rapidly, in current
prices, since the mid-fifties. The trend rate of growth,
1955-72, estimated by least squares, was 14.1 per cent p.a.
Column (B) shows that they have typically been of the order
of a third of all western exports to the USSR, though this
share has fluctuated from year to year. One element in this
fluctuation has of course been the sharp intrusion of
emergency grain imports. Column (C) shows that, at any rate
from 1960 to 1972, a fairly steady share of around two-fifths
of Soviet earnings from exports to the West (roughly
corresponding to hard currency earnings) less expenditure on
grain from the West, in any one year, could perhaps be
construed as being made available for buying western
machinery; the effect on machinery import figures would be
lagged by about a year because of the time that typically
elapses between the signing of a contract and the delivery of
machinery contracted for.

The implication of this is, of course, that the availability of
hard currency from visible export earnings limits machinery
purchases. In the period 1955-71, at least, variations in
western credit outstanding to the USSR, in Soviet gold sales,
and in the Soviet hard-currency invisibles balance do not
seem to have greatly altered the relationship between
merchandise export earnings, grain imports, and machinery
imports. Regression analysis supports this view. The lagged
effect of exports to, and grain imports from the West, in the
period 1955-71, provide a powerful explanation (in a purely
statistical sense) of changes in the level of machinery imports
from the West. This remains so even when the effects of the
strong upward time trends in Soviet exports to and
machinery imports from the West are excluded.

A number of relationships between the annual series MK
(the machinery import series of Table 2.1 Column (A)), X
(Soviet exports to 'industrially developed capitalist countries') and MG (Soviet grain imports from the West — see
note to Table 2.1 Column (C)), all in current millions of

dollars, were tested. For the period 1955-71 the equation that gave the best results of those tried was:

$$MK_t = \frac{-72.42 + 0.386\, X_t - 0.394\, MG_{t-1}}{(0.934)\ (8.086)\quad (-2.502)} \quad (R^2 = 0.916)$$

The bracketed figures under the coefficients are t statistics; the coefficients estimated for X_t and MG_{t-1} are both significant at the 1 per cent level.

The strong upward trend over time in both X and MG is a source of difficulty. It would be reasonable to posit some causal relationship between the two trends but their presence may still be a source of some spurious correlation. For the data with MK and X de-trended, which probably understate the influence of X and MG on MK, the best fit of the equations tested is given by the following:

$$MK_t = \frac{38.17 + 0.76 X_{t-1} - 0.27 MG_{t-1}}{(1.823)\ (2.475)\quad (-2.689)} \quad (R^2 = 0.544)$$

where the bracketed figures beneath the coefficients are again t statistics and the X and MG coefficients are significant at 5 per cent.[20]

With the *détente* moves in 1972, however, and the sharp increase in credit available from the USA, this pattern changed. In that year the Soviet Union increased sharply both grain and machinery imports, covering the large resulting deficit by much-increased borrowing. This was of course very sensible, since the Soviet credit rating in the West is good, government-supported credit terms were cheap, and rapid western inflation could be expected to erode the real burden of the debt. Then, in 1973, came the sharp increases in oil and commodity prices which brought windfall gains to Russia's -hard-currency earning capacity. In general, the hard-currency exports constraint on imports of western machinery has eased considerably since 1971, and not only because of US *détente* policies.

In the period from 1955 to 1971, however, the constraints on Soviet imports of western machinery were severe. A comparison of Columns (D) and (E) of Table 2.1 shows that the import of western machinery, in current prices, has none the less risen faster over the whole period than Soviet domestic investment in equipment in (allegedly) constant prices. In the mid-1960s, however, imports of western machinery levelled off (1962-7), apparently because grain imports following the 1963 and 1965 harvest failures were given a prior claim on available hard currency. Paradoxically, therefore, at a time of growing awareness among Soviet policy makers of the importance of increased negotiable technology transfer from the West, the main channel for such an increase ceased to widen.

The 'real' dimensions of what was happening are obscured by the weakness of machinery price indexes, especially of the index used to deflate the series of domestic Soviet equipment investment. The constant price series in Column (E) conceals an element of inflation in the prices of new machines. If we take it at face value, however, and try to relate the two 'real' flows (imports of western machinery and domestic equipment investment) simply by turning the former into constant prices, converting it to 1969 roubles at an appropriate conversion rate and then seeing how large a proportion this imported western machinery has been of all Soviet investment in machinery and equipment, we get the results shown in Column (F).

The figures in Column (F) are striking on two counts. First, because they show imported western machinery as a very small ingredient in the Soviet investment effort. Secondly, because they reveal no clear and substantial increase in the relative importance of that ingredient between the late 1950s and the beginning of the US-Soviet *détente*. Both these impressions must be rather imprecise because of the problematic nature of some of the figures, but it is unlikely that either impression is really misleading.[21]

The absolute size of the western import share in any one year is almost certainly larger than Column (F) indicates because the rouble-dollar conversion rate used to link dollar-value imports and domestic-rouble-value investment data (at 1964) is derived from conventional western comparisons of Soviet and western machinery prices. These comparisons largely neglect differences in the reliability, maintenance cost and service life of otherwise equivalent Soviet and western machines. Western engineering assessments of Soviet machinery suggest that it may well be generally and substantially inferior in these respects.[22] The share of western machinery, therefore, in Soviet investment in domestic rouble terms should almost certainly be higher than is shown here. Even if it should be twice as high, however, its aggregate share is still extremely small: not more than 4 per cent.

The failure of this share to increase much over the period can be attributed, it seems, primarily to hard currency constraints. These were more severe in real terms than they might otherwise have been because of (a) the exigencies of grain imports in the mid-1960s and (b) the acceleration, in the late sixties and early seventies, of the previously very slow inflation in western machinery prices. The more recent impact of US credits, Soviet gold sales, and an improvement in the Soviet terms of trade will probably have tended to increase slightly the share of imported western machinery in Soviet investment from 1973 onwards. At all events, imports of western machinery rose sharply in 1972 and again in 1973.

If we consider the whole period since the mid-1950s, however, the role of western machinery in Soviet investment seems small. What are we to make of this small share No doubt the value of these western machinery imports to the Soviet economy, if measured by the R & D and production costs which would have been required in their absence to achieve the same results in production, would be considerably greater than their cost at western export prices. But it is hard to see how this difference could be estimated.

One way of improving our understanding of the role of negotiable technology transfer is to look at the composition of Soviet imports of western machinery. What machinery was being imported, to produce what? Here the Soviet trade returns are more helpful than the western because they classify machinery more on the basis of user industry than on that of type of machine. They also enable us to compare Soviet imports from the West with Soviet imports from other sources. The machinery imports reported tend to run slightly higher (in dollars) than the western trade-partner figures (though both are fob) but they do not seem to be seriously inconsistent as a rule with the western data. Their main apparent weakness is the lack of consistently applied cut-off points for reporting at the three, four or five-digit levels. As a result, the shares that can be derived from them of different categories of machinery in total imports from the West will tend to be slightly understated, by unknown and varying margins.

Those categories of reported Soviet machinery and transport equipment imports that can be assigned to user branches for which investment data are available, form the basis of a comparison summarised in Table 2.2. The shares of the user branches in imported western machinery in 1955, 1960, 1965 and 1970 were compared with the shares of these same branches in 'productive' investment (all state and co-operative investment except in housing and social infrastructure) in 1956, 1961, 1966 and 1971, respectively. The aim of this comparison is to identify branches of the Soviet economy which seem to have had low, average and high degrees of dependence on imported machinery at different times. These are then grouped according to this apparent degree of dependence in Table 2.2. It must be borne in mind

TABLE 2.2 Apparent differences in dependence on imported western machinery of investment in selected Soviet industries, 1955-6, 1960-1, 1965-6 and 1970-1

A Consistently low dependence (investment shares in all cases clearly greater than import share of preceding year):
  coal industry; iron and steel; oil extraction and refining; building materials; agriculture

B Consistently high dependence (machinery import shares in all cases clearly greater than investment shares of succeeding year):
  light industry; timber, paper and pulp; shipping

C Changing dependence over time (in the sense specified in A and B):
  electric power: possibly somewhat dependent in 1955-6; thereafter not. Machine-building and metalworking: apparently 'high' dependence in 1955-6 and (much more markedly) in 1970-1. 'Low' dependence (though not markedly so) in 1960-1 and 1965-6.
  food industry: apparently high dependence in 1960-1; otherwise low.
  chemical industry: low dependence in 1955-6; very high dependence in 1960-1 and 1965-6; moderately high dependence in 1970-1

Source: Table 2 of a longer version of the present essay, available as a University of Birmingham Centre for Russian and East European Studies Discussion Paper, RC/B, no. 7. Sources and methods are explained in full in the Discussion Paper.

that 'high' and 'low' are here relative to a very low average utilisation of imported western machinery. Only perhaps in the chemical industry and shipping would the share of western machinery in branch equipment investment have been much over 10 per cent during this period; for the chemical industry in 1961 and 1966, using a conversion rate of $0.80 = 1r., the share of western machinery would have been of the order of 30 per cent. The share of western machinery in motor industry investment around the time of the Fiat deal, and now again with KamAZ, would also be substantial, but the motor industry is here submerged in the very large machine-building and metalworking sector.

As a way of getting at the importance of western machinery to different branches, the approach used in Table 2.2 is indirect and far from satisfactory. Direct comparison of import with investment figures for each branch would however require useable rouble-dollar conversion rates for machinery by separate branch user category, and these do not exist. It would be better to have branch shares in machinery and equipment investment, furthermore, than merely in total investment.

Looking at Table 2.2 with this qualification in mind, one can draw some tentative conclusions about the importance of western machinery to the growth of particular branches of the Soviet economy. Several industries show an apparent 'independence' of western machinery supplies. They include some of the traditional high-priority industries that one might expect to have relatively less need for infusions of western technology than more neglected branches: for example coal, iron and steel, and, except perhaps in the mid-1950s, electric power.[23] They also include, however, two industries that had been neglected before the beginning of the period and whose priority was subsequently raised: oil extraction and refining and (more strikingly) agriculture. The latter has in fact absorbed substantial machinery imports from East Europe rather than from the West. The generalisation that western machinery will be required in large quantities whenever a particular, previously neglected industry is being modernised does not seem to be correct.

On the other hand, light industry, timber, paper and pulp, and (especially) shipping and chemicals do seem to be instances of western machinery being introduced in large quantities in the course of a particularly sharp modernisation and expansion drive in an area of the economy previously neglected.

Machinery imports for the food industry, like those for agriculture, come to an important extent from East Europe.

Machine-building and metalworking is too large and internally diverse a branch to be considered in the same way as the branches discussed above. Its above par 'dependence' on western machinery in 1970-1 (and again from 1972 on) is largely the result of the major motor industry expansion at Tolyatti and on the Kama River. These projects however go far beyond the mere assembly of vehicles. A very wide range of equipment has been imported for them.[24] The potential spin-off to Soviet machine-building and metalworking unconnected with the motor industry must be considerable. At the same time it is clear that the direct input of western machinery is heavily concentrated in one part only of this extensive branch.

As a first approximation, then, we can say that negotiable technology transfer from the West, in its predominant form of machinery sales, has been not only a small ingredient in the Soviet investment programme in the post-Stalin period but one which has been concentrated in relatively few branches. (Though this does not preclude an important bottleneck role elsewhere.) These branches — chemicals, shipping, timber, paper and pulp, light industry, and the motor industry — all have in common the characteristic of low past priority and neglect, subsequently revised and, therefore, a particular need for modernisation. To them can be added the computer industry, a sub-branch not included in the above analysis for lack of investment data. Other branches, however — notably agriculture — which also share this characteristic of past neglect followed by an upgrading of their priority, have not in the period in question had much western machinery allocated to them.

It looks as though Soviet policy in the period 1955-72 was to concentrate hard-currency expenditure on western machinery for certain previously neglected branches in which problems of 'catching-up' were particularly acute and could not be resolved by other means. Shipping, the chemical industry, and the motor industry are the outstanding examples. Does it follow from this that the pattern of machinery imports for a particular branch tends to be markedly bunched in time, reflecting a once-for-all burst of catching-up rather than a continuing dependence on western supplies? A consideration of year-to-year changes over the period 1955-73 in imports for the MBMW, shipping, chemical, food and light industries does not support an expectation of short, once-for-all bursts of catching-up, at any rate for these fairly wide import categories. All of them fluctuated considerably but tended to increase over the period as a whole.

In none of these cases is there a clear once-for-all rise and fall in imports of western machinery within this period. Ships and marine equipment perhaps come nearest to such a pattern, and this is consistent with the very rapid early expansion of Soviet shipping, followed by slower growth in the fleet. It is also consistent with the assimilation, as opposed to mere acquisition, by the USSR, Poland and East Germany of advanced Western technology in ship-building and the manufacture of marine diesel engines. In the other cases, the process of negotiable technology transfer from the West seems to be of a long-term character.

Do these industries which show a *prima facie* 'relatively high dependence' on imported western machinery tend to exhibit particularly rapid technical progress in the period since the mid-1950s? Estimates of rates of technical change are, as was mentioned above, controversial; the best known to me for branches of Soviet industry in the period in question are those by Desai for 1955-71, for seven branches only.[25] She concludes that the chemical industry, machine-building and metalworking, building materials, and (subject to some doubt) food-processing appeared to be 'highly progressive' in this period, with the chemical industry outstanding; she found iron and steel, electricity supply, and light industry to be only 'mildly progressive'. The association of these results with the 'import dependence' of Table 2.2 is by no means clear, except that the outstanding major example of a branch acquiring relatively large amounts of western machinery, the chemical industry, is also the branch exhibiting the most rapid technical change in Miss Desai's estimates. This is suggestive, but to carry the argument further one would need to isolate and quantify the influence of negotiable transfer on branch rates of technical progress.

What can be concluded from this review of machinery trade is that there are large parts of the Soviet economy whose growth since the mid-fifties has not shown much obvious dependence on the import of western machinery. How are we to interpret this? The answer no doubt varies between branches. In armaments production the Soviet need for a secure indigenous production base and the western strategic embargo would seem obvious explanations. In some civilian areas Soviet technology may be broadly on a par with that of leading western producers and only relatively small injections of embodied western technology (like circuit breakers for high voltage transmission) may have sufficed to prevent the emergence of a substantial lag of Soviet behind western technical levels. Elsewhere, non-negotiable forms of technology transfer, such as prototype copying, espionage, and the screening of technical literature may suffice to produce results satisfactory to Soviet policy makers. In all branches indigenous research, development, and design work is important to technical progress even if its main role is to adapt foreign technology; in some branches there may have been, in addition, a deliberate choice of indigenous development over technology transfer of any kind.[26]

Soviet licence and know-how purchases from the West do not seem to be systematically reported in either East or West. A Soviet source states 'in the past eight years' (between 1965 and the end of 1973?) forty new processes and eighty new products were assimilated into Soviet production on the basis of licences purchased abroad. How this relates to the number of licensing agreements is not clear. Presumably, the few agreements made substantially before Soviet accession to the Paris Convention may be excluded. One of these is the 1959 Burmeister og Wain marine diesel engine licensing agreement, discussed at length by Sutton and constituting the standard approved success story to be trotted out in the Soviet literature. Later agreements which have not yet led to 'assimilation' may not be included. Indeed the same Soviet source gives an instance of failure to utilise a licence agreement within the contract period because of construction delays (blamed on Minavtoprom) affecting the start of production under the licence. The licence purchase in question was for production of disc brakes.[27]

Piecemeal evidence from press reports suggests a concentration of Soviet licence and know-how purchases in the chemical and motor industries (the latter extending into related metalworking technologies). These purchases are generally associated with the buying of related machinery. Their values tend to be carefully buried within the totals for large contracts, especially turn-key projects, and are probably largely included in the values of machinery sales. Information on their branch distribution and total value would probably not alter the conclusions reached above on the basis of machinery trade alone.

CONCLUSIONS

The review of Soviet public discussion suggested that great and increasing importance has been attributed by Soviet policy makers over the past decade and a half to technology transfer from the West. The general impression is one of a dawning feeling that 'catching-up' was harder than it had seemed in the late fifties, and that the Soviet Union was losing out by staying so much on the sidelines of technological exchange among developed nations.

The review of what has actually been happening since the mid-fifties, on the other hand, tended to suggest that the kind of technology transfer that is relevant to *détente* has been of limited importance in Soviet economic growth.

There need of course be no contradiction in this: Soviet policy makers have come to believe that the situation should change and that negotiable technology transfer from the West should be increased. No doubt it can be increased, and the Soviet-US *détente* may assist such an increase substantially. The effects of *détente* can already be seen in the large increases in Soviet imports of western machinery in 1972 and 1973 and especially in the enhanced share of the United States as a supplier: from a mere 1 or 2 per cent of the total in the mid-sixties to about 13 per cent in 1973. To the extent that large Soviet-US co-operation deals are actually implemented, *détente* may loosen the hard-currency constraints on

Soviet import of western technology to a very considerable degree. Large and long-term improvements in the Soviet terms of trade might prove to be even more important.

It could be, however, that the limits imposed by difference of economic system on the scale of negotiable technology transfer from the West may still prove to be severe. Even if the inconvertibility of the rouble and the Soviet shortage of convertible currencies became less of an obstacle, there would still be the problem of the barriers to the movements of people in and out of the USSR and of equity capital into it. True, there is the experience of Japan in rapidly absorbing US and West European technology while largely excluding (until recently) direct foreign investment from its territory; the ultimate question then arises of the capacity of the Soviet economic system to absorb foreign technology more rapidly and to procure indigenous innovation on a scale commensurate with the size of its economy. Systemic defects in innovation apart, invention itself — as well as international diffusion — often benefits from extensive personal contacts across international boundaries.[28]

The view taken above, however, about the limited role of negotiable technology transfer in recent Soviet growth, and therefore the doubts expressed about its future potential, should perhaps be qualified. Soviet policy makers have not been concerned exclusively with GNP or net material product growth figures as an end in themselves, but also with the composition of output. Growth figures could be propped up by an ever-increasing production of faulty tractors or short-lived standard machine tools, but Soviet policy has to some extent aimed at correcting past structural neglect including neglect of the consumer sector. The use of western machinery to expand and modernise the chemical and motor industries, in its effect on the composition and quality of output, may be important in ways not fully measured by aggregate output changes valued in established prices.

There is a hint, too, of a possible 'systemic comparative advantage' developing in some of the East-West trade we have been considering. The Soviet system tends to favour large-scale production units in engineering industries, suited to long production runs of relatively standardised products. This is the case, for instance, in the Soviet machine tool industry.

The system tends to neglect the development of efficient small and medium-sized engineering plants (outside the military sector, at least) producing more specialised machinery on a once-off or small-batch basis. Yet production units of the first type often require precisely the kinds of specialised machines produced by units of the second type (e.g. special purpose machine tools for a giant car-making complex such as Tolyatti). There is a systemic basis here for trade, at least in one direction — in both directions if the products of Soviet standardised large-scale plants can be marketed in the West.

I conclude, then, with no firm views about the future development of East-West economic interdependence but with at least some grounds for expecting it to increase, so far as Soviet interests are concerned. Whether the Soviet policy makers' interest in acquiring western high technology is fundamentally wise, is a question I have not asked. If one believes, with E. F. Schumacher, that in the world as a whole further technological advance on present lines is merely 'optimising the arrangement of deck-chairs on the Titanic', an increase in Soviet borrowing of western high technology simply compounds the catastrophe to come and is hardly worth the attention given it here.

Similar views have been expressed within the Soviet Union. In his *Letter to Soviet Leaders,* Solzhenitsyn pointed out that Russia's westernisers were, as usual, out of date in their pursuit of western fashions; they were still hot on the trail of high technology when the most advanced western thinkers had begun to denounce it as destructive. Russia should turn instead to its Siberian back garden and cultivate it with what a westerner would call alternative technology. The gap between 'advanced thinkers' and public policy, however, is a wide one everywhere, and this may well be a good thing for public policy.

NOTES

1 Research support by the Social Science Research Council and research assistance by Mr Iancu Spigler are gratefully acknowledged. A number of people made helpful comments on earlier drafts, and I would particularly like to thank Carl McMillan, Paul Marer and Hugo Radice. I am also indebted at several points in this essay to the ideas of Stanislaw Gomulka.

2 Robert Conquest and others, '*Détente:* An Evaluation', *Survey* (Spring-Summer 1974) p. 10.

3 The most extensive recent study of the post Second World War period is by A. C. Sutton, in the third volume of his polemical but informative study of Soviet acquisition of western technology, *Western Technology and Soviet Economic Development 1945-1965* (Standford: Hoover Institution Press, 1973). A number of studies are under way at the University of Birmingham of comparative Soviet-western technology levels in particular fields. The results so far seem to support the view that the USSR lags considerably behind the West in computer, control and instrumentation equipment, chemicals and some machine-tool technologies, but not in high-voltage power transmission.

4 *International Economic Report of the President* (Washington, 1974).

5 See J. M. Cooper, 'The Concept of the Scientific-Technical Revolution in Soviet Theory', Centre for Russian and East European Studies Discussion Paper, University of Birmingham (1973), and R. Amann, 'The Soviet Research and Development System', *Minerva* (Apr 1970).

6 Nearly all the analysis of Congressional speeches was carried out for me by Hugh Jenkins, for whose assistance I am most grateful. The translations used in the passages cited in the text are partly his and partly my own.

7 *XXII S"ezd KPSS, stenograficheskii otchet*, vol. 1 (Moscow, 1961) p. 63.

8 *XXIII S"ezd KPSS, stenograficheskii otchet*, vol. 2 (Moscow, 1966) pp. 60-1, 62. The reference is presumably to patent and licence trade with the West since free exchange of technical information was still practised in CMEA in 1966. The system of free exchange was beginning to break down by 1966 and apparently East Germany had already begun to insist on payments for licences but this was still the exception within CMEA. See Robert Campbell, 'Technology Transfer Among Communist Countries', *ASTE Bulletin* (Winter 1969).

9 The quotation is from M. Maksimova in *Mirovaya ekonomika i mezhdunarodnye otnosheniya*, no. 4 (1974) p. 15. Virtually the same statement is made by O. Bogomolov in *Kommunist*, no. 5 (1974) p. 89. Brezhnev himself makes the same point in his speech on 26 October 1973 to the World Congress of Peace-Loving Forces in Moscow.

10 M. L. Gorodissky, *Litsenzii vo vneshnei torgovle SSSR* (Moscow, 1972) pp. 135 (establishment of Litsenzingorg), 144 (Soviet accession to the Paris Convention; the imputation of motives is my own), 183 (planning of licence acquisition and use).

11 The IMEMO projection of world licence trade is cited by Maksimova, op. cit., p. 17. It is not clear whether the projection is of licence trade between western countries alone or between all countries. The analogy between western transnationals and the

Comecon international associations is made by Yu. Shiryaev in *Planovoe Khozyaistvo*, no. 4 (1974) pp. 35-6. Japanese experience is cited by S. A. Kheinman in A. I. Notkin (eds), *Faktory ekonomicheskogo razvitiya SSSR* (Moscow, 1970) p. 57, and at some length by N. Smelyakov, a deputy minister of foreign trade with special responsibility for machinery trade, in his fascinating article, 'Delovye vstrechi', *Novyi Mir*, no. 12 (1973) pp. 228-9.

12 Sutton, op. cit., p.205.

13 Sutton, op. cit., gives numerous examples of Soviet prototype copying. He argues that there has been a systematic Soviet practice of buying from the West large numbers of single items 'almost certainly for design purposes'. As an example he gives (p. 57) a list of twenty-three purchases of single items of machinery from the United States in the third quarter of 1960. If Sutton is right in his interpretation of these purchases, this is an illustration of a form of non-negotiable transfer at a time when the sort of negotiable technology transfer exemplified by the major US contribution to the Kama River truck complex, now under construction, would have been ruled out by US policy. Purchases of small total value, of the kind made in 1960, would be feasible in any situation short of total embargo and in that sense non-negotiable.

14 S. Gomulka, in his *Inventive Activity, Diffusion and the Stages of Economic Growth* (Aarhus, 1971) argues that the overall rate of technical progress of a country absorbing technology from another, more advanced country, will be produced by the joint impact of its own indigenous technical change and of technology transfer from abroad, but that in a middle-level industrialised economy the latter will be the dominant influence and aggregate technical change will tend to approach the rate which would be generated by diffusion from abroad alone. This convergence of the growth rates of overall technical progress and of diffusion from abroad will only occur, however, when the latter, by growing faster than indigenous innovation, has acquired an overwhelming weight in the determination of the economy's rate of technical progress. We cannot say, *a priori*, for the Soviet Union or any other 'middle-level' country, whether diffusion from abroad actually has at any given time an overwhelming role in technical change. The problem of identifying and measuring indigenous innovation and diffusion from abroad remains.

15 Gomulka, op. cit., p. 58, provides an experimental estimate of the growth of the 'effective research' output of the Soviet technology sector, 1926-66, of 3.8 per cent, which he contrasts with a labour productivity growth of 5-6 per cent. On his view, though, the difference would not amount to an estimate of the role of technology transfer. So far as expenditure directed towards technical change is concerned (in current prices), negotiable technology transfer, in the form of imports of Western machinery, and Soviet domestic spending on research, development, testing and evaluation (using the Stanford Research Institute estimates of

F. W. Dresch, W. T. Lee, M. M. Earle *et. al.*) have been growing at very similar rates. The trend rate of growth of the former from 1955 through 1972 was 14.1 per cent p.a. (see text). The average annual growth rate of the latter from 1955 to 1970 was 14.6 per cent.

16 The statistics in OECD, *Gaps in Technology, Comparisons between Member Countries* (Paris, 1970), and the case-studies in J. Jewkes, D. Sawers and R. Stillerman, *The Sources of Invention*, 2nd ed. (London, 1969), bring out this interdependence clearly. Mark S. Massell, 'The International Patent System', *Journal of Economic Issues*, no. 4 (1973) p. 646, notes that the percentage of US patents granted to non-residents rose from seventeen in 1961 to twenty-nine in 1971. The overall US dominance of international know-how trade is however beyond dispute. The chapter by J. H. Dunning in C. P. Kindleberger (ed.), *The International Corporation* (Cambridge, Mass, 1970) contains interesting evidence for the view that US subsidiaries in Europe contributed significantly to West European technical change and thus economic growth in the 1950s.

17 The data used for calculating the US import share in domestic equipment investment are from Department of Commerce, *Survey of Current Business* (Feb 1973) pp. S-2 (New plant and equipment expenditure, 1971, all industries) and S-23 (SITC 7 imports, 1970). Passenger cars were subtracted from the latter.

18 In 1963-4, in intra-OECD trade, equivalent to about 3.5 per cent of machinery trade, on the basis of data in OECD, op. cit., pp. 201, 277. This proportion has been tending to increase.

19 This formulation follows the approach used by S. Gomulka in some recent econometric work on technology transfer. S. Gomulka, 'Import of Capital Goods, Technical Change and the Rate of Development; A Generalised Capital-Vintage Model', paper delivered to the Oslo Econometric Meeting (Aug 1973), and S. Gomulka and J. D. Sylwestrowicz, 'Intercountry Embodied Diffusion and the Time Changes in the Factor Productivity Residual', paper presented to the Reisenburg Symposium (1974).

20 For a full description of the regression analysis and the other coefficients estimated see Appendix A of the University of Birmingham Centre for Russian and East European Studies Discussion Paper RC/B no. 7, which is a fuller version of the present essay.

21 A recent tentative western estimate of concealed inflation in Soviet official machinery price indexes suggests that this statement should be slightly modified. A. S. Becker, 'The Price Level of Soviet Machinery in the 1960's', *Soviet Studies* (July 1974), suggests that an approximate 25 per cent increase occurred in industry wholesale prices of machinery between 1958 and 1970. If we accept this provisional but well-documented assessment, the import share figure (column F) for 1970 becomes 2.1. The most plausible picture of the change in the 'true' share would then be from about

2 per cent in the mid-1950s to about 4 per cent in 1970. This should perhaps be described as a perceptible, though not substantial, increase.

22 M. R. Hill, 'Aspects of Quality Control Regulation in the USSR', mimeo (Loughborough, 1973).

23 W. G. Allinson, 'High Voltage Power Transmission in USSR', manuscript (Birmingham, 1974) p. 12, states that imports of high-voltage air-blast circuit breakers from France in 1957 may have been of critical importance to the Soviet move to 500 kV power transmission.

24 A detailed description of KamAZ contracts signed with western firms by the end of 1973, totalling almost $900 m. and occupying fourteen pages, is in Chase World Information Corp., *KamAZ the Billion Dollar Beginning* (New York, 1974) pp. 7-21.

25 P. Desai, 'Technical Change, Factor Elasticity of Substitution and Returns to Scale in Branches of Soviet Industry in the Postwar Period', mimeo (1974).

26 R. Amann, 'The Soviet Chemical Industry: Its Level of Modernity and Sophistication', CREES Discussion Paper, RC/C 11 (Birmingham, 1974), gives examples, however, of Soviet indigenous R & D which has got stuck at the pilot plant stage and then been succeeded by the import of foreign technology to achieve the end originally aimed at.

27 *Pravda*, 12 Mar 1974.

28 The case-studies of major twentieth-century inventions in Jewkes, Sawers and Stillerman, op. cit., provide several examples.

3 Foreign and Defence Policy

DAVID HOLLOWAY

The judgement which Khrushchev's successors pronounced on his foreign and defence policy was not essentially different from their assessment of his leadership in other fields. His 'voluntaristic and unrealistic approach to the phenomena and events of international life' was attacked for 'giving rise either to smug overconfidence or to weakness in the face of the military threat from imperialism'.[1] The military leaders denounced subjectivism in defence policy and called for greater attention to military advice and recommendations.[2] It was not the general objectives of Khrushchev's policies that were disputed, but the manner in which they were pursued. He was seen to be moving too precipitately towards better relations with the Federal Republic of Germany, and with unnecessary haste towards a complete break with China. His impending visit to Bonn was cancelled, and the tone of Soviet policy towards China was changed in an unsuccessful attempt to improve relations. The new leaders endorsed the policy of *détente* with the United States, but evidently felt that this did not lessen the need for military strength. Khrushchev's attempts to exploit Soviet military power for political ends — as for example in Cuba and Berlin — were condemned as adventuristic. The verdict on Khrushchev was that he had been guilty of the solecism of power: he had pursued ends he had not the means to attain.

1964 did not mark a sharp break in policy. The military build-up of the late 1960s derived very largely from decisions taken under Khrushchev. There was no major change in the strategic doctrine he had announced in January 1960, assigning the primary role in Soviet defence policy to the Strategic Missile Forces. It was in 1963, in the aftermath of the Cuban missile crisis, that the movement towards *détente* began and the first important arms control agreement was reached, with the signing of the Partial Test-Ban Treaty. The new leaders retained the same policy objectives and defined them in the same way: maintaining Soviet domination in East Europe, achieving a postwar settlement in Europe, avoiding war with the West while restraining western military power, containing Chinese influence, asserting Soviet authority in the world Communist movement, raising Soviet influence in the developing countries. This continuity is not surprising. The removal of Khrushchev from office was not accompanied by a purge. Replacement of those in charge of foreign and defence policy has been a gradual and slow process, with the passage of time the main agency of change.[3]

It is paradoxical that, in spite of this continuity, Soviet policy has, by the slow accretion of change, contributed to major shifts in international politics. The Soviet Union has attained strategic parity with the United States, and on that basis has entered into negotiations to halt the arms race. *Détente* has deepened so that relations between East and West are much more relaxed than in the early 1960s. Many of the outstanding issues of postwar Europe — most notably the German question — have been settled by treaty. The Soviet Union has reached a whole series of agreements with the western powers on military and economic matters, and trade and technology have assumed a much larger place in East-West relations. An era of negotiation has certainly begun, even if its outcome is by no means clear.

If under Khrushchev Soviet policy was marked by an imbalance in which foreign policy outreached military power, it now appears to many that a new imbalance has been created in which the strengthening of military power is out of key with the peaceful intentions proclaimed by the Soviet leaders. Soviet policy shares the ambiguity of East-West relations as a whole, for there now exists a clear disjunction between *détente* and the continuing arms race. It must be asked what contribution Soviet policy makes to this state of affairs and to the possibility of moving away from it. It will not be possible in this chapter to review the whole range of Soviet foreign and defence policy, or to look in detail at its domestic sources. I have tried to provide a broad survey of Soviet defence policy and of Soviet relations with East and West Europe, the United States and China in order to arrive at a clearer understanding of *détente* and of the Soviet conception of it.

DEFENCE POLICY

The strengthening of military power over the last ten years provides an essential backdrop to Soviet foreign policy. The Soviet Union has used armed force directly in Czechoslovakia and on the border with China, and military power has been used to further Soviet policies in various indirect ways, for example through military aid and presence in the Middle East. The defence policy of the present leaders appears to result not from any grand design, but from decisions taken before 1964 and from attempts to respond to military complaints about Khrushchev's policies. Khrushchev had sought to reduce defence expenditure by cutting conventional forces; and although he assigned to the Strategic Missile Forces the chief place in Soviet defence policy, he seemed at times to favour a strategy of 'minimum deterrence', whereby the Soviet Union would possess just enough missiles to be able to strike the United States if attacked first. Khrushchev's policies met with opposition from important elements in the armed forces who argued that they made it impossible for the Soviet Union to use military power flexibly.[4]

There seems to have been general agreement among the new leaders that numerical inferiority in strategic missiles was disadvantageous on both military and political grounds. Minimum deterrence was rejected, and it is possible that the new leaders took steps to speed up, or extend, the missile programmes. Nevertheless, the increase in missile numbers, which began in 1965, must have been based largely on decisions taken before 1964. In the last ten years the Soviet Union has moved from a five-to-one inferiority in ICBM's (intercontinental ballistic missiles) and SLBM's (submarine-launched ballistic missiles) to a lead of about 500 over the United States (see Table 3.1). By 1969 the Soviet leaders claimed parity with the United States and it was on this basis that the strategic arms limitations talks (SALT) began. By 1971 the Soviet ICBM build-up was largely complete, and

TABLE 3.1 US and USSR strategic nuclear forces 1965-74

	1965	1966	1967	1968	1969	1970	1971	1972	1973	1974
Strategic bombers										
USA	738	708	697	646	581	517	565	525	496	496
USSR	155	155	155	150	140	140	140	140	140	140
SLBM's										
USA	464	592	656	656	656	656	656	656	656	656
USSR	–	–	–	32	128	224	336	444	564	636
ICBM's										
USA	854	934	1054	1054	1054	1054	1054	1054	1054	1054
USSR	262	338	722	902	1198	1498	1527	1527	1547	1567
Independently-targetable nuclear warheads on missiles (estimated actual total)										
USA	1318	1526	1710	1710	1710	1874	3082	4146	5210	5966
USSR	262	338	722	934	1326	1722	1863	1971	2111	2203

Source: SIPRI Yearbook 1974 (Stockholm and London 1974), pp.106-7.

attention was focused on qualitative improvements in the ICBM and SLBM arsenal. Since the late 1960s the United States has concentrated on the deployment of multiple warheads on its strategic missiles and now has a three-to-one lead in this area. The Soviet Union, which began to test new ICBMs and a new SLBM in 1973, is trying to close this gap as it did the gap in missiles.[5]

The Soviet lead in missiles was codified in the Interim Agreement on Offensive Missiles which was signed by Brezhnev and Nixon in May 1972. This is to be followed by a new agreement to last until 1985, the guidelines for which were decided in November 1974 at the summit meeting in Vladivostok. This will allow the Soviet Union and the United States 2400 strategic delivery vehicles (missiles and bombers) apiece, and 1320 of the missiles may be armed with MIRV's (multiple independently-targetable re-entry vehicles). This agreement does not halt the arms race and seems to have been designed precisely to accommodate procurement programmes now in hand in the Soviet Union and the United States. There is little consensus on the relevant calculus for assessing the strategic balance. Neither side is now capable of delivering a 'disarming strike' against the other: 'rough parity' remains the best description of the present situation. But the Vladivostok agreement holds out the possibility that the Soviet Union, through a combination of MIRV's and throw-weight, and the United States, through a combination of MIRV's and missile accuracy, will acquire the capacity to destroy all the other's ICBM's in a single strike. Missile-carrying submarines are still immune from detection, although both sides are working strenuously to develop effective anti-submarine warfare techniques.

The Soviet strategic build-up was accompanied by a debate about nuclear strategy, although it is not clear whether this served as a guide to policy rather than a rationale for it. Soviet military doctrine has never accepted the deterrent balance as a foolproof device for preventing war or as a guide to force planning. Soviet doctrine has always taken account of the possibility that deterrence might fail and war break out. Consequently force structure has been based on the need to wage war should deterrence fail. Within this context numerical inferiority in strategic forces is disadvantageous, even where a relationship of mutual assured destruction exists; moreover, superiority short of a 'disarming strike' is desirable in so far as it will help to limit the damage to the Soviet Union.[6]

The pursuit of a more flexible military force, which could wage war as well as deter it, has embraced all aspects of the armed forces, and can be seen in the reassertion of the role of the ground forces and in the extended deployment of the navy. In September 1964 the Ground Forces Command was disbanded and the ground forces put under the direct command of the Ministry of Defence. In 1967 the command was reinstated and the possibility of a non-nuclear campaign in Europe accepted. The first test of the new command came in 1968 with the invasion of Czechoslovakia. This left four divisions in its wake, thus raising the number of Soviet divisions in East Europe by four to thirty-one, a level which has not since been reduced. Along the frontier with China the number of divisions has grown from fifteen to forty-five since 1967. The deployment of the ground forces has changed greatly over the last ten years, and the doubts about their role have vanished.[7]

The emphasis on the role of the ground forces has led to a shift in the military balance in Central Europe where the Warsaw Pact now has more forces than NATO, while reinforcements could probably be brought more easily from the Soviet Union than from the United States. The level of Soviet forces has prompted many to question the Soviet policy of *détente* and to ascribe an offensive military purpose to Soviet policy in Europe. The significance of Soviet force levels is, however, not as clear-cut as some critics of Soviet policy suggest. The comparison of military strengths is a notoriously complex exercise, which leaves a wide margin of uncertainty.[8] Besides, Soviet forces in East Europe have not only a strategic role *vis-à-vis* NATO, but also, as the invasion of Czechoslovakia shows, a police role in the area itself. Furthermore, Soviet doctrine assigns an offensive role to its forces in Europe in the event of a general war, but it does not follow from this that the Soviet Union wishes to start such a war, even though its forces are prepared for offensive operations. The emphasis on waging as well as deterring war means that superiority of any kind matters. At the negotiations on mutual force reductions in Central Europe the Warsaw Pact powers have pressed for the same percentage reductions on either side, which would preserve for them the numerical advantage they now enjoy. All this suggests an ambiguous rather than an offensive policy.

The Soviet Navy has also acquired a new pattern of deployment in the last ten years, and the Soviet Union now has a naval presence in the Mediterranean Sea and the Indian Ocean where its ships were not regularly to be found ten years ago. The development of the Soviet Navy in this period is marked not by an increase in size, but by this extended deployment, and also by a notable improvement in the design and armament of the latest ships. The shift to a new pattern of deployment has been a lengthy process, involving the acquisition of many new naval skills. The reasons for the new deployment are much disputed in the West, the central issue being whether it has been undertaken in order to counter western naval power or to implement an aggressive inter-ventionist foreign policy. If taken in the context of Soviet policy as a whole it seems most plausible to interpret the extended deployment as an attempt to counter the Western sea-borne nuclear force (aircraft carriers and Polaris) and to inhibit the West from using naval power in a limited way to pursue political ends. This is not to say that the Soviet Navy might not be used offensively, for example to interdict sea lanes, but this does not appear to have been the primary purpose of the new deployment. Moreover, offensive action against NATO ships would create a very high risk of general war. [9]

The dynamism of Soviet policy is evident, but its dynamic, its moving force, is not. Debates about military doctrine are not by themselves the key to policy, for doctrine does not appear to provide the criteria for decisions about force structure. There was, for example, apparent disagreement about the goals of the missile build-up: it was not clear whether superiority rather than parity was being pursued, and different kinds of superiority were advocated in the military press. Nor can Soviet policy be seen simply as the outcome of a close interaction with NATO policy. Inter-action of some kind obviously exists, but the evidence points to a persistent search for destinctive policies, as for example in deterrence and strategic weapons. Moreover, the armed forces and the defence industries are important components of the domestic political scene, and institutional and bureaucratic factors play a major role in determining the level of defence effort and the kind of policy pursued. The military debates reflect fairly clearly the desire of the different elements in the armed forces to secure their own position. The search for flexibility, for example, was not only a matter of military doctrine, but also a way of accommodating competing military interests.[10]

Soviet policy proposes a demilitarisation of the East-West conflict and a transition to peaceful coexistence under which the military confrontation would be ended and the conflict conducted on economic, political and ideological grounds. At the XXIV Party Congress Brezhnev outlined a peace programme which called for nuclear disarmament, the elimination of military trouble spots in South-East Asia and the Middle East, recognition of the territorial *status quo* and a move towards collective security in Europe, an end to the arms race and a reduction of the risk of war, an end to colonialism, and international co-operation in environmental and other areas.[11] But there are many Soviet statements about Soviet policy which do not indicate any awareness of a contradiction between high levels of military effort and the pursuit of *détente*. It has been argued in the military press, for example, that military strength is an essential ingredient in Soviet policy and contributes to its successes:

> there is no doubt that all the other factors of the struggle for peace would not have played their role if the powerful armed forces of the socialist countries had not existed, in the first place the Soviet Army and Navy. Consequently the special political role of the socialist armies, and in particular of the Soviet Armed Forces consists in the fact that they are an effective factor in the struggle to prevent world war. They exert their influence on the course of social progress firstly as a force which, together with the fraternal armies, reliably protects the socialist commonwealth and limits the actions of the imperialists in other regions of the globe. Secondly, the Soviet Army and Navy are a direct active force if the imperialists should attempt

to attain their aggressive goals in the struggle against
socialism . . . The struggle for international security comprises both peaceful initiatives and simultaneously the
strengthening of the economic and military might of the
Soviet Union.[12]

The relaxation of international tension is not thought to have
made military power redundant. Indeed, the growth of Soviet
power is presented as an essential element in *détente,* for it
makes it impossible for the West to deal with the Soviet
Union from a position of strength and forces the western
powers to base their relations with the Soviet Union on the
principles of equal security and peaceful coexistence. The
primary function of Soviet military power has thus been to
neutralise western military power and render it politically
ineffectual. The Soviet Union has not moved to an adventuristic foreign policy; military power is seen to provide its
own reward.[13]

It must be asked, in the light of this, what *détente* actually
means in military terms. Arms control is seen by its advocates
as a way of linking the relaxation of international tension to
a reduction of military forces on either side. This, however,
has not happened; arms control negotiations have not been
successful in reducing force levels or even limiting arms
procurement. The most notable achievement has been the
Anti-Ballistic Missile Treaty, signed in 1972, which limits the
deployment of ABM systems in the United States and the
Soviet Union. Important though this treaty is, partial steps of
this kind have had the effect not of slowing down the arms
race but of rechannelling it.[14] The technical complexity of
deciding on balanced reductions allows ample scope for the
domestic opponents of arms reduction to make their opposition felt, and in the wake of the Cold War these opponents
are very powerful. High levels of military force are justified in
terms of their political influence — as, for example, in the
Soviet arguments quoted in the last paragraph. It is, however,
extremely difficult to test these claims to political influence
against the realities of international relations.

Arms control negotiations have been more successful in
seeking to reduce the risk of accidental or inadvertent war,
for example through the 'Hot Line' Agreement, the Nuclear

Accidents Agreement, the Agreement on the Prevention of Incidents on and over the High Seas, and the Agreement on the Prevention of Nuclear War.[15] Although many people have an interest in the production and procurement of nuclear weapons, it is clearly not in anyone's interest to have a nuclear war. In spite of the emphasis on war-waging in Soviet military doctrine, it is difficult not to believe in the sincerity of Soviet efforts to prevent nuclear war with the United States. Thus in the military sphere *détente* has led to an institutionalised dialogue between the Soviet Union and the United States which helps to regulate their strategic relationship but has not halted the arms race.

THE WARSAW PACT AND EAST EUROPE

In the last ten years Soviet policy has achieved several of its major aims in East Europe. The existing frontiers have been accepted and the German Democratic Republic has gained international recognition. The Soviet Union has faced and weathered severe crises in Czechoslovakia in 1968 and in Poland in 1970, and consolidated its position as the dominant power in the area. Several of the East European countries have carried through major economic reforms without precipitating the fundamental political change that many had anticipated. Limited diversity has thus been possible in East Europe without undermining the Soviet position. The Soviet Union has made various concessions, for example on the status of West Berlin and the independence of Rumanian foreign policy. In general, however, Soviet policy has been more successful than might have appeared likely in 1964.

There seem to be three main reasons for the Soviet concern to maintain domination in East Europe: the defence arrangements in the area are an integral part of the Soviet defence system; control of East Europe helps to prevent the emergence of a powerful united Germany which might rival or challenge the Soviet Union; the societies of East Europe must not be allowed to regress on the path of socialist development. These three motives are interrelated. The military arrangements in East Europe are determined not only by Soviet policy towards NATO, but also by Soviet interests and aims in East Europe itself. The Soviet motives for invading Czechoslovakia were no doubt complex, but among them were the desire to maintain the party's monopoly of power in Czechoslovakia and also the determination to prevent Soviet defence arrangements from being undermined. The crucial point is that it is impossible to separate the two motives, for a Czechoslovakia in which the party has lost its 'leading and directing role' would be seen as a weak link in the chain of Soviet defence.

The Soviet Union maintains its domination through a complicated structure of multilateral and bilateral relationships. The two most important international agencies of control and co-ordination are the Warsaw Pact and the Council for Mutual Economic Assistance (CMEA). The military organisation and policy of the Pact are decided in Moscow: the Joint Command is dominated by Soviet officers, and there is no Pact military doctrine distinct from Soviet doctrine. The Warsaw Pact is seen in the Soviet Union not only as a military-political alliance of sovereign states, which is how it is presented in the treaty, but also as an instrument of socialist consolidation: it derives its substance as much from the social systems of its members as from the purposes and obligations set out in the treaty. As Soviet interests in East Europe have been threatened the Soviet Union has resorted to this latter interpretation of its military arrangements in order to justify intervention. This is to be seen most clearly in the Brezhnev doctrine which was used to vindicate the occupation of Czechoslovakia. This declared that the socialist states could not 'remain inactive in the name of some abstract idea of sovereignty when they saw how the country [Czechoslovakia] was exposed to the danger of anti-socialist degeneration.'[16]

The Pact, although it is the most disciplined instrument of Soviet domination, is not of course designed solely for that purpose. In the last ten years the Soviet Union has attempted to strengthen the Pact as an instrument of policy *vis-à-vis* NATO by raising force levels and modernising equipment. In 1969 the military structure of the Pact was reformed. A committee of Defence Ministers was set up to advise the Political Consultative Committee, and a Military Council of the Joint Command was created, which is akin to the Military

Council of a Soviet Military District. The importance of this reform lies in the fact that the non-Soviet defence ministers are no longer subordinate to the commander-in-chief of the Pact (who is himself a Soviet first deputy minister) but constitute, together with the Soviet minister, the highest military body in the alliance. The non-Soviet contingents assigned to the Pact are commanded by deputy defence ministers who are also deputy commanders-in-chief of the Pact. These changes have made it possible to streamline the Joint Command by giving better training and equipment to the assigned troops. At the same time they have made several concessions to the national susceptibilities of the Pact's non-Soviet members, although these are largely symbolic.[17] The Soviet Union remains firmly in control. In the event of war the Soviet High Command would take over the Pact's forces; the occupation of Czechoslovakia was commanded by the commander-in-chief not of the Pact but of the Soviet ground forces.

In the co-ordination of economic and foreign policy Soviet control has been less tight. The new leaders had to accept the failure of Khrushchev's ambitious schemes for multilateral economic integration, and to accommodate different national aspirations in their policy towards the West. Nevertheless, economic integration and the co-ordination of foreign policy have retained their high priority. The most important single step within CMEA has been the long-term programme of co-operation and integration adopted in July 1971.[18] Although vague in parts, this embodies an ambitious policy of integration. But the Soviet Union has to take more account of national interests in economic than in defence policy, and this makes piecemeal and bilateral approaches more appropriate than grand designs, even though some multilateral arrangements are required to facilitate bilateral links. In the co-ordination of foreign policy the Political Consultative Committee (PCC) of the Warsaw Pact has come to play a crucial role. It has issued a series of major declarations and proposals on co-operation and security in Europe. It has also provided a forum in which differences between Pact members can be discussed and settled; the number of meetings has increased greatly in the last ten years. There is much more real debate and consultation here than on the military side of the alliance.

While Soviet troops may provide a 'safety net' under the regimes of East Europe it is clearly to the advantage of the Soviet Union to secure its domination in other ways than by military force. The occupation of Czechoslovakia, while it was very successful as a military operation, was evidence of political mismanagement. Besides, it did great harm to Soviet policy towards the West. Since 1968 Soviet policy has put more emphasis on close supervision of developments in East Europe. The Hungarian New Economic Mechanism, which is similar to the abortive Czechoslovak economic reform of 1966-9, has been watched carefully since it was introduced in 1968. When the political crisis erupted in Poland in December 1970 the Soviet leaders took the view that this was not fomented from outside, that the grievances of the workers were genuine and that their economic, if not their political demands ought to be met as far as possible.

There are limits to diversity, however, and these were set out in the Warsaw letter of 15 July 1968 from the five Communist and Workers' Parties to the Central Committee of Czechoslovak Communist Party.[19] Besides expressing fears about Czechoslovak foreign and defence policy the letter demanded that the party retain control of the mass media, that it remain united and avoid factional splits, and that it retain its monopoly of power. The ground rules for the leaders of East Europe thus appear to be: remain in the Warsaw Pact and ensure that the party retains its 'leading and directing role' in society. The Soviet Union has consolidated its position in East Europe: the territorial *status quo* has been recognised, and the Czechoslovak crisis belied the Soviet fear that political crisis in East Europe would prompt NATO military intervention. All this has made the process of *détente* easier; but there is no sign that *détente* will lead to any immediate relaxation of the limits on political development in East Europe.

WEST EUROPE

Soviet policy towards West Europe has passed through several distinct phases in the last ten years. Many of the objectives of that policy have however remained unchanged: preventing the emergence of a powerful West European military bloc; seeking recognition of the territorial *status quo*; gaining access to western trade and technology. The first major initiative of the new leadership was the 'Declaration on Strengthening Peace and Security in Europe', which was issued by the Political Consultative Committee of the Warsaw Pact in Bucharest in July 1966.[20] This called for a European Security Conference and for the creation of a collective security system in Europe. This has provided the framework for Soviet policy in Europe, and has proved flexible enough to accommodate more specific objectives — preventing West German possession of nuclear weapons or gaining acceptance of the invasion of Czechoslovakia, for example.

The Bucharest Declaration called for the dissolution of NATO and the Warsaw Pact in favour of a new European security system in which the two German states would play a part; a European Security Conference would initiate the transition to the new system. This policy had both defensive and offensive uses. It served as a way of countering the *Ostpolitik* of the Federal German Grand Coalition by demanding recognition of the GDR and existing frontiers as the basis for improved relations; the Soviet Union was not wholly successful in this, for early in 1967 Rumania broke rank and established diplomatic relations with the Federal Republic. The policy was used also to reduce the disruptive effects of United States efforts at 'bridge-building' with the East European countries. In a more offensive vein Soviet policy attempted to exploit West European resentment of United States economic and military power. De Gaulle's decision to withdraw from the military side of NATO in 1966 seemed to hold out the hope that anti-American sentiment in West Europe might help to dissolve NATO on its twentieth anniversary in 1969, and this hope was strengthened by European reaction to the Greek *coup d'état* and the war in Vietnam. The diplomatic offensive was intensified at the Conference of Communist and Workers' Parties in Karlovy Vary in April 1967. The Soviet Union attempted to portray itself as *the* European great power; it did not think that the United States or Canada should take part in the European Security Conference.[21]

The invasion of Czechoslovakia left this policy in ruins. It was not until the Budapest Appeal of the Political Consultative Committee in March 1969 that Soviet policy returned to the themes of *détente* and European security.[22] The invasion had confirmed many doubts about the Soviet conception of security. In trying to revive the momentum of its policy the Soviet Union now adopted more modest goals — for example, recognition of the territorial *status quo* rather than a transformation of the security system — and a more amenable attitude to United States and Canadian participation in the European Security Conference. In spite of these inauspicious circumstances, however, the Soviet Union has since 1969 achieved many of its major objectives in Europe. Treaties have been concluded between the Soviet Union, Poland and the German Democratic Republic on the one hand, and the Federal Republic of Germany on the other. These treaties recognise the territorial *status quo* and the existence of two German states, both of which became members of the United Nations in 1973. A four-power agreement has almost completely removed Berlin as a contentious issue in European politics. Economic and technological relations between East and West have grown closer. 1973 saw the opening of the Conference on Security and Co-operation in Europe (CSCE) and of negotiations on mutual force reductions (MFR) in Europe.

These changes have resulted not only from Soviet policy, but also from political developments in the West. The new SPD government, which took office in October 1969, pursued a more active and radical *Ostpolitik* and thus made possible the various treaties with the East European powers, while the Nixon administration's activist foreign policy helped to lay the basis for better Soviet-American relations. China was beginning to emerge from the diplomatic isolation induced by the Cultural Revolution, and it was soon clear that the Nixon administration would be willing, and able, to use its improved relations with China to counter offensive diplomacy on the part of the Soviet Union. The Soviet Union has not altered its policy in a fundamental way, but there have been important shifts of emphasis since 1969. Greater stress has been laid on economic and scientific-technical relations with the West, and on the political conditions which would make those relations possible. There is much less insistence on the dissolution of NATO and the Warsaw Pact and the transition to a new security system. Moreover,

American withdrawal from Europe seems to have lost its priority in Soviet policy.

The new emphases in Soviet policy which emerged in the years 1969-71 were influenced by factors other than the changes in the West. Western technology has always played an important part in Soviet economic development, but in the two years before the XXIV Party Congress — while the ninth Five-Year Plan was being drawn up — the decision seems to have been taken to make more vigorous efforts to acquire western capital and technology. Resource allocation has become more contentious since the draconian simplicities of Stalinist policy, and the priorities of the present leaders are more complex even than those of Khrushchev, for they have sought to raise the level of consumption without cutting defence expenditure (see Table 3.2). The events in Poland in December 1970 showed the political dangers of not raising living standards, and when it was finally adopted the Five-Year Plan promised for the first time a higher rate of growth for consumer goods industries than for producer goods industries. Although, as Hanson's chapter suggests, the evidence is ambiguous, it is not implausible to assume that the new emphasis on economic and technological co-operation with the West — whether translated into reality or not — was related to problems of Soviet economic policy.

The most important changes to have taken place are those which amount to a recognition of the political settlement that emerged in Europe after the Second World War, and to an acceptance of new institutions such as CMEA and the European Communities. There has undoubtedly been a reduction of tension in Central Europe, but the efforts to create new military and political relationships have not been very successful. In 1973 the CSCE and MFR talks opened. The former had been a Soviet objective since 1966, while NATO had proposed the latter in 1968. The NATO powers had argued that the Soviet proposal for a European Security Conference was inadequate because it did not include any specific military measures on the agenda: Europe's security problems would not be solved merely by a renunciation of the use of force and better economic and scientific-technical relations. In June 1968 NATO proposed to the Warsaw Pact that negotiations be held on mutual and balanced force

TABLE 3.2 Soviet defence expenditure

	Defence budget[a] (m. rubles)	SIPRI estimate[b] (m. rubles)
1964	13,300	17,300
1965	12,800	16,600
1966	13,400	17,400
1967	14,500	18,800
1968	16,700	21,700
1969	17,700	23,000
1970	17,900	23,300
1971	17,900	23,300
1972	17,900	23,300
1973	17,900	23,300
1974	17,650	

[a] *SIPRI Yearbook 1974* (Stockholm and London 1974), pp.210-11, and 1975 budget speech.

[b] Op. cit., p.191.

The Soviet Union publishes a figure for the defence budget each year, but most analysts agree that this does not represent total defence expenditure, since it does not include, for example, all outlays on military research and development. There is, however, no agreement on the way to estimate total expenditure. The ruble estimate given here is subject to a wide margin of error, and is probably lower than the average estimate made. Moreover, it is not altogether clear what the ruble figures mean, nor is it easy to translate them into dollars. Thus for 1973 SIPRI gives a dollar estimate of $63,000m., while IISS gives $87-91,000m.

(Cf.*SIPRI Yearbook 1974*, p. 200; *The Military Balance 1973-74*, p.9.)

reductions in Europe. The Soviet Union at first resisted this proposal on the grounds that it was intended only to divert attention from the Security Conference; besides, in the wake of the invasion of Czechoslovakia the proposal was embarass-ing to the Soviet Union. In 1971, however, the Soviet government declared its willingness to enter these talks, probably because it saw that there would be no CSCE without them and because, after the reorganisation of the Warsaw Pact, it realised that such negotiations need not be dis-advantageous. In the negotiations the Warsaw Pact powers are seeking a proportional reduction so that the numerical advantage they enjoy in Central Europe will not be des-troyed. They propose also that national ceilings rather than a common ceiling should be established; in this way a limit would be set to the growth of the armed forces of the Federal Republic of Germany.

By 1972 many of the contentious issues in the postwar settlement in Europe had been resolved and the process of normalising East-West relations completed; the centre of tension was now the Mediterranean rather than Central Europe. Most of the original Soviet objectives in calling for a European Security Conference had been achieved. Indeed the Conference has been embarrassing for the Soviet leaders in so far as they have come under pressure to grant greater civil rights to their own citizens. When the CSCE began its work in 1973 it faced the problem not of resolving old disputes but of working out the principles which would govern the peaceful development of Europe. Whether it can do more than set the seal on the normalisation of relations and move towards the creation of something new remains to be seen. The Soviet Union still attaches importance to the Conference as a symbolic affirmation of *détente*. But the absence of progress towards disarmament in Europe sets a limit beyond which the improvement of relations cannot go since the high force levels embody, and have to be justified by, a belief in the hostile intentions of the opposing side. Neither the experience of arms control negotiations so far, nor the reports coming from the MFR talks, offer much hope of a transformation of military relationships to match the relaxation of political tension.

THE UNITED STATES

The most spectacular development in Soviet foreign policy since 1964 has been the improvement of relations with the United States. The most dramatic changes have taken place since 1969, but the present period of *détente* can be traced back to 1963 when, in the aftermath of the Cuban missile crisis, the 'Hot Line' Agreement and the Partial Test Ban Treaty were signed. During the mid-1960s Soviet relations with the United States were marred by the war in Vietnam, by United States attempts at 'bridge-building' in East Europe, and by Soviet efforts to exploit anti-American feeling in West Europe. The situation was later made worse by the Six Day

War and the Invasion of Czechoslovakia. In spite of this, however, it was clear that during this period the Soviet leaders wished to minimise the risk of war with the United States, even while attempting to restrain American power.

Soviet-American *détente* is based on an apparent acceptance by the leaders on both sides that they have common interests in preventing nuclear war, in halting the arms race, and in extending their economic relations.[23] While the common interest in preventing nuclear war was made clear by the Cuban missile crisis, it was in the late 1960s that the Soviet Union came to agree to talks on limiting strategic arms and to put greater emphasis on trade and technology in its foreign policy. The reasons for these changes have already been outlined: the attainment of strategic parity with the United States, the emergence of a triangular relationship between Moscow, Washington and Peking, and the problems of economic development. These factors did not, however, exert an automatic and immediate influence on Soviet policy; it was only during the years 1969-71 that their implications were worked out. Nor were these decisions straightforward. It was not clear what position to take at SALT: ballistic missile defence fitted well into the Soviet war-waging conception of nuclear strategy, and it was therefore difficult to agree to limit the deployment of ABM systems. There was the danger that the pursuit of credits and technology might give the western powers a lever with which to influence Soviet policy. *Détente* might encourage dissent and create problems of social control in the Soviet Union.

Nevertheless, the major policy choices seem to have been made by the time of the XXIV Party Congress in April 1971: the Peace Programme was presented and great stress put on foreign trade and technology. In May it was announced that the United States and the Soviet Union had agreed in principle to conclude an ABM Treaty and an Interim Agreement on Offensive Missiles. In the same month Brezhnev declared that the Soviet Union was willing to engage in talks on mutual force reductions in Central Europe, and thus weakened Congressional Pressure on the Nixon administration to reduce United States forces in Europe unilaterally. The turning-point in Soviet-American relations was marked by the Nixon visit to Moscow in May 1972; three further summit meetings have taken place and numerous agreements have been concluded.

During the first summit meeting various agreements were signed: the ABM Treaty; the Interim Agreement on Offensive Missiles; Agreements on Co-operation in Environmental Protection, Medical Science and Public Health, the Exploration and Use of Outer Space, Science and Technology, and on the Prevention of Incidents on and over the Sea. Nixon and Brezhnev also signed a document on the Basic Principles of Mutual Relations in which they agreed to observe the principle of peaceful coexistence and to work towards their three common interests: the prevention of war and crises, arms limitation, and the extension of economic, scientific-technical and cultural relations.[24] The momentum flagged, however, during Brezhnev's visit to the United States in June 1973. Agreements were signed on agriculture, transportation, the peaceful uses of atomic energy, and in other fields. But in arms control the two sides did no more than decide on the Basic Principles of Negotiation in which they declared their intention to conclude a permanent treaty on the limitation of offensive missiles in 1974.[25] They also signed an Agreement on the Prevention of Nuclear War, which embodies an intention rather than concrete measures; the Soviet Union has claimed that the new United States doctrine of 'limited strategic options', which envisages the possibility of a limited nuclear exchange, contravenes this agreement, but there is no mechanism for adjudicating or preventing contravention.[26] The momentum slowed even further in 1974: Nixon's visit to Moscow in June produced no arms limitation treaty; in November Ford and Brezhnev decided on the guidelines discussed earlier in this chapter.

Progress towards better economic relations has also been far from easy. In May 1972 the Nixon administration agreed to remove restrictions on trade by granting the Soviet Union Most Favoured Nation status, and to make large credits available to the Soviet Union in order to finance the expansion of trade; in return the Soviet Union began to settle the Lend Lease debt inherited from the Second World War. It took the United States administration more than two years to fulfil its promise, because Congress refused to pass the Trade Bill unless the Soviet Union made emigration easier for

Soviet Jews. In September 1974 a rather mysterious understanding was reached between Kissinger and Gromyko. This
was interpreted in the United States as a willingness to allow
freer emigration, and Congress passed the Trade Bill, but with
provision for only $300 million in credits and a clause
demanding a review after eighteen months. In January 1975
the Soviet Union abrogated the Trade Agreement, while
declaring its intention to continue the policy of *détente*. This
episode shows both that the Soviet Union was willing to
make concessions in order to acquire American credits and
technology, and that there was a point beyond which such an
agreement ceased to be advantageous. The improvement of
Soviet terms of trade in the last three years would make credits
of $300 m less attractive, while the eighteen months clause
would mean that Soviet adherence to a very vague understanding would come up for review during the 1976
presidential election and the vaguencess of the agreement
might be used to the disadvantage of the Soviet policy.[27]

Thus, in two of the most important areas — economic
co-operation and arms control — Soviet-American *détente* has
achieved very little. The Soviet leadership has had a clear
interest in economic co-operation, but has been unwilling to
pay the price of outside interference in internal affairs. Soviet
arms control policy is ambiguous inasmuch as there is a
contrast between the expressed desire for disarmament and
the arms policies actually pursued. It is likely that this is the
result not of a deliberate attempt to attain strategic superiority, but of the difficulty of securing the domestic political
support needed for effective measures when international
competition, technological change, and bureaucratic pressures create a fluid and uncertain environment. In the third
major area — the avoidance of war and of crises — *détente*
appears to have been more successful in so far as tension
between the Soviet Union and the United States has clearly
relaxed. But, as the situation in the Middle East shows, this
has not eliminated the rivalry between the two powers. Both
powers have an interest in preventing an escalation of the
Middle East crisis into a Soviet-American war, but short of
that they pursue their interests vigorously. The October War
of 1973 demonstrated that *détente* has clear limits, that it
provides a new, and perhaps safer, framework of Soviet-

American rivalry, but does not transform that rivalry into all-round co-operation.[28]

CHINA AND THE WORLD COMMUNIST MOVEMENT

One of the great failures of Khrushchev's leadership was the emergence of a deep split between the Soviet Union and the People's Republic of China. Although there is no doubt that Khrushchev's own behaviour helped to embitter relations with China, the basic causes of the split went much deeper than personal animosities. There were two major differences between Soviet and Chinese theory and practice: China had chosen her own path of socialist development and was not prepared to follow in Soviet footsteps; and China took a more militant attitude to United States imperialism and placed much greater emphasis on violent revolutionary struggle. The conflict was fought not only in polemics but also within the world Communist movement, where Communist parties were now presented with two alternative strategies of revolution and socialist development. The new Soviet leaders attempted at first to cool down the conflict by refraining from polemics, but they soon reverted to attacking Chinese policy since the Chinese had not followed suit. They also resumed the efforts which Khrushchev had been making to convene an international conference of Communist and workers' parties in order to rally support for the Soviet position.[29]

The intensification of the American war effort in Vietnam provided a focus for Sino-Soviet differences in 1965 and 1966. When the Cultural Revolution broke out in 1966 it confirmed the Soviet leaders in their belief that Mao and his colleagues were irrational and unscientific. Although it produced incidents such as the harassing of Soviet diplomats in Peking which further embittered relations, the Cultural Revolution also led China to turn inwards, away from the concerns of foreign policy. In spite of this the Soviet Union did not find it easy to convene the international conference; it did not take place until June 1969. Many of the Communist parties seem to have feared that the Soviet Union would use such a conference to lay down a single line and create a monolithic movement; this would deprive them of independence in adapting to local conditions and sharpen the tensions within their own parties. The Chinese Communist Party and many of the Asian parties, including those of North Korea, North Vietnam, Laos and Cambodia, refused to attend.

In his speech to the conference Brezhnev declared that the Chinese leaders had attacked scientific Communism and the Communist movement for about ten years and had intensified those attacks since the IX Congress of the CCP earlier in 1969. In this way, he said, they aided imperialism by splitting the world Communist movement. He accused them of seeking hegemony in the world Communist movement in order to realise their great-power aspirations. He criticised them also for preparing their own people for a war against the Soviet Union. In spite of the absence of many of the Asian parties the Soviet position did not win very much support, and no specific criticism of China appeared in the conference resolutions.[30]

Brezhnev's attack on the Chinese leadership at the International Conference of Communist and Workers' Parties came only three months after Soviet relations with China had reached their lowest point. In March clashes on the Ussuri river had led to the death of thirty-one Soviet border guards and an undisclosed number of Chinese. During 1969 the Soviet leaders let it be known that they were contemplating a nuclear strike against China. This may have been no more than a way of putting pressure on China, but it did of course further embitter relations.[31] The tension eased after Kosygin visited Peking in September 1969, and in the next two years relations improved when negotiations opened on the border issue and ambassadors were exchanged. But the tension and the rumours of war have returned.

The Chinese are not asking for the return of the territories acquired under the 'Unequal Treaties'; the border is a symbol of the conflict as a whole rather than a substantive issue in itself. Neither side shows any willingness to yield on the political, economic or ideological matters that divide them. Soviet policy has been directed very largely towards containing Chinese influence in the world, and in Asia in particular. The improvement of relations between the United States and China created a new factor in Soviet policy towards the West, inasmuch as the danger of a Chinese-American or Chinese-West German axis had to be prevented. This seems to have encouraged the Soviet Union to pursue a policy of *détente* towards the West. But it is clear that Soviet economic and military power makes it very unlikely that the United States or West Europe would choose good relations with China as an alternative to good relations with the Soviet Union, as long as the latter were possible.[32] Soviet relations with China are not improved by the constant Chinese warnings to West Europe that Soviet *détente* policy is a fraud and serves only to mask great-power ambitions.

The Soviet desire to restrain Chinese influence is evident in both the Soviet 'Peace Programme' and the proposal for a collective security system in Asia. The former attempted to portray Chinese nuclear weapons policy in a hostile light by making disarmament proposals that the Chinese leaders would not accept, while the latter, which was first mooted at the Conference of Communist and Workers' Parties in 1969, is designed to limit the possibilities of an expansion of Chinese power in Asia. Soviet policy gives priority not to Communist or revolutionary parties but to established regimes, more or less irrespective of their political complexion. In the last ten years this tendency has grown stronger, while the revolutionary appeal of Soviet socialism has grown weaker. The Soviet Union is trying to use its economic and military power in a more flexible way to acquire political influence in the developing countries. With the extended deployment of the navy the Soviet Union has been led in effect to abandon its political objections to foreign bases, and the search for facilities tends to reinforce Soviet relations with existing regimes. Military power has assumed a new importance in limiting western and Chinese influence in the developing world. The Egyptian expulsion of Soviet military advisers in July 1972 shows, however, that as an instrument of policy military presence is not invariably successful.

CONCLUSION

The picture that emerges from this survey is of *détente* as a continuation of the East-West conflict by other means. The

area of co-operation and common interest has widened, and
international tensions have relaxed. Many of the issues in
dispute between the Soviet Union and the western powers
have been settled and this has created an easier and more
co-operative political climate. This is a necessary first step
towards a demilitarisation of the conflict and new security
arrangements. But there has been no movement in this
direction, and rivalries, whether real or imagined, remain.
Soviet policy is of course only one piece in a complex pattern
and is to be seen as the product not merely of Soviet designs
but also of the whole configuration of international politics.
The Soviet leaders declare that they would like to see a
demilitarisation of the conflict with the West, but they do
not consider military power redundant. They ascribe political
and military utility to both nuclear and conventional forces.
The common interest which the Soviet Union and the United
States say they have in halting the arms race has not been
translated into effective action. Moreover, despite *détente*,
the danger remains that if the arms race continues unabated
it will by its very momentum create enormous tension and
increase the risk of war.

Although Brezhnev has emerged as the prime mover,
especially since the XXIV Party Congress, policy appears to
be arrived at through a regular process of advice and
consultation. A greater role is now given to military advice
and recommendations in making defence policy and in
deciding on the use of military power in support of foreign
policy. The Politburo appears nevertheless to be the final
arbiter and has met during summit meetings to consider
specific proposals advanced by the United States delegation.[33] The inclusion in April 1973 of the Ministers of
Defence and Foreign Affairs and the Head of the KGB as full
members of the Politburo strengthens its role as the supreme
foreign policy-making body. The emphasis on consultation
suggests that the policy pursued by the Soviet Union is based
on a consensus among the leaders rather than the support of
a single faction. It suggests also that the policy is responsive
to domestic pressures. In the last ten years there has been
strong domestic pressure to maintain a high level of military
effort and to acquire foreign capital and technology. The
military effort is justified in part by stressing that it

contributes to *détente*, while *détente* provides the necessary climate for better economic relationships. Thus, the present foreign policy reduces the need for major reforms or changes in power relations in Soviet society.

Soviet policy has played a great part in creating the present relaxation of tension, and there is little doubt that it is in the Soviet interest to remain committed to *détente*. This is true even in the present crisis of capitalism. But, partly because of internal pressures, Soviet policy does little to resolve the contradiction between *détente* and the continuing arms race. As a result, Soviet policy does not make easier the transition to new and safer military relations between East and West.

NOTES

1 *Dvizhushchie sily vneshnei politiki SShA* (Moscow, 1965) p. 507. Quoted in H. Adomeit, *Soviet Risk-Taking and Crisis Behaviour: From Confrontation to Coexistence?*, Adelphi Paper No. 101, International Institute for Strategic Studies (London, 1973) p. 12.

2 See Marshal M. V. Zakharov in *Krasnaya Zvezda*, 4 Feb 1965.

3 For example, Gromyko has been Minister of Foreign Affairs since 1957, while Marshal Grechko succeeded Marshal Malinovsky, Minister of Defence, on the latter's death in 1967. Malinovsky had held the post since 1957.

4 For analyses of Soviet defence policy under Khrushchev see R. Garthoff, *Soviet Military Policy* (London, 1966); R. Kolkowicz, *The Soviet Military and the Communist Party* (1967); T. W. Wolfe, *Soviet Strategy at the Crossroads* (Cambridge, Mass, 1964).

5 See 'Developments in strategic nuclear weapons since SALT I', in *World Armaments and Disarmament, SIPRI Yearbook 1974* (Stockholm and London, 1974) pp. 103-122.

6 For an analysis of the strategic debate and the missile build-up see John Erickson, *Soviet Military Power*, Royal United Services Institute for Defence Studies (London, 1971) pp. 41-52.

7 See T. W. Wolfe, *Soviet Power and Europe, 1945-70* (Baltimore and London, 1970) ch. 17; *Strategic Survey 1973*, International Institute for Strategic Studies (London, 1974) pp. 65-9. The divisions in Eastern Europe are at Category 1 combat readiness, i.e. at between three-quarters and full strength, whereas on the Chinese frontier they are largely in Categories 2 or 3, i.e. between half and three-quarters strength, or at one-third strength. See *The Military Balance 1974-1975*, International Institute for Strategic Studies (London, 1974) p. 9.

8 See Carola Bielfeldt, Gert Krell, Stephan Tiedtke, 'Aufrüstung durch Rüstungsvergleiche: Europäische Sicherheit: ein Rechenkunststück?' in C. Bielfeldt *et al.*, *Frieden in Europa?* (Hamburg, 1973) pp. 8-47.

9 See Barry M. Blechman, *The Changing Soviet Navy*, Brookings Institution (Washington, 1973); the series of articles by Admiral S. G. Gorshkov, Commander-in-Chief of the Soviet Navy, in *Morskoy Sbornik* between February 1972 and February 1973.

10 For an analysis of some of the domestic sources of Soviet defence policy see David Holloway, Technology and Political Decision in Soviet Armaments Policy, *Journal of Peace Research* no. 4 (1974).

11 See L. I. Brezhnev, *O vneshnei politike KPSS i Sovetskogo gosudarstva. Rechi i stat'i* (Moscow, 1973) pp. 349-51.

12 S. Tyushkevich, Sootnoshenie sil v mire i faktory predotvrashcheniya voiny, *Kommunist vooruzhennykh sil*, no. 10 (1974) p. 16.

13 For an interesting analysis of the role of military force in international relations see V. M. Kulish *et al.*, *Voennaya sila i mezhdunarodnye otnosheniya* (Moscow, 1972).

14 For an analysis of the SALT I agreements see Dieter Senghaas, *Aufrüstung durch Rüstungskontrolle* (Stuttgart, 1972).

15 See *The Implementation of International Disarmament Agreements* Stockholm International Peace Research Institute (1973). For the Agreement on the Prevention of Nuclear War see *'To Build Peace'. A Summary of Agreements and Statements during the Visit to the United States of General Secretary Leonid Brezhnev of the Soviet Union*, US Information Service (Washington, 1973).

16 *Pravda*, 26 Sep 1968.

17 See Robin Alison Remington, *The Warsaw Pact* (Cambridge, Mass., 1971) p. 130; Marian Jurek and Edward Skrzypkowski, *Uktad Warszawski*, 2nd ed (Warsaw, 1971) p. 67; A. S. Bakhov, *Organizatsiya Varshavskogo Dogovora* (Moscow, 1971) p. 86.

18 *Comprehensive Programme for the Further Extension and Improvement of Co-operation and the Development of Socialist Economic Integration by the CMEA Member-Countries* (Moscow, 1971).

19 *Pravda*, 15 July 1968.

20 See Remington, op. cit., pp. 209-21 for the text.

21 See T. W. Wolfe, *Soviet Power and Europe 1945-70*, ch. 12, 13.

22 See Remington, op. cit., pp. 225-8 for the text.

23 See G. A. Arbatov, 'O Sovetsko — amerikanskikh otnosheniyakh', *Kommunist*, no. 3 (1973) pp. 101-13.

24 *USSR Peace Program in Action. On the Results of the Soviet-American Talks* (Moscow, 1972).

25 *'To Build Peace'. A Summary of Agreements and Statements during the visit to the United States of General Secretary Leonid Brezhnev of the Soviet Union*, US Information Service (Washington, 1973).

26 See M. A. Mil'shtein and L. S. Semeiko, 'Problema nedopustimosti yadernogo konflikta', *SShA*, no. 11 (1974).

27 Senator Jackson, one of the leading contenders for the Democratic nomination in 1976, had declared that 60,000 visas a year would be the 'minimum standard of compliance'. If this figure were

reached he could claim success in forcing concessions from the
Soviet Union; if it were not reached he could say that the Soviet
Union was not fulfilling its side of the agreement. In fact, between
1969 and 1973 the annual rate of Jewish emigration rose from 400
to 33,500. See the *Financial Times,* 16 Jan 1975.

28 See *Insight on the Middle East War,* by the Insight Team of the
Sunday Times (London, 1974).

29 For a Soviet account see O. B. Borisov and B. T. Koloskov,
Sovetsko-kitaiskie otnosheniy (Moscow, 1971).

30 See *International Conference of Communist and Workers' Parties*
(Moscow, 1969).

31 For an account of the clashes, with maps, see *Strategic Survey
1969,* International Institute for Strategic Studies (London, 1970)
pp. 66-72.

32 See the analysis by V. P. Lukin, 'Amerikano-kitaiskie otnosheniya:
kontseptsii i deistvitel'nost'', *SShA,* no. 2, pp. 12-23

33 On military decision-making see M. Gallagher and K. Spielmann Jr,
Soviet Decision-Making for Defence (New York, 1972); David
Holloway, *Technology Management and the Soviet Military Estab-
lishment,* Adelphi Paper, no. 76, Institute for Strategic Studies
(London, 1971); on Politburo meetings see J. Kraft, 'Letter from
Moscow', the *New Yorker,* 29 July 1974.

4 Demographic Developments

J. A. NEWTH

The total population of the USSR increased from 226.7 millions at the beginning of 1964 to 250.7 millions at the beginning of 1974. The increase was by no means uniform over the interval, as Table 4.1 illustrates:

TABLE 4.1

(1 Jan)	Total	Urban (millions)	Rural	Births	Deaths (rates per 1000)	Nat. Increase
1964	226.7	117.7	109.0	19.5	6.9	12.6
1965	229.6	120.7	108.9	18.4	7.3	11.1
1966	232.2	123.7	108.5	18.2	7.3	10.9
1967	234.8	126.9	107.9	17.3	7.6	9.7
1968	237.2	129.8	107.4	17.2	7.7	9.5
1969	239.5	132.9	106.6	17.0	8.1	8.9
1970	241.5	135.9	105.6	17.4	8.2	9.2
1971	243.9	139.0	104.9	17.8	8.2	9.6
1972	246.3	142.5	103.8	17.8	8.5	9.3
1973	248.6	146.1	102.5	(17.3)	(8.8)	(8.5)
1974	(250.7)	(149.6)	(101.1)			

Note: Population data for 1 Jan 1970 estimated from 1970 census; bracketed data are estimates.

Source: Nar. khoz. SSSR v 1972 g., pp. 7, 46.

The period clearly divides into two five-year periods; in the first, the birth rate falls steadily, while in the second it is stable or tending to rise a little; in the first period, the death rate rises, with some tendency to stability in the second. The joint effect of these factors is a rapid drop in the rate of natural increase between 1964 and about 1969-70, with stability at a rather low level thereafter. Of the total increase of 24 millions, one-half comes in the first four and one-half years; the remaining half taking five and one-half years. As against the general deceleration in growth, the urban sector has been growing at an increasing rate, adding 15.2 millions in the first five years, and 15.8 millions approximately in the

TABLE 4.2

	(thousands) 1964	1974 (in boundaries of 1972)	1974 as % of 1964
Total	226,669	250,737	110.6
RSFSR west	85,502	91,420	106.9
Kaliningrad	669	770	115.1
Northwest	11,563	12,584	108.8
Centre	26,453	28,138	106.4
Volga-Vyatka	8,295	8,280	99.8
Central B. Earth	7,996	7,856	98.2
Volga	17,414	18,861	108.3
N. Caucasus	13,112	14,931	113.9
Other west	73,653	81,860	111.1
Ukraine			
Don. Dnepr	19,095	20,651	108.2
Southwest	19,960	21,174	106.1
South	5,609	6,752	120.4
Belorussia	8,480	9,263	109.2
Estonia	1,267	1,420	112.1
Latvia	2,227	2,450	110.0
Lithuania	2,917	3,265	111.9
Moldavia	3,243	3,769	116.2
Armenia	2,097	2,721	129.8
Azerbaijan	4,369	5,514	126.2
Georgia	4,389	4,881	111.2
RSFSR east	39,677	41,415	104.4
Urals	15,184	15,180	100.0
West Siberia	12,060	12,238	101.5
East Siberia	7,125	7,710	108.2
Far East	5,308	6,287	118.4
Other east	27,837	36,042	129.5
Kazakhstan	11,469	13,905	121.2
Kirgizia	2,458	3,210	130.6
Tajikistan	2,383	3,276	137.5
Turkmenistan	1,804	2,421	134.2
Uzbekistan	9,723	13,230	136.1

Sources: 1964: *Nar. khoz. SSSR v 1963 g.*, p.12, adjusted by reference to *Vestnik statistiki*, no. 2 (1971) pp.85-6; 1974: *Nar. khoz. SSSR v 1972 g.*, p.16, extrapolated to estimated 1974 total population.

second; while the decline in the rural sector has also accelerated (a fall of 2.4 millions between 1964 and 1969; one of about 4.6 millions between 1969 and 1974).

The total increase of 24 millions has not been distributed evenly as between the various republics and regions. There has been a good deal of adjustments in territorial boundaries during the interval, and the estimates in Table 4.2 cannot be guaranteed to be exact.

The relative weights of the four divisions of the country have changed as follows:

	1964 (%)	1974 (%)	change (%)
RSFSR west	37.72	36.46	−1.26
Other west	32.49	32.65	+0.16
RSFSR east	17.50	16.52	−0.98
Other east	12.29	14.37	+2.08

This denotes in effect a relative movement to the periphery of the country, whether the increase be due to an excess of births over deaths or to the actual migration of people; all the non-Russian republics in Transcaucasia and the East have increased at a rate above the average, as have Estonia, Lithuania and Moldavia, with the southern part of the Ukraine. On the other hand all regions of the RSFSR have lost ground except the remotest areas of Kaliningrad and the Far East, plus the largely non-Russian North Caucasus region; and so has the greater part of the Ukraine.

The three salient features of the demographic developments of the post-Khrushchev era are thus:

(1) a declining rate of overall growth;
(2) an accelerating rate of urbanisation; and
(3) territorial redistribution away from the Slav core towards the periphery.

The first of these factors is dependent upon changes in both the birth and death rates, which are in their turn dependent upon changes in the age structure of the population, and also upon autonomous and independent changes in the age-specific rates of fertility and mortality. I shall deal first with the matter of the age structure as it has evolved during the decade under review. The only firm and official data at our disposal are the distributions published in the censuses of 1959 and 1970 (setting aside those published since 1970), and these are limited at best to five-year groupings. These are not fully adequate to specify the variations in successive annual groups, and attempts to interpolate for single years have encountered the apparent difficulty that the two census tabulations do not appear to be entirely consistent. The principal difficulty is that the number of births (and hence of children observed at a later date) seem to have been systematically under-measured at least during the early sixties (and probably earlier also), and the rate of growth indicated in Table 4.1 represents a revision on earlier estimates to take account of this. It is, however, sufficiently clear that the single year age distribution as we find it in the contemporary Soviet population shows enormous fluctuations deriving from the historical experience of the people of the USSR: a sufficient approximation for our present purpose will be given by the bald statement that (as at 1974) survivors born around 1918, 1933, 1943 and 1968 are fewer in numbers than those born in adjacent years; while the peaks come among survivors born in or about 1928, 1938 and 1960. A very rough computation of the numbers involved would be (single year age groups in millions):

1918	1.6	1938	4.7
1928	4.0	1943	1.8
1933	2.8	1960	5.3
		1968	4.0

It will be clear from these figures that the size of a contingent at some single year point (e.g. the age for entering school, of reaching legal maturity, of retirement from work) may well fluctuate violently, that the age composition of a larger body (e.g. women of childbearing age, the working population) may also vary to a considerable extent, and that the total size of these larger groups may also vary, although more slowly. Two particular aspects of this question will be examined below: the age distribution of the school and higher education sector and of the population of working age. With a particular eye to the course of the birth rate let us set out the age distribution of the sector of women of childbearing age over the interval 1964-74 (figures in millions):

Age:	15-19	20-4	25-9	30-4	35-9	40-4	45-9	Total
1964	7.5	8.2	10.2	9.1	10.3	7.0	6.3	58.6
1966	9.4	6.2	11.1	8.4	10.5	8.4	5.8	59.8
1968	10.5	6.4	9.7	9.2	9.7	9.7	6.3	61.5
1970	10.8	8.5	7.0	10.7	8.5	10.3	7.5	63.3
1972	11.4	9.9	5.8	10.8	8.3	10.2	8.8	65.2
1974	12.0	10.5	7.4	8.1	10.0	8.8	9.9	66.7

Source: US Dept. of Commerce, 'Estimates and Projections of the Population of the USSR', series P-91, no. 23 (Mar 1973).

These data illustrate the point of the variability of age structure very forcefully: the proportion of women aged 25-9 in the total was 18.6 per cent in 1966, but only 8.9 per cent — less than half — in 1972.

The age-specific fertility rates in 1964 (the number of children born annually to women of the specified age) were:

	15-19	20-4	25-9	30-4	35-9	40-4	45-9
No. per 1000	24	158	139	96	52	21	4

If this fertility schedule had persisted unaltered throughout the decade, the number of births would have been as follows (in millions — the actual number is inserted in brackets):

1964	1966	1968	1970	1972	1974
4.5	4.3	4.2	4.3	4.4	4.5
(4.5)	(4.2)	(4.1)	(4.2)	(4.4)	(n.a.)

Assuming a constant fertility schedule, we would have expected a fall in the number of births followed by a recovery, the amplitude of the changes not being very large, in spite of the substantial increase in the number of women 'at risk'. The curve of the actual number of births follows this pattern, but both the fall and the recovery seem to have been somewhat sharper than expected. This can however be accounted for by the reported changes in the fertility schedule: the latest data available are for 1971-2 and show a progressive concentration in fertility towards the younger ages, with a corresponding fall among the older women:

(1971-2)	15-19	20-4	25-9	30-4	35-9	40-3	45-9
	32	174	137	84	49	15	2

This shift towards an increase in specific fertility among younger women combined with a relative decline in older women is sufficient to account for the discrepancy; but it then raises a point of profound importance for the future development of the Soviet population. The average age of the mother at the time of birth has tended to fall steadily throughout the period; the implication of this is that families are tending to be formed earlier, and that the total final size of the family is falling. This is corroborated by the figures for the proportion of births which are of a third or higher-order child, which fell steadily from a maximum of 38 per cent in 1965 (37 per cent in 1964) to 29 per cent in 1972. It is not possible to explore here the full potentialities of the argument as to the long-run capacity of the Soviet population to reproduce itself; but we must discuss the variations which seem to be becoming more apparent as between one part of the country and another. The most commonly used measures of this potential are the Gross and the Net Reproduction Rates, i.e. the average number of daughters born per woman during her reproductive life in total (gross) and taking account of mortality (net). The following values from 1969-70 show the enormous disparities between republics in this regard:

	GRR	NRR		GRR	NRR
Latvia	0.94	0.91	Azerbaijan	2.29	2.09
RSFSR	0.97	0.93	Kirgizia	2.43	2.23
Ukraine	1.00	0.95	Uzbekistan	2.79	2.60
Estonia	1.05	1.02	Tajikistan	2.95	2.66
Belorussia	1.13	1.09	Turkmenistan	2.95	2.69

The implication of these data is clear enough: that the long-run ability of the western ('European') parts of the USSR to sustain their existing numbers is in doubt; while the 'eastern' republics, in which a huge reduction in mortality during the Soviet period (and particularly of infant mortality) has not been offset by a reduction in fertility, are in the classical phase of population explosion. Two more sets of data (out of many now available on this issue) may be adduced to reinforce this point. The distribution of births by order is known for the Ukraine (1966) and for Uzbekistan (1963). The figures show the enormous differences in social attitudes between these two republics:

	Ukraine (%)	Uzbekistan (%)
First	44	14
Second	35	16
Third	12	17
Fourth	4	17
Fifth and higher	5	36

Under 10 per cent of births in the Ukraine were of fourth or higher-order children; more than one half of those born in Uzbekistan were in these categories.

A slight indication of preferences as to family size (which has a rough correspondence to what actually happens) is given by these data based on an enquiry in the Tselinograd *oblast* of Kazakhstan in the late sixties:

Preferred number of children (%)

| | Urban | | Rural | |
	Russians	Kazakhs	Russians	Kazakhs
None	0	0	0	0
One	3	0	2	0
Two	51	17	27	2
Three	41	33	48	34
Four and over	5	50	23	64
Average	2.7	3.7	3.0	4.3

Again, quite different sets of attitudes towards the family are indicated.

Before exploring the extent to which these differences (which for convenience we lump together into western and non-western, or even more dubiously, Slav and non-Slav) are reflected in other population developments during the decade, we must return to the rise in the death rates over the decade. The table of age-specific death rates is now published almost annually, and two features emerge. There has been, as we might well expect, a progressive improvement in mortality in infancy and childhood, and among young adults; but from about the age of thirty the death rates seem to have risen at all ages. It would appear that this is rather a reflection of improved techniques in the collection of data than a genuine deterioration in the conditions of life in the USSR; but in view of the rather strange rates published in association with the 1959 census (which gave the USSR curiously favourable rates for the elderly compared with broadly analogous countries in East Europe), it is difficult to be fully satisfied even with the data as they now appear. In any case, the steadily aging composition of the population (as exemplified by the great increase in the number of pensioners) is sufficient to account for the reported deterioration of the overall death rate.

We now pass from the demographic data which are published annually and exhibit a dynamic picture to the examination of such data as derive from the two population censuses of 1959 and 1970, most of which cannot be directly compared with current statistical series. As indicated above, there appears to be copious evidence of differences between

Slavs and non-Slavs (terms used *faute de mieux*) with respect
to demographic indicators; and these differences can be
traced in a number of other respects also. We begin with the
question of migration from the countryside to · the towns.
The number of Slavs (Russians, Ukrainians and Belorussians)
increased from 159.3 millions to 178.8 millions, increased in
towns from 83.0 to 111.4 millions, and fell in rural districts
from 76.3 to 67.4 millions. If we assume that the natural
increase rate was the same for urban and rural, this implies a
natural increase among 1959 town dwellers of 10.2 millions
with a migration from the countryside of 18.2 millions, those
in the countryside having a gross natural increase of 9.3
millions, and after migration, a net loss of 8.9 millions.
About two-thirds of the urban increase among Slavs thus
came from immigrants from the countryside. The corresponding figures for non-Slavs are: total increase from 49.6 to
62.9 millions; urban increase from 17.0 to 24.6 millions — of
this 7.6 millions 4.6 came from existing inhabitants, 3.0
millions from the countryside. The countryside increased
from 32.5 millions to 38.3; this net gain of 5.8 comprised 8.8
millions natural increase of which 3.0 millions moved to the
towns. Somewhat under one-half of the increase in urban
non-Slavs came from internally generated natural increase.

A further indicator of social differences is found in the
share of women in the labour force. We have no satisfactory
data on the basis of nationality, and we are obliged to use the
data for specific areas, bearing in mind that all areas have
substantial numbers of Slav settlers, which will tend to
reduce the differences which are due to national peculiarities.
We note, however, that whereas for the USSR as a whole the
share of women in the increase of the employed population
between 1959 and 1970 amounted to 61 per cent, the share
in the corresponding increase of the group consisting of the
four Central Asian republics plus Azerbaijan amounted to a
little less: 58 per cent. It would seem very probable that the
proportion of women of the Slav nationalities who live in
these areas and go out to work is higher than the corresponding proportion for women of the local nationality. We have
now in fact a good deal of information on the difference
between Slav families and indigenous ones, and also some
clues as to the extent of mixed marriages — in the national

sense. In 1970, out of approximately 59 million families, somewhat under 8 millions contained members of more than one nationality (as an interesting sidelight on the present-ation of Soviet statistics, we also have the number of families of the same and mixed social groups — *rabochiye, sluzhash-chiye* and *kolkhozniki* — and it is not without interest that the number of marriages across the class line, so to speak, was more than twice as great as those across the national line (something over 17 millions).

These figures on ethnically mixed marriages are not complete, primarily in that there is a considerable fraction of the total population who are either completely isolated individuals — *odinochki,* to use the official term — who have no family ties at all, or who live away from the group that they consider to be their family. These two categories are likely to be relatively large among migrants of recent settlement, but they can also be shown to be of significant importance in such republics as Estonia, where the propor-tion of elderly people (mostly women) without family ties is also large. Nevertheless, as a starting point for further analysis, and as the basis for a rough assessment, these figures are of some value. As we would expect, there is substantial variation between republics, partly at least due to the varying proportions of the basic indigenous population and the range of non-indigenous types; for example, in Kazakhstan, where in addition to the native Kazakhs and the large (indeed greater) number of immigrant Russians whose date of establishment in the area ranges over a full century there is an extraordinary range of settlers, the proportion of mixed families is 21 per cent; while in Armenia, with some 90 per cent of the population Armenians, only 4 per cent of the families are mixed. There is also in all republics a great difference between the urban and the rural population: in Azerbaijan, for example, the proportion of mixed families in the cities is 13 per cent, while in the countryside it is only 2 per cent.

Again, the explanation is partly the different national composition of the towns and countryside respectively, and partly the degree of contact which is presumably much greater in the cities, and particularly such big cities as Baku. One small clue as to average family size is a slight

contribution to the difficulty that we are often obliged to use
territorial data as a substitute for ethnic data: there is a small
but significant correlation between the family size of pure
Russian families in a given republic, and the size of pure
families of the local nationality. The union-wide average size
of Russian families is 3.4 persons; but this average conceals a
range as shown in Table 4.3.

TABLE 4.3

	Russian families	Local national families
Ukraine	3.2	3.4
Belorussia	3.2	3.6
Georgia	3.2	4.0
Moldavia	3.2	3.9
Latvia	3.2	3.1
Estonia	3.2	3.1
Lithuania	3.3	3.4
Turkmenistan	3.3	6.0
Uzbekistan	3.4	5.9
Azerbaijan	3.4	5.6
Tajikistan	3.4	6.1
Kirgizia	3.5	5.5
Armenia	3.5	5.0
Kazakhstan	3.6	5.5

This range — basically low in the west, high in the east — may
suggest that there is some degree of social assimilation to the
background; but the great disparity between the average
Russian family size which varies over the comparatively
narrow range of 3.2 to 3.6 and the great values found, for
example, in Central Asia (5.5 to 6.1) suggests that the
assimilation is very slight. The impression that we are dealing
with two types of society is very strong: the majority society,
Russian predominantly, with other national groups of European type associated with it, particularly outside their home
areas (within the home areas of the western nationalities, and
especially in the Ukraine, it is a different story); and what we
tend to regard under a blanket designation as non-Russian,
but which closer examination will show to be a set of
mutually independent or nearly so sub-societies.

We have, unfortunately, no data on the key issue of

occupational structure by nationality, but a further illustration of this apparent division can be derived from the
data on nationality and language. The number of persons
who are Russian by nationality but who speak some other
language as first choice is negligibly small in the first analysis
— 204,000 out of 129 millions; if we add in those who
speak Russian as a second language (122 thousand) we
are almost justified in claiming complete identity between
nationality and language in the case of the Russians. But if
we are particularly interested in this phenomenon of the
margin at which assimilation may be taking place we may
look at the proportion of non-Russian speaking Russians in
each republic and the fraction of them whose first language is
that of the local republic. (See Table 4.4.)

TABLE 4.4

	(A) Russians by nation-ality whose mother tongue is not Russian	*(B)* of which, those whose mother tongue is the local republic language	*(B)* as % of *(A)*
Ukraine	136,790	135,324	98.9
Belorussia	14,762	14,512	98.3
Estonia	5,268	5,029	95.5
Latvia	8,950	8,351	93.3
Lithuania	5,940	5,291	89.1
Moldavia	3,669	2,446	66.7
Armenia	356	328	92.1
Azerbaijan	583	343	58.8
Georgia	2,419	1,974	81.6
Kazakhstan	2,912	281	9.6
Kirgizia	381	26	6.8
Tajikistan	269	61	22.7
Turkmenistan	233	47	20.2
Uzbekistan	1,228	514	41.9

Source: 1970 census, vol. 4 *passim.*

The proportion of Russians by nationality who have some
other language as their first choice declines from west to east,
and at the same time the proportion even of this small
fraction who are in some sense linguistically associated with
the local majority declines from west to east. If we were

justified in proceeding from this kind of evidence to an estimate of intermarriage, we would hazard the view that marriage contact between Russians and non-Russians is confined almost entirely to the Western nationalities — Slavs and Balts, with minor contact in Georgia and Armenia.

Let us pass on to the question of migration during the decade with which we are most directly concerned. Here we encounter for the first time a complete and direct contradiction between the two types of information at our disposal: the first of these being the evidence of the 1970 census, the second being derived from the officially published annual figures for population, births and deaths in each district. Dealing first with the second element, several scholars have for some years now followed the practice which is also employed by Soviet writers (who are after all dependent on the same published material that we also receive), namely to assume that if the population of a given district at the beginning of one year is A, and at the beginning of the next year is B, and that the recorded number of births and deaths in that district during the interval is respectively C and D, then the number of migrants to (positive) or from (negative) is: $B - A - C + D$. For example, let the number of inhabitants of a given region at 1 January 1964 be 1,296,000, and a year later 1,342,000. The published birth and death rates are 22.4 per cent and 8.9 per cent respectively. The natural increase in the interval is thus 13.5 per cent of the mid-year population (1,319,000) or 18,000 approximately, implying net immigration of 28,000. In fact, since the yearly totals derive specifically from the reverse of this process (they start with a beginning-year total, and then derive their end-year total by adding and subtracting the births, deaths and movements which are documented in their ZAGS offices), there should be nothing wrong with this unless somebody has lied by commission or omission. We now know that the number of births which occurred annually during the intercensal period was understated, and that the totals for some districts are therefore in error by an amount which no one has yet published, but the general effect of gains and losses should not be wildly out.

The other method, however, depends on the tables of volume 7 of the census, which are based on statements of the public during the census, in that persons who had changed their address during the two years before 15 January 1970 were asked to specify their old address. On the basis of these replies, migration data for 1968-9 were compiled. The results are startlingly inconsistent with the original picture. We had got used to the idea of people moving out of the RSFSR, at a steadily declining rate over the years, as the birth rate fell; to overall migration into the western republics — again at a somewhat declining rate; to transfer between Georgia and Azerbaijan on the one hand and Armenia on the other, to the net advantage of the latter; and to net migration into Central Asia as a whole, with the former heavy migration into Kazakhstan turning into a net outflow in the last years of the sixties. On the census data, we find a net inflow into the RSFSR, not an outflow; the gain of the western republics and the movement within Transcaucasia both stand; but Kazakhstan and the Central Asian republics all show a significant outflow, not an inflow. Precisely what has gone wrong is still unclear; but it is not without interest to note that the data for 1972, with the local units presumably corrected as to their total populations in the light of the census, show a continuation of the trends as indicated by the same methods which seemed to produce a consistent result in the sixties. It would of course be a great pity to have to jettison the census data, which are copious, as subject to grave error, and it seems that the effort of reconciling the two methods, laborious though it might well be, would be time well spent.

Even if they do contain gross inaccuracies, presumably due to biased reporting, some features emerge which conform to the general picture as originally built up by other methods. The most conspicuous feature of the figures is the evidence that they provide as to the volume — gross — of migration (the other methods producing only a net figure). They indicate that during two years, at least 13 million people changed their address, this of course being an underestimate, since some people must have moved from district *A* to *B* and back again and thus would be recorded as stationary. This figure of 6 to 7 millions a year, or around 2½ to 3 per cent of the total population, implies that the mobility of the population is rather high (implying, indeed, an average change of district once in a generation) and this at a time when the rate of new development in fresh areas is at a historically rather low level. Most of the movement seems to be restricted in range, however; although there are sharp local differences, something over one-half of all movements are within the same *oblast,* and something like another quarter with the same economic region. An experimental study has in fact been undertaken (although not yet published) by the present author, in which the matter of national attitudes again forms an element; it consists essentially of using the reported migration data to produce for each region a schedule of preferences, i.e. to establish for each region on the basis of what people actually do in the way of migration a ranking of all other regions: the greater the number moving to region *A,* the higher its rank in the preference schedule. This set of preference schedules is then amalgamated into an all-Union compound preference schedule, as a result of which there emerges an image of the hierarchy of desirability as seen by the population as a whole, as well as a measure of the degree to which the preferences of given areas agree with the general opinion.

The results as they emerge for the USSR are rather strikingly different from those for these other countries for which studies of a broadly analogous kind have been undertaken. Whereas they in general have a fairly clear ordering of preferences — i.e. some regions stand out as universally desirable and others as universally undesirable — there seems to be in the Soviet case no clear pattern at all. A whole range of factors may of course contribute to this kind of result, but two may be suggested: the first, that the average Soviet citizen has for some reason not formed anything like as clear a mental map of his country as has say the average citizen of the UK — that is, there are no areas which are conspicuously desirable or the reverse; and secondly, that mobility is inhibited to a very substantial extent by the factors of language and other cultural elements. There seems to be some reason to believe that more detailed analysis along the lines indicated above would confirm this reluctance, which takes the form of canalising movement broadly along the east-west line from the western border to the Pacific, with Kazakhstan as part of this system, while leaving the southern republics as isolated sub-systems. Along this main sequence, so to speak, there seem to be three nodes: the extreme west and north-west; the south-centre (basically the North Caucasus region); and the Far East. The less urbanised regions of the west-centre (Volga Vyatka, Central Black Earth, most of the Volga region) and the urbanised but stagnating regions of Western Siberia both are tending to lose migrants to the nodal points indicated.

This analysis must, however, be taken as extremely tentative at this stage, and requiring much further development to fit it for publication or even for very detailed discussion at pre-publication level. Similarly, we can build up a picture of the nature and trends of migration between the countryside and the cities. Here again there are local variations, but there seems to be reason to suppose that at least over the interval 1959-70 towns between about the 10,000 or 15,000 level and around 75,000 tended to grow faster the larger they were, whereas for towns above this kind of critical size (around 76,000) relative growth tended to taper off: as it were, a kind of logistic pattern. The explanation of this may well lie in the migration of fully rural population first to the smaller towns and then to the larger ones, where a certain degree of training and skill are required, but that the process of filtering from the medium-sized town to the real giants is somewhat more difficult. It seems quite certain that a substantial part of the differential growth of the large cities is brought about by movement from one major city to another. The analysis of urban growth as it differs between one region of the USSR and another is hampered, however, by the facts that cities of European type are of relatively recent growth in the more backward parts of the country and that their function also differs from region to region. It would seem that much useful information would emerge from an analysis of the effects on the general employment position of this very rapid turnover of labour, but the materials presented in the 1970 census concerning the distribution of labour are curiously defective (although some further data have since been released). To a limited extent, we can reconstruct the outline of the position (see Table 4.5).

TABLE 4.5

(A) Population aged 15-69 (thousands)

	1959 Total	Males	Females	1970 Total	Males	Females
15—	16,471	8,259	8,212	21,999	11,225	10,774
20—	38,533	18,973	19,560	30,875	15,440	15,435
30—	30,590	13,139	17,451	37,738	18,548	19,190
40—	22,672	8,704	13,968	31,259	13,502	17,757
50—	10,447	4,010	6,437	9,078	3,430	5,648
55—	8,699	2,905	5,794	12,013	4,273	7,740
60—	11,736	4,099	7,637	17,595	5,922	11,673
Total	139,148	60,089	79,059	160,557	72,340	88,217

(B) Employed (thousands)

	Total	Males	Females	Total	Males	Females
15—	9,806	5,109	4,697	8,723	4,695	4,028
20—	31,965	17,274	14,691	26,960	13,821	13,139
30—	24,968	12,465	12,503	35,600	18,100	17,500
40—	17,251	8,062	9,189	28,680	12,954	15,726
50—	6,893	3,490	3,403	7,253	3,065	4,188
55—	4,074	2,338	1,736	5,220	3,398	1,822
60—	4,173	2,787	1,386	2,651	1,735	916
Total	99,130	51,525	47,605	115,204	57,828	57,376

(C) Activity rates (per cent)

	Total	Males	Females	Total	Males	Females
15—	59.5	85.8	60.2	39.6	41.8	37.4
20—	83.0	91.0	75.1	87.3	89.5	85.1
30—	81.6	94.9	71.6	94.3	97.6	91.2
40—	76.1	92.6	65.8	91.8	95.9	88.6
50—	66.0	87.0	52.9	79.9	89.4	74.2
55—	46.8	80.5	30.0	43.4	79.5	23.5
60—	35.6	68.0	18.2	15.1	29.3	7.8
Total	71.2	85.8	60.2	71.8	79.9	65.0

Sources: All data in (A) from 1970 census, vol. 2; 1959 data in (B) by adding fifteen republics in 1959 census; 1970 data from *Naseleniye,* booklet issued by TsSU (Moscow, 1974) p.143.

Total employment in the age range 15-69 has gone up a very little faster than population. The age and sex composition of the latter altered materially between the two censuses, principally by a sharp decline in the number of persons in their twenties, but also by a slight improvement in the proportion of men to women. As to employment, the age-specific activity rates have fallen at the lower end and again at the upper end of the age scale; more people in 1970 were staying at school or receiving some form of tertiary education than in 1959 (changes in the conscription rules are immaterial here, as the employment figures include military personnel under the head of their civilian occupation); and a greatly increased number of the elderly who were recorded as deriving their income from employment in 1959 (including *kolkhoz* members, but not persons living off their private plots) were by 1970 keeping alive on their retirement pensions — the number of this latter group had rocketed since the extension of the state pension scheme to collective farmers in 1964.

On the other hand, the activity rate has increased sharply in the middle ranges of life; the rate for men was nearly 100 per cent by 1970, while that for women has increased by over 20 per cent in the approximate age range 30-55. The peak age for male employment remained at about 35, but that for women moved forward by about a decade (1959, c. 25; 1970, c. 35). Women already at work in 1959, some of whom might have been expected to leave in order to attend to their families, have remained at work, and their numbers have been greatly augmented by new recruits to the labour force. The shift from the *kolkhoz* to employment in state enterprises is underlined by the accentuation of the relative drop in the activity rate for women aged 55-9 as against 50-4 (1959 difference, 22.9 per cent; 1970, 50.7 per cent). This shift is further corroborated by the structural changes in the composition of the labour force affecting and reflecting the employment of women: the great majority of the increase in the number of employed women (56.2 millions in 1959; 64.8 millions in 1970) went to the non-manual sector (12.0 million women in 1959; 18.8 million in 1970), in spite of the change in the industrial classification by which shop assistants and some other smaller groups — very much dominated by women — have been reassigned to the manual sector.

The course of developments in the field of education since the 1959 census tends to confirm the picture outlined above, but it is noteworthy that the principal change lies in the Khrushchev period rather than in the decade since his departure. In 1960 the number of pupils in classes I to VII (the then obligatory period) was 31.1 millions; in classes VIII and above (principally, pupils of working age), 5.1 millions. By 1965 the younger group had expanded to 35.5 millions (demographic growth accounts quite adequately for this) but the number in classes VIII and over had shot up to 12.1 millions, due principally to the introduction of the compulsory eighth year. Growth thereafter has been slow. By 1970 the numbers were 36.5 and 12.9 millions, respectively; and by 1972, 35.1 and 14.3 millions. Over and above this, there has been an expansion of the numbers attending special secondary schools (corresponding to the senior age groups of the ordinary school) and also higher educational establishments (students, of course, being rather older than this). It seems probable, however, that the size of the appropriate age group has expanded somewhat more rapidly than that of the senior school population in the last decade, and one is tempted to speculate upon the possibility of a juvenile unemployment problem in the immediate future. It must, however, be stressed that the demographic data at our disposal are simply inadequate to assess this possibility with any confidence, and it seems prudent to leave the question open for future analysis.

A NOTE ON SOURCES USED

The principal sources used in this chapter are the population censuses of 1959 (sixteen volumes) and 1970 (seven volumes), supplemented where necessary by the (nearly) annual statistical publication, *Narodnoye khozyaistvo SSSR*. The latest volume of this last available to the writer was that for 1972. A good deal of material is published first, or only, in the monthly journal of the Central Statistical Administration, *Vestnik statistiki.*

An excellent analysis of Soviet demographic problems has recently been published: B. Ts. Urlanis, *Problemy dinamiki naseleniya SSSR* (Moscow, 1974). Much of the data cited on pp. 81-4 of this chapter come from this study. There is a series of projections of the population of the USSR published by the US Department of Commerce, of which the 1973 issue has also been used.

5 The Changing Composition of the Communist Party

PETER FRANK

Leonard Schapiro has identified six main features in the Communist Party of the Soviet Union as it appeared to him in 1952 on the eve of Stalin's death. In the first place he put the fact that while retaining its selectivity the CPSU had become a 'mass party'. This was at a time when there were slightly over 6,700,000 party members. Shortly after the political demise of Khrushchev (1 January 1965) the party had a membership of 11,758,000. By 1974 party membership stood at well over 15,000,000. Of course, the population of the USSR has increased considerably since 1953 (from 184.8 millions to 248.6 millions in 1973). As Table 5.1 shows, party membership more than doubled in the same period,

TABLE 5.1

	Population of the USSR	Party membership	Party membership as a percentage of population
	(Millions)		
1952	184.8	6,707,539	3.62
1957	201.4	7,494,573	3.72
1964	226.7	11,022,369	4.86
1973	248.6	14,330,525	5.76

Note: all data relate to 1 January of the given year.

although expressed as a percentage of the population the increase in party size was far less dramatic. Moreover, comparison would be more realistic had we full information on percentages of party size in relation to that part of the Soviet population aged eighteen and over. Brezhnev at the XXIV Congress mentioned that the figure (March 1971) stood at 9 per cent, or one out of every eleven adults.

These reservations notwithstanding, it is clear that under Khrushchev there was a big influx of new members and in the period 1957-64 there were annual increases in the overall size of the party ranging from 4.5 per cent to 6.6 per-cent. Under the present leadership the annual percentage increase has in recent years dropped to below 2 per cent.

If we look at the percentage rate of increase in party membership, it is evident that there has been a steady deceleration under the present leaders. But, as we have noted already, the absolute size of the party is increasing quite rapidly. The explanation is that whereas a 1 per cent increase in 1965 was 'worth' 67,075, in 1973 it was worth 148,210. At the present time, given the age structure of the party, recruitment would have to be practically halted in order to keep party numbers static.

The two apparently contradictory trends in fact reflect a contradictory dilemma which faces the leadership. Continuing recruitment, even at the unusually low rate of around 1.3 per cent, means that the party is reinforcing an existing expectation in many socio-occupational groups that party membershp is virtually an adjunct of their jobs. The implications of such a dangerous tendency, which had developed rapidly under Khrushchev, are too obvious in the Soviet context to need spelling out. Conversely, however, to cease recruitment, even temporarily, would be to deny party membership to those who genuinely deserve it, as well as alienating those who perhaps do not deserve it but who none the less expect it. Moreover, such a policy would play havoc with the age structure of the party which, in time, could cause considerable tensions within the membership.

Consequently, although the period 1964-74 has been *relatively* uneventful and characterised at the leadership level by considerable 'immobilism', so far as the demography of the party is concerned, there are signs that Brezhnev is seeking to control a process which was quietly and unobtrusively getting out of hand. What follows is an attempt to describe and evaluate this process in terms of political generations. One justification for such an approach is that the USSR is now perhaps the most politically stable of all the great powers and we do not think it likely that the CPSU's primacy will be successfully challenged. It may be, however, that the subtle changes occurring within the mass party membership will have profound consequences. Certainly, Brezhnev has approached the problem with skill and circumspection. It remains to be seen, though, whether or not he can control what may turn out to be inexorable trends towards permanent growth in the mass membership and the 'democratisation' in sheer quantitative terms that this would imply. The alternative, it may seem, would be a growing social isolation of the party — something, surely, which no party leader dare contemplate.

POLITICAL GENERATIONS

A great many factors contribute to the formation of political attitudes, and it is probably safe to assume that the outlooks of any two individuals are unlikely to be exactly the same over a range of issues, even though they may be in agreement over one or more. Yet it is equally true that a given age group with direct experience of an event is likely to have been influenced by that event, albeit in different ways. To take an example of this from British politics: the 1920s and 1930s, with their poverty and mass unemployment, left a deep imprint on the political consciousness of a generation of Labour MP's; yet it would be a mistake to suppose that Conservative MP's of the same generation remained unscathed by their experiences during those two decades. Certainly, perceptions of the period differ, and the differences are no doubt attributable, at least in part, to factors such as social origin, education, and even, perhaps, to geographical location at the time. The impact of the 'Great Depression' on many Labour MP's is too well-known to need documenting; but Harold Macmillan's response to the industrial North-East in 1923 may well characterise the feelings of a significant number of Conservatives: 'For Macmillan, the discovery of the desolation of Stockton gave a focal point to his vague radicalism.'[1] Macmillan's reaction was paternalistic and lacked the bitterness of many of those who were to enter Parliament as Labour MP's in 1945, but it could not be said that he was unaffected by his experiences: '. . . the discovery of Stockton had (as he liked to put it) the same kind of impact as going to the front line of the trenches after living in headquarters.'[2]

It is almost impossible to find a political autobiography which does not contain some reference to factors which the author deems to have awakened his political consciousness or to have helped to create a lasting political outlook. Again, Emanuel Shinwell's belief that the spur to his desire to enter politics was 'the violent contrasts between poverty and wealth which existed fifty years ago' runs like a *leitmotif* through the recollections of many of his generation.[3] Our first point, then, is quite simple: events in the individual's social and political environment are likely to contribute to his political make-up. It goes without saying, of course, that events and circumstances occurring in the narrower environment of the family are also powerful factors in establishing political attitudes.

So far we have drawn examples from the British scene. But the argument applies to the individual in any polity. However, the obvious qualification needs to be made that while certain events (such as a major war) may be common to the experience of more than one polity, on the whole most societies from time to time experience events which are uniquely their own. In the USSR the 1930s was, to say the least, an eventful decade and it is unlikely that anyone who lived through the collectivisation of agriculture, the beginnings of rapid industrialisation, and then the purges remained untouched by their impact. But the causes of crisis in the two polities — Britain and the Soviet Union — and their impact were radically different. As Alec Nove points out in the conclusion to his chapter on the 1930s in his *Economic History of the USSR,* 'It should be added that morale in Russia itself, and the impact of her achievements internationally, were affected by the co-incidence of the Great Depression. Russia was growing, the Western capitalist system was apparently collapsing, with massive unemployment and social disruption, . . .'[4] Thus, in Britain widespread misery, bitterness and resentment were caused by lack of work. In Russia the same feelings were widespread, but 'at least Russia's troubles could be seen as growing pains,'[5] and no one would seriously suggest that the political responses to the decade were the same for Soviet and British citizens alike.

None the less, with these reservations in mind, our point stands that personal experience plays a major role in the formation of political attitudes. To that extent, it is possible to hypothesise political generations on the basis of life span and the events encompassed by it. The use of the categories of pre-war, wartime and postwar generations is a classic example of a convenient method employed by many commentators to differentiate between age groups within a single polity and to accord to each group an inferred set of attitudes. In such a case, the term 'generation' does not imply a regular, equal span of time; it suggests, rather, that the momentousness of the event distorts life experiences with the result that 'generations', in terms of time, become irregular and uneven.

A large, organised body of people such as a political party is bound to contain segments of the total membership which correspond broadly to generations. What we must be clear about, however, is what we mean by a 'generation' in this context. One approach is to delineate 'biological generations', that is, groups of party members differentiated according to age alone. Thus, with either a single individual or a specific generation one can set life span against events which have occurred within the polity during that span of time and from such a juxtaposition infer likely attitudes and political stances. If, moreover, additional data, such as social origin, are available, then the likelihood of making correct inferences is enhanced. Hence, a Russian of poor peasant background born in 1915 would be fifteen years old when the collectivisation drive was at its height and his perception of events would almost certainly differ from one of his peers who was the child of a *kulak,* or from one who was the son of an urban industrial worker. The age datum alone would permit only the broadest conclusions to be drawn, but, as we have said, additional information might reasonably allow us to make fairly accurate inferences.

Not all events in the life of a polity have the immediacy of the impact of collectivisation on the child of a Russian peasant. And, as we have seen, in the Britain of the 1920s and 1930s widespread poverty and unemployment could make its mark on more fortunate individuals than the poor and unemployed. Similarly, it is important to take into account the possibility that an event which lies within the recollection of one person may be not even a vague memory for another of the same age. Most of us can recall domestic events set in early childhood, but, usually, these are scattered, and in that sense incoherent, recollections. At some point in one's life, however, memory becomes coherent and events are connected in the mind. Wherever that point may be, we shall describe it as 'the age of conscious recollection'. It may be that psychologists could agree on an age of conscious recollection which would hold good for most people. Somewhat arbitrarily, we shall fix it at the age of ten. Although ten might be considered too late, it has at least the advantage that it encompasses the age of conscious recollection for all or most persons. A point fixed arbitrarily lower would run the risk of excluding significant numbers of a population.

Age of conscious recollection is a relevant factor in that if an event is sufficiently momentous, even so early in life, it is likely to have lasting consequences so far as the attitudes of the individual are concerned. Given the importance of the 1917 revolution, and the sanctity accorded to it in the Soviet Union, it is highly improbable that a Soviet citizen aged ten in 1917 would remain uninfluenced by the fact that the revolution lay within the bounds of his conscious re-collection. However, to speak about 'conscious recollection' is not the same thing as to speak about 'political conscious-ness'. Indeed, most would agree that the two are far from synonymous and are separated by an interval of years. The question is: how many?

A recent attempt to apply a 'generational model of social change' to the Soviet political elite begins by addressing itself to precisely this problem: 'Generation theory asserts that in the maturation process of individuals, there is a 'most probable' time when political events are most 'impactful' on the developing political consciousness of the individual, and that it is during this period that the basic political orientation is stabilised.'[6] After pointing out that one scholar deems the 'most probable' time to be in the age range fifteen to twenty, while another prefers 'around 20', the author of the study settles for the range seventeen to twenty-five:

Substantively, the generational model asserts that (modally) between the ages of 17 and 25, the basic formation of political consciousness ... takes place; that after this period, the changes in broad political outlook are relatively smaller and represent marginal revisions, or attempts to adapt, within the general framework already established.[7]

While we have no scientific or empirically based grounds for objecting to this age range within which political consciousness is said to be established, we will, nevertheless, record three reservations. First, the quotation above appears to concern the fixing of political allegiance or orientation whereas we should be inclined to argue that political consciousness *precedes* the establishment of political allegiance in many cases. Second, we should argue that momentous events such as war, revolution, famine and so on, if they occur early in the life of an individual or a generation, may well hasten the acquisition of a political consciousness. Conversely, a prolonged period of uneventful stability in a polity might equally delay a generation's acquiring a political consciousness (although this point we should press less strongly than the first). And, third, it seems to us slightly odd that, when psychologists and educationists stress the importance of the years up to five as being the most formative period in the individual's life in so many aspects of his subsequent behaviour, *political* consciousness should be allocated to a point in the life span as late as seventeen to twenty-five. In this connexion, it is interesting to note that the psychologist Erich Fromm has this to say when discussing what he calls 'the social character':[8]

The social character is reinforced by all the instruments of influence available to a society: its educational system, its religion, its literature, its songs, its jokes, its customs, and, most of all, its parents' methods of bringing up their children. This last is so important because the character structure of individuals is formed to a considerable extent in the first five or six years of their lives.[9]

As we remarked earlier, we have none but intuitive grounds for rejecting the age range seventeen to twenty-five as the time when political consciousness is established. However, for the reasons just given above, our inclination is to take the lower end of the range (age seventeen) as being nearer to the mark than twenty-five.

So far discussion has centred on 'biological age', the 'age of conscious recollection', and the age of political consciousness. What is needed now is a delineation of generations in terms of events. Figure 5.1 is a time chart of events in Russia and the USSR begining with the 1905 revolution. In some cases, the entries specify momentous events (the 1917 revolution, collectivisation, the Second World War, and so on). Other events are more symbolic (for example, the completion of the Dnieper hydro-electric station in 1932), while yet others are little more than minor landmarks (in comparison with momentous events), the XXIV CPSU Congress being a case in point. If, however, using the same time scale, we place alongside the chart the lifespan of an individual, or of a generation, we can see the degree to which the ages of conscious recollection and acquisition of political consciousness correspond to certain events in the life of the polity. Figure 5.1 depicts also, in simple biological terms, the coincidence of Brezhnev's life (A) and his aide Katushev's life (B) with events in the life of the Soviet polity and also *vis-à-vis* each other.

On the basis of Figure 5.1 we can see that the 1917 revolution lies within the range of Brezhnev's conscious recollection, that he was twenty-three when mass collectivisation began, thirty-five at the outbreak of war between the USSR and Germany, and so on. Katushev (born 1927), on the other hand, attained the age of conscious recollection at the height of the purges and was too young for military service during the war. These observations, interesting though they may be, are curiously flat and one-dimensional if only the individual's age and the events are described. To round out the picture, and to enhance the validity of any inferences which might be drawn, what is needed also is some indication of events personal, or peculiar, to the individual. At this juncture, we introduce the factor of 'political', as opposed to simply 'biological' age.

In the context of the USSR, 'political age' we would define as being the 'age' of an individual calculated from the

FIG 5.1 USSR – time chart

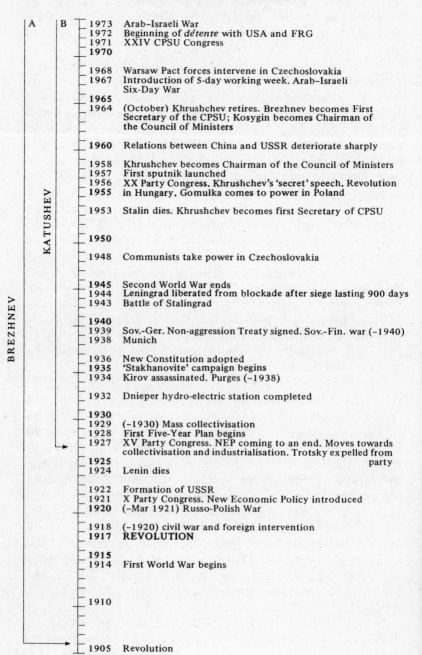

		1973	Arab–Israeli War
		1972	Beginning of *détente* with USA and FRG
		1971	XXIV CPSU Congress
		1970	
		1968	Warsaw Pact forces intervene in Czechoslovakia
		1967	Introduction of 5-day working week. Arab–Israeli Six-Day War
		1965	
		1964	(October) Khrushchev retires. Brezhnev becomes First Secretary of the CPSU; Kosygin becomes Chairman of the Council of Ministers
		1960	Relations between China and USSR deteriorate sharply
		1958	Khrushchev becomes Chairman of the Council of Ministers
		1957	First sputnik launched
		1956	XX Party Congress. Khrushchev's 'secret' speech. Revolution
		1955	in Hungary. Gomulka comes to power in Poland
		1953	Stalin dies. Khrushchev becomes first Secretary of CPSU
		1950	
		1948	Communists take power in Czechoslovakia
		1945	Second World War ends
		1944	Leningrad liberated from blockade after siege lasting 900 days
		1943	Battle of Stalingrad
		1940	
		1939	Sov.-Ger. Non-aggression Treaty signed. Sov.-Fin. war (–1940)
		1938	Munich
		1936	New Constitution adopted
		1935	'Stakhanovite' campaign begins
		1934	Kirov assassinated. Purges (–1938)
		1932	Dnieper hydro-electric station completed
		1930	
		1929	(–1930) Mass collectivisation
		1928	First Five-Year Plan begins
		1927	XV Party Congress. NEP coming to an end. Moves towards collectivisation and industrialisation. Trotsky expelled from party
		1925	
		1924	Lenin dies
		1922	Formation of USSR
		1921	X Party Congress. New Economic Policy introduced
		1920	(–Mar 1921) Russo-Polish War
		1918	(–1920) civil war and foreign intervention
		1917	**REVOLUTION**
		1915	
		1914	First World War begins
		1910	
		1905	Revolution

BREZHNEV KATUSHEV A B

time when he joined the Communist Party of the Soviet Union. The first and most obvious observation is that the concept of political age as defined here applies to only a small percentage of the population of the USSR. More relevantly, however, we must explain the reasons for believing that 'political age' is distinct from biological age and age of acquisition of political consciousness.

For that minority of the population of Great Britain who become members of one of the major political parties the act of enrolment implies no doubt an act of political participation which marks them off from the majority of their fellow citizens. We would argue, however, that becoming a member of one of the major British political parties has nothing like the impact on the British individual that joining the CPSU has on the Soviet citizen. The requirements of CPSU membership are in comparison extremely stringent, and, once admitted, the party member is obliged to maintain a high level of activeness [*aktivnost'*] and participation.[10] Moreover, in a single-party system the aura of exclusiveness surrounding party membership enhances the individual's consciousness of political commitment. Nor does the apparent prevalence of passiveness [*passivnost'*] amongst many CPSU members detract from this proposition, since periodically the party engages in membership purges[11] for the purposes of weeding out passive members or at least reactivating them. In either case, the demands of party membership are kept constantly in the forefront of the individual member's consciousness.

Another important distinction is that the history of the USSR since the beginning of the century has been far more turbulent than that of Britain. Since 1917 the CPSU has been the dominant political party, and for most of that time the *only* political party involved in the running of the polity. Consequently, all events in the Soviet Union's development are inextricably linked with the party. Successes are attributed to the party, and also failures (though in this case, rarely publicly). Especially in the early years of Soviet power, to be a party member meant very often to risk one's life. In the civil war (1919-21) and then again in the Second World War (1941-5) Communists were mobilised and sent into the front line, suffering heavy casualties in the process. Again, many party members endured harrowing experiences during collectivisation, and it is well-known that Communists were far from immune to the predations of Stalin's purges. In short, it is our view that the act of becoming a member of the CPSU (even today) is a matter of greater moment than is the case in most West European societies (excluding, of course, the act of joining a western Soviet-type Communist party), and that the individual's responses to situations are likely to differ depending upon whether or not he is a Communist. Also, we suggest that the membership of the CPSU may be subdivided into generations, with 'political age' taking precedence over 'biological age'.

It is evident that the CPSU itself recognises the existence of political generations within its ranks, and it is interesting to note that it is length of party service [*partiinyy stazh*], rather than biological age, which determines the boundaries of generations. What is *not* publicly acknowledged is the possibility that there exists a potential for conflict between different generational groups. The following extract from Brezhnev's main speech to the XXIII Congress (1966) ilustrates both these points:

> Length of party service in terms of entry into the CPSU's ranks merits attention. We can see party veterans, who have experienced three revolutions; communists tempered in the struggle for the industrialisation of the country and the battle for the collectivisation of agriculture — for the great socialist transformation of the Motherland; we see here also those who linked their lives to the party in the terrible years of the Great Patriotic War and who after the war raised up again the Soviet Motherland from ruins and ash. All of these are today actively building the communist society as members of the united army of political fighters.[12]

It would be a mistake to imagine that Brezhnev's optimistic, emotional and somewhat idealised view of the CPSU membership is not shared by large numbers of Communists. On the other hand, it quite obviously ignores the more negative aspects of being a party member in some of the periods enumerated. It may indeed be the case that many Communists who participated in the collectivisation process were uplifted by the belief that their cause was a right one, and that the 'socialist transformation of the Motherland' justified the methods employed in that transformation. But to hold such beliefs did not necessarily render the individual insensible to the horrors being perpetrated, and these must surely have left their mark on the political consciousness of many participants:

> Those of the *Communists* who had been directly immersed in the horrors of collectivisation were thereafter marked men [recalled one participant[13]]. We carried the scars. We had seen ghosts. We could almost be identified by our taciturnity, by the way we shrank from discussion of the 'peasant front'. We might consider the subject among ourselves . . . but to talk of it to the uninitiated seemed futile. With them we had no common vocabulary of experience [emphasis added].

Events such as war and revolution, collectivisation and the purges obviously merit the designation 'momentous'. Willy-nilly, they involved the participation of masses of people. But events involving in a direct sense only a small number of people may have an enormous impact on the populace in general and on party members in particular. Such an event was Khrushchev's 'Secret Speech' to the XX Party Congress in 1956 when many of Stalin's 'excesses' were spoken about openly for the first time. The revelations attracted world-wide attention, but the effect on members of the CPSU was probably unique. Evtushenko's recollections of the 'Secret Speech' are interesting on two counts. First, they give an idea of the shock wave which Communists, and others, experienced at the time; and, second, they provide a useful and necessary caution against conceptualising generations in wholly horizontal terms. That is, while in general it may be proper to isolate generations — biological or political — according to a linear time scale, it is also wise to bear in mind that, in terms of attitudes and responses, vertical divisions may occur which encompass all or a number of generations: 'The older generation split in two: the genuine, dedicated communists who continued to work without losing courage but ready to remember past mistakes in order to correct them; and the dogmatists who naturally regarded themselves as the most dedicated communists of them all.'[14] Moreover,

Evtushenko adds, 'There are many communists old enough to be my father whom I have always felt to be my contemporaries — and I have contemporaries who reek to me of mothballs.'[15]

The death of Stalin and his subsequent exposure by Khrushchev in 1956 are probably the last events in Soviet political life to merit being described as 'momentous'. The ousting of Khrushchev from the party and state leaderships, party congresses, Czechoslovakia in 1968 — all these are important landmarks in recent Soviet history, but none bears comparison with the upheavals and strains of earlier periods. Indeed, should this relative stability continue for another decade or longer, then it will be necessary to revise one's views about generational differences in CPSU composition. Already, more than three-quarters of the total party membership joined the party in the postwar period. In terms of members' political lives, the 1973 composition may be divided as in Table 5.2.

TABLE 5.2 CPSU membership (1973): length
of party service

Length of party service	Time interval in which joined party	Percentage of total membership
All members and candidate members		100.0 (14,821,031)
By *stazh:*		
up to 5 yrs	since 1967	19.1
6-10 yrs	1963-7	22.5
11-20 yrs	1953-62	26.9
21-30 yrs	1943-52	22.1
31-40 yrs	1933-42	6.2
41-50 yrs	1923-32	2.9
More than 50 yrs	Up to 1923	0.3

Source: Adapted from 'KPSS v tsifrakh', *Partiinaya Zhizn'* no. 14 (July 1973) 9-26, p.19.

As Table 5.2 indicates, 68.5 per cent of the CPSU membership have joined the party in the post-Stalin period, and a further 8.3 per cent between the end of the war and 1953 (76.8 per cent in all). Even if one allows for the fact that many of these party members will have been influenced by events occurring in the pre-party part of their lives, it is none the less striking that approximately seven out of every ten communists have no first-hand experience of intra-party life under Stalin's personal leadership. Similarly, well over 90 per cent of today's members of the CPSU were recruited in the post-purge period.[16] As we shall see below, this is in marked contrast to the political experience of men who currently occupy senior office in the party apparatus.

Table 5.3 depicts the composition of the CPSU in 1973 in terms of biological age. We have adapted the official data in such a way as to express not simply age cohorts, but also the years in which each cohort is estimated to have reached the age of conscious recollection and the age of political consciousness (ages ten and seventeen respectively). We have assumed that the mean age for joining the party is twenty-five[17] and the year for each cohort's estimated time of joining is given, too.

Assuming that the age when political consciousness is attained is seventeen, we can see from Table 5.3 that over 70 per cent (73.3) of today's party members attained the age of political consciousness in the post-1939 (or, post-purge) period. Even on the basis of 'conscious recollection', some 44 per cent of party members fall into the post-1942 bracket, and, of course, this percentage would increase significantly were we able to estimate those who attained the age of conscious recollection in the period 1939-42. In short, our chief point is that, whether one takes the criterion of biological age or of political age, a very large proportion of the party membership is highly unlikely to have participated directly, or to have been directly affected by (in descending order of probability) the Purges, collectivisation, the first industrialisation drive, the intra-party struggles of the twenties, NEP, War Communism and the civil war, and, least likely, the revolution.

On the other hand, many of the men who now constitute the central party leadership and, *inter alia,* determine policy possess life experience which includes all or many of the above-mentioned events. This in itself is insufficient evidence to suppose that there exists within the party a 'generation conflict', but, circumstantially at least, it does suggest that the potential for such a conflict is present. The possible issues

TABLE 5.3: CPSU membership (1973): age

Age	Years when born	Absolute no.	As % of total no.	Yrs when attained age of 'conscious re-collection' (10)	Yrs when attained age of political consciousness (17)	Yrs when joined CPSU (assuming mean age of joining to be 25)
All members and candidate members CPSU (1973)		14,821,031	100.0			
By age:						
up to 25 yrs	Born since 1948	834,166	5.7	1958	1965	1973
26-30 yrs	1943-7	1,101,794	7.4	1953-7	1960-4	1968-72
31-40 yrs	1933-42	4,588,939	31.0	1943-52	1950-9	1958-67
41-50 yrs	1923-32	4,329,005	29.2	1933-42	1940-9	1948-57
51-60 yrs	1913-22	2,425,048	16.3	1923-32	1930-9	1938-47
Over 60 yrs	Born before 1913	1,542,079	10.4	Before 1923	By 1930	By 1938

Source: Compiled from data in 'KPSS v tsifrakh', *Partiinaya Zhizn'*, no. 14 (July 1973) 9-26, p.19.

over which conflict might arise lie outside the present
discussion, but Nove's assessment of Khrushchev as a political
leader is apposite to the general point:

> [He achieved] considerable successes, especially in his first
> five years, and his defects are explicable by his background
> and experience. He was politically 'educated' under
> Kaganovich, in the dramatic years of the early thirties. He
> inherited many perplexing problems, and his methods of
> tackling them belonged to a different epoch, and were now
> obsolete. . . . He showed that he knew better than anyone
> how the bureaucratic apparatus of party and state could
> distort policy and paralyse desired initiative. But in the
> end he knew only the traditional methods.[18]

At the present time (April 1975), twenty-five men
constitute the central CPSU leadership — the Politburo and
Secretariat of the All-Union Central Committee. Their
average age is sixty-two. Taking the Politburo alone (full and
candidate members together) the average age rises to sixty-
four, while the average age of full members of the Politburo
(of whom there are fifteen) is sixty-five. General Secretary
Brezhnev is sixty-eight (born 1906) and has been a
Communist since 1931, and Premier Kosygin is seventy-one
years old and joined the party in 1927. Podgorny, President
of the USSR, is seventy-two and became a party member in
1930. In terms of biological age, then, all three men belong to
the 10.4 per cent of the CPSU's total membership which was
born before 1913 (see Table 5.3). In political terms, they
belong to the 3.2 per cent of Communists who joined the
party before 1933 (see Table 5.2). The pattern is much the
same if we take the 'average' full member of the Politburo;
although extremes naturally differ from the mean, with
Pel'she, who was born in 1899 and joined the party in 1915
at one end of the continuum, and Kulakov, born 1918 and a
party member since 1940, at the other.

The generational gap between the central party leadership
and the mass rank and file is a frequent source of comment
by political scientists specialising in Soviet affairs. In his
analysis of the Central Committee elected at the XXIII
Congress in 1966, Michael P. Gehlen noted that in that year
over half the party's members were under forty years old.

Taking into account that 'they had matured and begun their careers after the great purges' and that 'they represent a better educated and more highly specialised generation than the older party generation', Gehlen concludes that 'in a sense they constitute a real threat to the older generation. The more conservative apparatchiki are particularly suspicious of their career-oriented, advancement-conscious juniors.'[19]

Now, this seems to us to be a reasonable inference to make on the basis of the available statistical evidence. However, simple generational discrepancies such as those we have mentioned above (and also those mentioned by Gehlen and others) require additional support of a less circumstantial nature in order to reinforce the validity of any generalisations concerning generation conflict (actual or potential). To some extent, support for this view was provided by Brezhnev himself in his main report to the XXIV Congress in 1971 when he devoted a section of his speech to what in western political-science teminology would be called 'elite circulation'. He began by noting that 'During the period under review [1966-71] many new people have been promoted to Party, government and economic work in the centre and in the localities, and the cadres have been renewed or augmented with fresh blood.'[20] Brezhnev is saying, in effect, that in the middle to upper levels of leadership new personnel have been brought in to replace others who have been moved up from, or out of, these levels. Who has gone up?

'The secretaries of some territorial and regional [party] committees, the chairmen of some regional executive committees [of Soviets] and other functionaries from republican, territorial and regional organs have been promoted to posts in central bodies such as ministers, chairmen of state committees and other leading positions.

Who, then, has come in to replace the promotees?

Many new comrades with an excellent political and specialist training have been promoted to the leadership of Party and government bodies in the localities, including the posts of first secretaries of the Central Committees of the republican Communist Parties, and of territorial [*krai*] and regional [*oblast*] committees.

The aim governing the leadership's cadre policy is, added Brezhnev, 'to promote young, promising functionaries while maintaining a considerate attitude to veteran cadres and making maximum use of their experience and knowledge.'

Several points emerge from Brezhnev's remarks. First, it must be remembered that in most political systems, for most of the time, there is an inevitable discrepancy in age between party and government leaderships on the one hand, and the rank and file on the other. Quite simply, it takes time for the individual to work his way up a hierarchy before attaining a top leadership position. Second a leader, or *the* leader, may be relatively old, yet he may manage to infuse the leadership group with younger blood and new ideas. Macmillan's dismissal in 1962 of seven members of his Cabinet is perhaps an example of this; and Brezhnev's remarks fairly explicitly acknowledge the need for periodic renewal of leading cadres. Yet the irony here is that, although Brezhnev is clearly aware of the need to do this, and, indeed, has been as good as his word so far as the upper levels of the local party apparatus are concerned, when it comes to the central party leadership itself there has been considerable 'immobilism' since 1964.[21] Moreover, the very group to which he paid most attention in his 1971 congress speech is precisely that sector of the party apparatus which is most likely to have ambitions to move into the central leadership, that is, the party *obkom* first secretaries. The fact that approximately two-thirds of the twenty-five men who currently constitute the central party leadership were *obkom* first secretaries immediately prior to being promoted into leadership positions at either republic or all-Union level is evidence enough that the *obkom* first secretary tier constitutes the most important single reservoir for recruitment into the top party leadership. The question is: how long will this group remain satisfied with ministries and chairmanships of state committees so long as the Politburo and Secretariat are dominated by men who, in the main, are over sixty, with several aged seventy and over? It is in this sense that 'immobilism' and 'generation gaps' can cause blockages in the promotion pipeline with their resultant frustrations and conflict. To that extent, the *obkom* first secretaries would appear to be a key group in any examination of the problem of intra-party generations, and it is to that group that we now turn our attention.

Table 5.4 shows the years when four generations of CPSU *obkom* first secretaries were born. The ranges are the same as those used for Table 5.3 when summarising the age of generations within the total CPSU membership. The most appropriate column in Table 5.4, therefore, for the purposes of comparison, is that relating to the 1970 generation of *obkom* first secretaries, which may be compared with the data presented in Table 5.3 which relate to 1973.

There are obvious risks inherent in a comparison of a population of approaching 15 million (CPSU membership in 1973) with a sub-group of that population as small as 141 (the number of *obkom* first secretaries in 1970), and, also, of course, with the three-year discrepancy involved. None the less, it is equally clear that a sub-group of officials within a structured organisation might reasonably be expected to reflect trends within the total party membership, especially with respect to generation differences. The first and most striking observation, then, is that 100 per cent of the 1970 *obkom* first secretaries are drawn from 56 per cent of the total party membership. Conversely, 44 per cent of CPSU members have no 'peer representation' at the *obkom* level. Since, as we shall see, *obkom* first secretaries constitute an important segment of Central Committee membership, the implications of this discrepancy go beyond symbolic representation and bring into question once more the possibility of at least latent generational conflict, but now with the additional dimension of occupancy of party office. To reinforce this point and linking it with the question of 'immobilism', we can see from Table 5.4 how that group of *obkom* first secretaries born in the period 1913-22 is holding its dominant position into the 1970s. In 1958 just under a quarter of *obkom* first secretaries had been born in those years, while the majority (98 out of 132) were older. Then they represented the younger cohort of first secretaries, whereas by 1962 they were evenly balanced with the older generation. But the most striking feature is that, reaching their peak in 1966, the 1913-22 group maintained their position in absolute numbers in 1970, and even proportionately their share fell by less than 1 per cent between 1966 and 1970, from 53.2 per cent to 52.5 per cent. The fact that the *obkom* first secretary generation born between 1923 and 1932 improved its position from zero representation in

TABLE 5.4: CPSU *obkom* first secretaries: date of birth

When born	1958 generation (N = 132 = 100%)	1962 generation (N = 140 = 100%)	1966 generation (N = 139 = 100%)	1970 generation (N = 141 = 100%)
Before 1913	98 (75.4%)	66 (47.1%)	39 (29.0%)	23 (16.3%)
1913–22	32 (24.6%)	66 (47.1%)	74 (53.2%)	74 (52.5%)
1923–32	Nil	8 (5.7%)	26 (18.7%)	44 (31.2%)

TABLE 5.5: CPSU *obkom* first secretaries: length of party service

When joined the party	1958 generation (N = 132 = 100%)	1962 generation (N = 140 = 100%)	1966 generation (N = 139 = 100%)	1970 generation (N = 141 = 100%)
Before 1923	1 (0.8%)	Nil	Nil	Nil
1923–32	65 (49.2%)	39 (27.9%)	22 (15.8%)	11 (7.8%)
1933–42	62 (47.0%)	77 (55.0%)	63 (45.3%)	53 (37.6%)
1943–52	4 (3.0%)	24 (17.1%)	48 (34.5%)	62 (44.0%)
1953–62	Nil	Nil	6 (4.3%)	15 (10.6%)

1958 to 31.2 per cent in 1970 is clearly important in itself (in that it represents, at least in age terms, what Brezhnev described as a renewal of cadres 'with fresh blood').[22] Yet the renewal has obviously been exclusively at the expense of the older, pre-1913 generation. There are two possible interpretations of this trend. First, it might be argued that the continued primacy of a political generation in so small a group as the *obkom* first secretaries is likely to exacerbate intergenerational tensions. Second, it may be that, given the present leadership's clear desire to stabilise and regularise elite circulation, the trend observable in Table 5.4 is simply a reflection of a more measured and rational distribution of senior party cadres: that, indeed, we can envisage a stable career structure in which there is a fairly predictable tenure of office. For the ratio 23:74:44 which we find in 1970 describes a much more regular curve than in any other year except 1966. It remains to be seen whether or not the curve is skewed in the future. If it is, then it would tend to confirm our first hypothesis (that intergenerational tensions are likely to increase). If the curve remains normal, then our second suggestion (that career patterns are being deliberately stabilised) would seem to be more accurate.

Turning now to length of party service (cf. Tables 5.2 and 5.5), we can see that 100 per cent of the 1970 generation of *obkom* first secretaries are drawn from 58.4 per cent of the total CPSU membership (with, therefore, nearly 42 per cent not 'represented' at the *obkom* level). Again, it is worth repeating that there is an inevitable and 'natural' discrepancy between rank and file of a party and its senior functionaries; but in the case of the CPSU the difference seems to us to be unusually great.[23]

Taking the two variables together, the situation in 1970 was for *obkom* first secretaries aged between forty-eight and fifty-seven to predominate (over 52 per cent of the total); while in terms of party service the biggest single group consisted of those first secretaries who had joined the party between 1943 and 1952 (44 per cent). In terms of biological age, therefore, the most numerous group of 1970 *obkom* first secretaries, taking the mean year of birth for this cohort to be 1918, were reaching the age of conscious recollection just as collectivisation and the First Five-Year Plan were getting under way, and the age of political consciousness at the height of the purges. Their promotion up the party hierarchy coincided with the postwar reconstruction period preceding the death of Stalin in 1953 (as we have noted, they joined the party between 1943 and 1952). Even allowing for statistical distortion (in fact, it is most probable that a majority of this cohort joined the party in the period 1939-42), the picture which emerges is of a group of party functionaries whose life experience coincides with the most vicious period of Stalin's rule. It should not, however, be assumed automatically that these men are necessarily 'neo-Stalinists' simply on the strength of this chronological coincidence. We have noted already Evtushenko's caution against such over-simplification, and there is also the important point that few of these men held offices of importance at the time of Stalin's worst excesses (even though they were the beneficiaries of Stalin's depredations on party cadres in the 'thirties). That apart, however, there is a risk that these *obkom* first secretaries might be imbued with Stalinist work styles. Alec Nove pinpointed Khrushchev's weakness in this respect and we find a strong echo of his words in Brezhnev's 1971 congress speech where he observed:

> It sometimes happens that a leading cadre gets the idea that all secrets of life are open to him, that he knows everything. That is when he begins issuing instructions on all questions, ordering people about, instead of skilfully using the experience and knowledge of others. We have long had skilled cadres capable of correctly resolving the problems within their competence. We must put more trust in them, and, correspondingly, more must be asked of them.[24]

What *are* the qualities the leadership is now looking for to meet the demands of the technological age? According to Brezhnev, these:

> We need people who combine a high level of political consciousness with a sound professional training, people who can knowledgeably tackle the problems of economic and cultural development and are well-versed in modern methods of management.

In cadres the Party has always highly valued such a quality as the feeling for the new. To have this feeling means to see the prospects of development, to look into the future and find the surest ways of resolving problems as they arise. This quality is particularly important today, when swift and far-reaching changes are taking place in social life and production.[25]

Obviously, to meet these requirements is a matter not simply of age. More than anything else, perhaps, it is a question of type and level of education. But to the extent that educational facilities in general and quality of instruction in particular have improved enormously in the USSR in the post-Stalin period, age alone is a fairly reliable indicator to use for estimating the qualities of those who received their formal education in the Stalin era, and these include, of course, the group of *obkom* first secretaries under discussion. By 1970 over 10 per cent of all *obkom* first secretaries had joined the party in the post-Stalin period, and, while they obviously received their education before 1953, they are less likely to have been affected by the initiative-stifling atmosphere to which their older and longer-serving colleagues had been exposed. It should be remembered, incidentally, that Brezhnev may wish to infuse younger blood into the *obkom* first secretary tier at a somewhat faster rate than is evident from the statistical data, but that he dare not force the pace for fear of antagonising unduly a group of men who, although few in terms of total CPSU membership, are an important major element in the Central Committee.

Our conclusions on the matter of intra-party generations are these:

(1) That there is ample circumstantial evidence to lend support to the proposition that there is a fairly high degree of 'immobilism' in the upper echelons of the party hierarchy. That Brezhnev, at least, its aware of the risks inherent in such a situation and is taking active steps to ameliorate the situation by speeding up elite circulation on both political and pragmatic grounds, but that so far he has failed to open up the key Politburo group to younger men to any significant degree. So long as this remains the case, the blockage in the career pipe line is

likely to persist, or grow worse, and this in turn could aggravate latent or actual intergenerational conflict.

(2) That the age and party-service composition of the total CPSU membership and the senior cadre group are out of jig with each other, but that there are some signs that the leadership is trying to correct these imbalances to produce a more regular situation.

(3) That a very large proportion of the CPSU mass membership (some 70 per cent) has no direct experience of party membership under Stalin, and while the fact of not having belonged to a political party during the period of leadership of a particular individual might not normally be regarded as a significant factor in the political outlook of a party member, in the Soviet context, for the reasons outlined above, we should argue that it is.

NOTES

1 Anthony Sampson, *Macmillan. A Study in Ambiguity* (London, 1967) p. 22.

2 Sampson, *Macmillan*, p. 21.

3 Emanuel Shinwell, *Conflict without Malice* (London, 1955) p. 29.

4 Alec Nove, *An Economic History of the USSR* (Harmondsworth, 1972) p. 223.

5 Nove, *Economic History of the USSR*, p. 223.

6 John D. Nagle, 'The Soviet Political Elite, 1917-1971: Application of a Generational Model of Social Change', a paper presented at the annual meeting of the American Political Science Association, New Orleans, Louisiana, mimeo (1973) p. 3. Nagle cites the views of three scholars on the question of political consciousness (see his footnotes 5, 6, 7).

7 Nagle, 'The Soviet Political Elite', p. 3.

8 Erich Fromm, 'The Application of Humanist Psychoanalysis to Marx's Theory', in Erich Fromm, *Socialist Humanism: An international symposium* (London, 1967) pp. 207-22, 210-11. Fromm defines the 'social character' as: 'that particular structure of psychic energy which is moulded by any given society so as to be useful for the functioning of that particular society'. We are not suggesting that this is directly equatable with 'political consciousness'.

9 Fromm, 'Application of Humanist Psychoanalysis', p. 211.

10 See *Ustav KPSS*.

11 We have in mind here 'purges' — *chistki* — in their non-violent sense. The exchange of party documents which began in 1973 is an example of such a membership purge.

12 *XXIII S''ezd KPSS, Stenograficheskii otchet* (Moscow, 1966) vol. 1, p. 87.

13   Victor Kravchenko, *I Chose Freedom. The Personal and Political Life of a Soviet Official* (London, 1949 ed.) p. 107.
14   Yevgeny Yevtushenko, *A Precocious Autobiography* (Harmondsworth, 1965) p. 109.
15   Yevtushenko, *Autobiography*, p. 111.
16   90.6 per cent of party members joined the party after 1942. Since the years 1939-42 saw considerable recruitment, even allowing for war losses, the figure for the post-purge period must be significantly higher.
17   Twenty-five may be too high a mean age. However, it is difficult to find reliable evidence on this. The mean age of joining the party for all generations of *obkom* first secretaries investigated by us was in the range twenty-four to twenty-five years. Older and longer-serving Communists may on average have been recruited at a younger age, although the *obkom* first secretary data would not bear this out.
18   Nove, *Economic History of the USSR*, p. 368.
19   Michael P. Gehlen, *The Communist Party of the Soviet Union. A Functional Analysis* (Bloomington, Indiana, 1969) p. 39.
20   These quotations are from Leonid Brezhnev, *Report of the CPSU Central Committee to the 24th Congress of the Communist Party of the Soviet Union* (Moscow, 1971) pp. 116-17.
21   See T. H. Rigby, 'The Soviet Leadership: Towards a Self-Stabilising Oligarchy?', *Soviet Studies*, vol. 22, no. 2 (1970) pp. 167-91. On 'immobilism' and the generational problem, see especially pp. 190-1.
22   Brezhnev, *Report*, p. 116.
23   We have no empirical evidence to support this supposition. So far as we know, there are no studies providing information on the ages of political leaderships and the mass membership of political parties.
24   Brezhnev, *Report*, p. 117.
25   Brezhnev, *Report*, p. 117.

6 The Development of Dissent and Opposition

PETER REDDAWAY[1]

INTRODUCTION

Under Stalin Soviet society was effectively atomised by the application over two decades of mass terror. In an important if paradoxical sense, it was depoliticised.[2] Since his death in 1953 a process of incipient repoliticisation has begun, affecting both the *apparat* which rules the country and many groups outside it. The process was encouraged in various deliberate and non-deliberate ways by Khrushchev, but has developed much faster under his successors. This has been partly in reaction to their tendency to try to *discourage* it and, in important respects, to reverse it. One could also perhaps say that in the absence of a return to mass terror such a process has been inevitable. In any case, most of the groups outside the *apparat* have developed increasingly dissenting features, a trend which seems sure to continue.

Today the leadership of the *apparat* possesses enormous power, but probably decreasing authority (at any rate at home). A similar situation existed, we might note in passing, in the last decades of the tsarist period. Today's leadership cannot, however, try to increase its authority by adopting a new ideology or seriously atoning for the past, as such a course appears to it much more risky — cf. Khrushchev's partial attempts — than 'clinging on'.

Why is this so? First, perhaps, because the post-Khrushchev leadership has systematically suppressed the issue of the mass crimes of Stalin, which involved, among other things, the death of some 20 million Soviet citizens through shooting, concentration camps, deportations and artificial famine in the period 1930-53. The leadership is therefore widely, if often subconsciously, linked with those crimes and with all the personal, social and economic suffering which accompanied them, some of which persists to this day. A second reason is that Soviet Marxism-Leninism has become ossifield, ritualised and almost universally — except within the party apparatus, where it is the obligatory language — discredited or ignored. In this way an ideological vacuum has been created in society and even, potentially, within the *apparat*. It is this vacuum which the dissenting forces show some signs of beginning to fill, much to the alarm of the *apparat*.

Not surprisingly, therefore, the Soviet leaders continue firmly to reject the idea of 'ideological coexistence' (as opposed to 'peaceful coexistence'), as such coexistence would tend to facilitate and, even worse, legitimise the growth of domestic dissent and opposition. When dissent none the less appears they often label it subversion, as will be seen below.

DEFINITIONS OF DISSENT AND OPPOSITION

This brings us to the problem of defining dissent and opposition. In any autocracy where such activities are illegitimate, or only semi-legitimate, and where the true aims of the dissenters and oppositionists are often therefore disguised, this problem is difficult. Under an autocracy with totalitarian goals, like that of the CPSU,[3] it is especially difficult. Broadly, though, opposition implies an aspiration to rule in place of the existing rulers, whereas dissent implies no such aspiration, just an objection to certain of the rulers' actions or policies and a determination to 'articulate demands' not only through approved, but also through non-approved channels. Thus Trotsky and his followers openly called themselves an opposition, even when exiled abroad. But the 2000-odd documents and books of *samizdat* which have reached the West in the last decade from extra-systemic sources contain very few references to any 'opposition' in the USSR today. Their authors use most frequently about themselves and their colleagues the word dissenters [*inakomyslyashchie*]. And such people are usually regarded as expressing dissent [*inakomyslie*], either in their writings or by their 'actions in defence of human (or national) rights'.

None the less, Soviet dissent should still be viewed as a seed-bed for opposition, and some of the dissenters as proto-oppositionists. For although most dissenters do not form conspiratorial groups or draft political programmes, and thereby at least imply a desire to change the system and play a leading part in a new one, there are some who do,[4] and the borderline between the two categories is often blurred. Also, there is the ambiguous phenomenon of those writings — like some of Sakharov's and Roy Medvedev's — which virtually amount to oppositional programmes, but whose authors show little or no inclination to court arrest by participating in oppositional (rather than dissenting) activity. This phenomenon could, perhaps, be called intellectual opposition.[5]

OPPOSITION WITHIN THE REGIME

Although the regime's greatest weakness is the inflexibility of itself and its *apparat* (terror no longer being available to cut through the various powerful vested interests), opposition can and does, as Conquest and others have shown,[6] exist at the higher levels. It is different in character from extra-systemic opposition, being, despite the party's ban on factionalism, less illegitimate and also more shifting and fluid. It occurs on particular issues and groups of issues, but, as with the 'anti-Party group' in the mid-1950s, it can quickly develop and embrace broad trends of policy. It is especially likely to appear when a power struggle is producing instability in the leadership.

Opposition within the *apparat* is, of course, when it occurs, the only significant and fully political opposition to exist in the contemporary Soviet Union. But it constitutes a big and largely separate subject, and therefore falls outside the bounds of this chapter. We might only note here that in a system as inflexible as the Soviet one, and in a world where change occurs with increasing rapidity, either opposition factions or established leaders could well in future feel compelled to look outside the Establishment for new ideas. Thus they could easily make contact with the dissenters in a way that most of the latter would welcome. Already one can infer that certain sorts of unorthodox ideas attract at any rate small sections of the *apparat*. Roy Medvedev, although a rather isolated figure among the active dissenters, has evidently enjoyed enough protection from *apparatchiki* sympathetic to his brand of 'socialism with a human face' to enable him to continue writing and publishing abroad. And, probably of greater significance, the Russian nationalist dissenters outside the *apparat* clearly enjoy high-level protection, as they have been virtually immune from arrest.

SOVIET LAW AND KGB PRACTICE IN THE AREA OF DISSENT

The traditional Soviet tendency has been to see, or pretend to see, actual or potential opposition in almost all forms of persistent dissent. Yet it should be stressed at this point that the Criminal Code, in defining different types of political offence, does make a distinction between dissent and opposition, even though not in those terms. Opposition is punishable under, notably, articles 70 and 72, which concern 'anti-Soviet agitation and propaganda' and 'anti-Soviet organisation', both conducted with the aim of weakening or overthrowing the Soviet system as a whole. The penalties are correspondingly severe. Article 190-1, by contrast, in practice concerns dissent. It penalises the possession or propagation (in written or oral form) of 'deliberate fabrications which discredit the Soviet political and social system'. It is not concerned with agitation against the system as a whole, and so the penalties are relatively light (up to three years' imprisonment or five years' exile).

The fact that 'deliberate fabrications', rather than 'views objectionable to the state', are specified in article 190-1 can presumably be explained by an official desire not to contradict too blatantly the constitutional guarantee of freedom of conscience. Yet, partly due to the dissenters' efforts, this fact has a definitely inhibiting effect on the KGB in some cases. In others, however, the well-documented pleas of defendants that they have propagated no fabrications, let alone deliberate ones, are simply ignored by the courts (acting on party or police instructions), which sentence them regardless. The dissenters' only satisfaction then is that they have clearly revealed the kangaroo nature of the proceedings.

Similarly, the KGB has to consider carefully, in some cases, whether it has enough evidence to prosecute under, say article 70, or whether it must content itself with article 190-1. The strength or weakness of their inhibitions in any particular case depends on many factors: are they operating in Moscow (under the eyes of activists and foreigners), or in the provinces (where arbitrariness knows fewer restraints)? Is the defendant skilful in his own defence and would he be able effectively to expose evidence they might fabricate? Has he managed to outmanoeuvre them and secure the services of one of the few lawyers who will vigorously defend him? And what are the operational guidelines of the moment from their political masters?

The KGB is, then, subject to certain political and legal restraints in its handling of dissent. More than this, ever since the arrest of Beria, the reduction of his empire, and this empire's subordination to close party control, the regime has taken pains to bureaucratise the KGB and thus to ensure that it can never again be used to destroy the party leadership as it did in the 1930s. The regime has achieved this partly through introducing (in the 1950s) laws to limit the KGB's powers, and partly through appointing men from the party apparatus to head the organisation, to follow Politbureau guidelines, and to prevent the re-emergence of any tendencies to autonomy.

The dissenters, too, impose restraints. As discussed above, they try to take full advantage of the more liberal laws. They also, with equal skill, use the weapon of publicity through *samizdat,* foreign news media, and western radio stations broadcasting to the USSR. In this way they increase the political cost of planned KGB repressions and sometimes mitigate or even prevent them.[7]

MAINSTREAM DISSENT OUTSIDE THE *APPARAT*

Manifestations of 'mainstream' dissent first appeared in the mid-1950s.[8] But a genuine human rights movement, in which different groups consciously co-operated with each other, began to emerge only in 1965-7. The main catalyst was the Ukrainian and Moscow arrests of 1965. These alarmed the more critical minds among the professional classes, which had become accustomed since 1953 to a significant degree of security and stability in their lives, to an at least embryonic rule of law. These minds had also been pondering for some years the phenomenon of Stalinism and drawing the lesson that unless one resists tyranny firmly from the start, the tyrant will soon eliminate the chance of any resistance at all. They therefore felt that the 1965 arrests, coming as they did at the same time as the tightening of the censorship and the banning of public discussion of Stalinism, might well signal a regeneration of Stalinism and that they must resist at once before it was too late.

This attitude of 'Never again!', stimulated by further political arrests in 1967 and the trial of the young intellectuals Galanskov and Ginzburg, brought the human rights movement to maturity in 1968.[9] In this year the *Chronicle of Current Events* began to appear, every two months, and to act as a forum and 'information center' for all the main groups.[10]

The most important prerequisite for this achievement by the dissenters — and also for all others — was the breaking of a series of social and political taboos, which were several decades old, and the creation of a certain atmosphere among a small section of the intelligentsia in various large cities. In this atmosphere people dared to think and act independently of the authorities, to create formal and semi-formal associations, to intercede for persecuted individuals and groups, to send information and texts of intercessions to the editors of the *Chronicle* in Moscow, to give similar material to foreign journalists, tourists and diplomats, to listen systematically to foreign radio stations and then circulate the information obtained, to turn *samizdat* into a large-scale cottage industry, to stage demonstrations, to propose to the authorities carefully drafted proposals for law reform,[11] and so on. In this atmosphere the *Chronicle* could appear and, with luck, survive.

What were its editorial principles? It avoided value judgements, it reported factually and objectively on events connected with human or national rights, and it summarised new works circulating in *samizdat*. Its liberal political position was implied by the article of the Universal Declaration of Human Rights (no. 19), which it carried regularly on its masthead: 'Everyone has the right to freedom of opinion and expression; this right includes freedom to hold opinions without interference and to seek, receive and impart information and ideas through any media and regardless of frontiers.' Its economic position was not stated, but its overall attitudes showed clearly enough in the atmosphere of enthusiasm (then mourning) for the 'Czechoslovak Spring' which some of its pages reflected.

The *Chronicle's* editors were, and still are, anonymous, as are the news items and articles, but not usually the documents, which it carries. But much is now known of its methods of compilation. Its editors have changed and rotated quite often, and very few people have known for sure who they were at any particular moment. Material for inclusion has been passed to these few people along chains which have developed on the basis of personal friendship and trust. The method of distribution has been the standard one for *samizdat:* typescripts passed from hand to hand, constantly being retyped in ten copies on onionskin paper.

Throughout its first two or three years the *Chronicle* steadily expanded its geographical coverage and its size. By 1971 it had published material from most of the major population centres of the European and Central Asian parts of the Soviet Union, and from a few labour camps and cities in Siberia. The most prominent cities over the years have been Moscow, Leningrad, Kiev, Lvov, Vilnius, Kaunas, Riga, Tallin, Gorky, Novosibirsk, and Tashkent.

The *Chronicle's* subject matter, apart from the *samizdat* summaries, can be categorised as information on: the judicial or extra-judicial persecution of individuals for expression of their views; the severe conditions in the labour camps and mental hospitals used to imprison dissenters;[12] the persecution of minority nationalities and religious believers; the activities of the censorship[13] and a few other oppressive institutions; and reactions to the dissenters' situation in the outside world. Underlying all the *Chronicle's* reporting has been an insistent concern for legality, for the observation of Soviet laws (in their more liberal interpretation), and for the subtle education of its readers in how to use their legal rights to promote the democratisation of society. Other notable features have been the *Chronicle's* size and also the accuracy, concreteness and detailed nature of its information: an average issue is 10-15,000 words long; the first thirty-two issues contain nearly 4000 different names (about half belonging to dissenters and a third to officials and their collaborators); it has made no reporting errors of substance; and it has corrected most of its minor errors in subsequent issues. In the underground conditions of its compilation and editing, clearly unusual care has been needed to attain this level of accuracy.

The 'mainstream' dissent movement, as opposed to the related but largely separate national and religious movements, has so far been supported at various times by only some 2000 people whose names we know.[14] But it has a considerably larger number of sympathisers, who read *samizdat* publications, help it in various ways, but prefer not to put their names to documents or protests. Socially, the movement is overwhelmingly middle-class. Among its informal leaders are a high percentage of people from research institutes, including a disproportionately high number of mathematicians and physicists. Other leaders and supporters are engineers, teachers, lawyers, writers, artists, journalists and students, with a very small number of workers and military men.

The movement has only been organised in the loosest sense, through personal contacts and a feeling of common purpose in difficult and often dangerous circumstances. That it would lose much of this unity if the regime were one day to liberalise and to ease the pressures on it is certain. The moral concerns which hold it together are a common humanitarianism, a common insistence on legality, and a common moral opposition to the oppressive methods of the regime. Hence it views itself not as a political but as a human rights movement, a movement which asserts the worth of the individual *vis-à-vis* the omnipotence and frequent brutality of the state.

This said, we may now look more closely at the main political, ideological and philosophical tendencies within it.

Neo-Leninists and neo-Marxists

A small and apparently declining sector consider (or considered) themselves neo-Leninists or neo-Marxists.[15] Some of these have formed groups with names like 'True Communists', which the KGB has usually broken up without much difficulty.[16] People such as the late writer Alexei Kosterin and ex-Major General Pyotr Grigorenko have tried to promote a return to Leninist ideals within the party, but have found little response and been expelled. Kosterin died in 1968, and Grigorenko was imprisoned in a psychiatric hospital.[17] The historian Roy Medvedev has pursued a similar line in a very different and less idealistic style, but also with little apparent success.[18] The absorbing *Political Diary,*[19] produced in his circles, shows in some detail how the *apparat* reacted over the years 1964-70 to this political trend and how it moved against it with increased decisiveness after seeing what a similar (if much stronger) trend could produce in Czechoslovakia in 1968. None the less, Medvedev has so far been allowed to keep the small flame of liberal Communism alight in the USSR, perhaps because elements in the *apparat* believe that the regime might one day need to turn in that direction.

Liberals and humanitarians

The second trend in the mainstream, and much the most important, can be described as liberal and humanitarian. Many people in it might call themselves apolitical supporters of ordinary human decency. Their more politically minded friends would probably not reject the western labels liberal, liberal socialist, or, in the case of the Orthodox layman Anatoly Levitin, Christian socialist. This is the trend which has produced the *Chronicle of Current Events* and which includes people like Pavel Litvinov, Larissa Bogoraz, Natalya Gorbanevskaya, Victor Nekrasov and Andrei Sakharov.[20]

Sakharov, one of the more politically minded adherents of the trend, regards himself as having moved since the mid-1960s from neo-Marxism to liberal socialism to liberalism. But since 1970 he has been typical of the trend in his tactics and his values. Skilfully using his semi-protected position as a famous scientist, he has sought more than anyone else to legitimise in practice the constitutional right to communicate truthful information at home and abroad. Such communication has now been performed so often with impunity by Sakharov, and by others operating to some extent under his wing, that it has become increasingly difficult for the KGB to prosecute producers of the *Chronicle,* which regularly does exactly the same thing. Naturally, though, the KGB's guidelines could be changed in future, to obviate this dilemma.

The humanitarian trend believes in the liberal principle of helping any individuals or groups which are being persecuted for their beliefs. Thus it maintains links with a wide variety of national, religious and cultural groups, studies their problems, transmits their petitions, journals and appeals abroad, gives these documents to foreign visitors and journalists, and publishes them in full or in summary in the *Chronicle.* It also runs an unofficial 'red cross' system of welfare and support for political prisoners and their families. Money and clothing are collected from well-off sympathisers and distributed to those in need. Money also comes from Sakharov and Solzhenitsyn, who have set up funds abroad out of income from their publications and from literary and humanitarian prizes. In addition to much *ad hoc* activity, regular meetings are held in Moscow flats, where relatives of political prisoners congregate, often from distant corners of the country, to exchange information and experiences, obtain legal advice, and, as their family incomes have often become nil, communicate their material needs.

Liberal Russian nationalists

The third and last broad trend can be labelled liberal Russian nationalist. The label distinguishes it from more chauvinistic varieties, which will be discussed later in a broader review of recent forms of dissenting Russian nationalism. This trend is not particularly strong or influential, but the presence in it of one man, Solzhenitsyn, however uncomfortably he fits, suggests that it may become stronger. Solzhenitsyn belongs in part, in fact, in the previous category, to which many of his friends also belong, as humanitarianism and human rights (especially opposition to censorship) figure strongly among his preoccupations, alongside his predominant concern for the moral regeneration of the Russian nation and the rebirth of Russian culture.[21] But his 'Open Letter to the Soviet

Leaders', published in 1974, clarifies matters and puts him indisputably among the liberal nationalists.

Vladimir Osipov, for three years the chief editor of the *samizdat* journal, *Veche,* calls himself a 'liberal patriot'. He has friends among the liberals, but strongly supports Solzhenitsyn's political position, and has consistently propagated in *Veche* the virtues of the nineteenth-century Slavophiles, whom Solzhenitsyn also admires. In early 1974 Osipov was ousted from the *Veche* editorship by less liberal elements, but soon founded a new journal of his own, *Zemlya,* only to be arrested in November of that year. It remains to be seen how strong support for his position will be in the future, and also whether the KGB will ultimately regard the liberal or the right-wing nationalists as more dangerous. The question of why it regarded Solzhenitsyn as more dangerous than any other dissenter, and therefore deported him abroad by force, is much clearer. His *Gulag Archipelago,* in particular, undermines the regime in passionate language at what, as noted earlier, are probably two of its most vulnerable points: its past record of mass crimes and its now widely discredited ideology.

THE RELATION OF THE MAINSTREAM DISSENTERS TO THE WEST

The values of the dominant trend in the mainstream dissent movement are, broadly speaking, similar to western democratic ideals. The dissenters have therefore, with one or two exceptions, expected that the western democracies will support them, and have sent a continuous stream of appeals to them to do so. Much less has been done from the West than the dissenters have hoped, but more than nothing. Most important have probably been, first, the contribution of western radio stations (especially Radio Liberty, which devotes up to a quarter of its broadcast time to transmitting *samizdat* texts) and, second, the determination of some governments and newspapers to try to defend the limited rights of western journalists in the USSR. However, *'détente'* has worried some dissenters, notably Sakharov,[22] because, while they support it fully in principle, they fear that the regime will succeed in conducting it on its own selfish terms and in exploiting what they see as western opportunism and naïveté. In this way, they fear, the West may be lulled into a false and dangerous sense of security, and the regime may be able both to postpone reform (especially economic) at home and to suppress more easily the growth of democratic trends.

To some extent their fears may, so far, have proved justified. Governments which have spoken out about the South African, Brazilian, Greek, Spanish, Chilean, and other authoritarian regimes, have preferred not to criticise publicly (or even, apparently, privately) the USSR's suppression of human rights and its treatment of political prisoners in forced labour camps and mental hospitals. In particular, the silence of the Nixon-Kissinger administration on these issues probably enabled the KGB to be considerably more repressive than the Politbureau would otherwise have permitted.

The one occasion on which a few governments spoke up was in the autumn of 1973, when a virulent campaign against Solzhenitsyn and Sakharov was launched in the Soviet media. This episode did, however, see a certain breakthrough in non-governmental, liberal opinion in the West, and this opinion, by its interventions, succeeded in acting as an at least temporary brake on KGB repression. An important lead was given by a statement of America's National Academy of Sciences in defence of Sakharov, and much liberal opinion — in the press and in organisations like the International PEN Club, the American Academy of Arts and Sciences, Amnesty International, and so on — followed suit. Thus, we might note, the situation of the late tsarist period may have been recreated. At that time equivalent opinion was strongly critical of the autocracy, while western governments generally held their fire, not apparently realising sufficiently that the noble causes of constitutional government and international stability would not be served if the autocracy reformed itself too little and too late.

MAINSTREAM DISSENT AND ITS IMPACT ON THE REGIME

The dissenters have not claimed that they constitute a powerful pressure group, nor that they make a continuous impact on the regime's policies. Yet we have seen the danger which the regime ascribes to Solzhenitsyn's writings, and the Politbureau must often have taken the dissenters into account when deciding, for example, how much to re-habilitate Stalin, how far it could afford to tighten political control, whether to make the censorship more severe (which would divert still more works into *samizdat*), whether to continue its internment of dissenters in mental hospitals (a convenient device internally, but politically embarrassing abroad), whether to ease its emigration policy, and so on.

Above all, perhaps, the mainstream dissenters have had an impact on the regime in two indirect but powerful ways. First, their writings and their example have probably had a considerable effect in persuading western opinion of the continuingly authoritarian nature of the Soviet system. In a period when, in reaction to the prolonged tensions of the Cold War, some western opinion has felt inclined to take Soviet assurances and intentions at face value, this role could not have been filled as effectively by anyone else. And second, the dissenters have, by breaking out of 'the inertia of fear', provided a powerful example to other oppressed groups in Soviet society of how to act. Their books and protests, and the *Chronicle,* have been systematically sent abroad and then broadcast back to the USSR and listened to by several millions of people. Some of the latter have belonged to groups which, as we shall see below, have gradually found the means and the resolution to imitate the dissenters' methods and take advantage of their services.

MAINSTREAM DISSENT AND ITS PROSPECTS

But however much impact the dissenters have or have not made, in late 1971 it became too much for the regime to continue tolerating at the then existing level. A high-level decision was taken to suppress the *Chronicle* and other major *samizdat* activities at all costs. A contributory factor in the decision, many dissenters believe, was an assurance allegedly given by the Nixon administration, as it laid the ground-work for '*détente*', that it would not make a public issue, or even protest, about the Soviet suppression of dissent. There is no proof that such an assurance was given, but, as mentioned above, no protests were in fact made.

In any case, in January 1972, as preparations were being made for Nixon's first visit to Moscow as President, the KGB struck at the *Chronicle* and its Ukrainian equivalent, the *Ukrainian Herald.* In the course of the year several hundred flat-searches and interrogations were conducted in the case against the *Chronicle,* in a variety of cities, and a dozen or so arrests were made. The breakthrough came late in the year, when two well-known Moscow dissenters, Pyotr Yakir and Victor Krasin, began to collaborate with the investigators after several months in prison. With a mass of detailed information from these men the KGB eventually succeeded in silencing the *Chronicle,* driving some of their associates into emigration under threat of long-term imprisonment, jailing others, and intimidating yet others. Much of the intricate network of *Chronicle* correspondents and distributors was uncovered, and 1973 was a year of reduced and less co-ordinated activity. Indeed, the movement *as such* sank to a low ebb, as the *Chronicle* had, in effect, been its principal collective expression. None the less, many networks continued to function, funnelling information and documents to the outside world in as large quantities as before, partly perhaps in response to the founding of a 'substitute' publication, *A Chronicle of Human Rights in the USSR,* in New York.[23]

In September 1973 the KGB launched its media campaign against the two most formidable dissenting figures, Sakharov and Solzhenitsyn, presumably planning to arrest or deport them and thus bring dissent under better control. At this moment, however, when, ironically, mainstream dissent was in considerable confusion, western opinion at last spoke up. As a result, over the next few months the KGB presumably received new guidelines from the Politbureau, the remaining dissenters took courage, a new co-ordinated network gradually took shape, and in May 1974 the *Chronicle* re-emerged with four large issues to fill in most of the backlog since its suppression.

To sum up, at least half the leaders of the 'first generation' of mainstream dissent had, by the end of 1974, been more or less neutralised through imprisonment, emigration, exhaustion, intimidation or death. But a second generation had begun to appear, and it seemed to be heartened by the increased vigour and co-operation of a wide range of dissenting groups outside the mainstream. If, though, as may be surmised, the humanitarian mainstream is too western-oriented, too apolitical, and too rational ever to develop widespread support in the USSR, then, if the politicisation of society should gather speed, more politically minded dissenters may divert an increasing amount of their energies elsewhere. But the services of a basically humanitarian movement seem likely to be needed for a long time to come, and the moral strength of the present movement will probably prove to be more than the KGB can break.

DISSENT AMONG THE NATIONAL MINORITIES

It is questionable whether the KGB has become more concerned over the last decade about mainstream dissent or nationalities' dissent. For the latter might eventually, as Amalrik has predicted, lead to the fragmentation of Russia's border lands, as happened in 1917-21.

The evidence suggests that significant and growing currents of opinion in a number of the Union republics feel that their nations did not achieve after 1917 (or 1944) the liberation from Russification and Russian imperialism which the Bolsheviks appeared to promise them and which was justified by their growing national consciousness (similar to that of many other peoples in the world's disintegrating empires). Such currents of opinion have been strongest in those republics and areas which the USSR annexed during the Second World War: here the brutality of the annexations ensured that there were fewer illusions about Soviet intentions.

National dissent in the republics has opposed, mainly, two separate but interconnected policies: first, the camouflaged but persistent policy of Russification, which manifests itself in the promotion of things Russian and in discrimination against minority languages, traditions, literatures, cultures and religions, and also in the officially sponsored settlement of Russians (or other Slavs) in minority areas. And secondly, this dissent has opposed the policy in practice — despite the façade of a federal structure which enshrines the sovereignty of the national republics — of dictating all important political and economic policies from Moscow. The national dissenters have based their protests and demands on the law and the constitution, and thus, not surprisingly, have had much in common, and important contacts, with the mainstream dissenters. They have also found sympathy on occasion from the local party leaders, whose loyalty to the centre — particularly over economic exploitation by Moscow — has apparently sometimes become weaker than their loyalty to their nation. If this last phenomenon should become more common in future, involving, as it does, a major potential vulnerability of the Soviet system, then it could probably be said that the nationalities problem would definitely become the regime's first preoccupation in the area of dissent.

The Ukraine

Ukrainian dissent has a long and complex history, but stems, in its contemporary form, mainly from Khrushchev's policy of increased Russification, introduced at the end of the 1950s. This stimulated dissent in literary and other circles, but, although several groups were arrested each year and their members sentenced, in a few cases to death, little suppression of socially more established dissenters occurred until 1965. Then, concurrently, with the arrests of Sinyavsky and Daniel in Moscow, twenty Ukrainian intellectuals were also arrested and sentenced to up to six years each. Their cases were documented in *The Chornovil Papers* (New York, 1968), the compilation of a young Lvov journalist, Vyacheslav Chornovil.[24] In his long introduction, written in early 1966, Chornovil skilfully deployed the juridical approach developed in subsequent years by the mainstream dissenters. With the latter the Ukrainian dissenters maintained close ties from the start, and as a result their problems have been well covered in the *Chronicle*.

For his book Chornovil served eighteen months in a labour camp, but with this and one other exception there were no arrests of well-known people in the Ukraine from 1966 until December 1971. This was the period when the First Party Secretary, Petro Shelest, tried to establish a *modus vivendi* with the Ukrainian intelligentsia. The other exception was the historian Valentyn Moroz, who served four years in 1965-9, and who in 1970 was re-sentenced to fourteen years of prison and exile for his writings. These powerfully written essays are concerned with human and national individuality and especially with the rebuilding of Ukrainian nationhood.[25]

But, as noted above, the KGB's major move came in January 1972. At this point, with Shelest's political position slipping fast and Shcherbitsky replacing him in May, the KGB arrested at least fifty dissenters and had them sentenced to an average of nearly ten years of prison and exile each. In this way the *Ukrainian Herald,* which had published six large issues in *samizdat* over two years, was soon suppressed, and with it, for a period, articulate national dissent. In 1974, however (following the Moscow *Chronicle*) it re-emerged.[26] None the less, Ukrainian dissent sustained in 1972 the heaviest single KGB assault since 1953 of any dissenting group, and so it remains to be seen how quickly it will recover. When it does so, it will probably be the stronger for its roll call of new martyrs and will have more chance of extending its roots from the intelligentsia down into the working class, which may, especially in the West Ukraine, prove to be more fertile soil than can at present be demonstrated from documents.

Lithuania

For whatever the potential strength of Ukrainian dissent, it has at no stage (since the 1940s) been a mass movement. The only republic whose national movement has achieved this status so far is Lithuania. Here the interlocked national and Catholic traditions, reminiscent of Poland, and the relatively small number of non-Lithuanians in the population of 3 million have facilitated the growth of a movement which the KGB seems powerless to stop. The movement began in the late 1960s among groups of Catholic priests, who protested against the restrictions on the printing of Bibles and religious literature, on the admission of students to seminaries, and on the freedom of action of the hierarchy. In 1971 the arrest of two priests stimulated the unrest, and although they received only one-year sentences,[27] in early 1972 the *Chronicle of the Lithuanian Catholic Church* began to appear in *samizdat* and 17,000 signatures were collected on an appeal to Dr Waldheim to intervene and bring religious persecution to an end. In May 1972 riots broke out in Kaunas, Lithuania's second city, after a student had burned himself to death in protest against the persecution of religion and national traditions.[28]

Since then the situation has remained tense, with the *Chronicle of the Lithuanian Catholic Church* appearing regularly, and with occasional arrests and trials. By late 1974 eleven large issues of the *Chronicle* had come out, edited in a more militant style than most other *samizdat* journals and calling repeatedly for support from the Vatican and from Christians abroad.[29] The most determined KGB drive against it was launched in November 1973 with a large wave of searches and interrogations, and some arrests, in various cities and villages. To date, though, evidently in deference to the mass nature of the dissent, the authorities have refrained from imposing sentences longer than six years at political trials.

Armenia, Latvia, Estonia, Georgia and Moldavia

In Armenia, Latvia and Estonia national movements clearly exist, but are much weaker than those in Lithuania and the Ukraine. Their exact strength is still difficult to gauge, as too few documents are yet available. Those to hand suggest that the Lithuanian example may have started to infect Latvia and Estonia, where small dissenting groups have been arrested, but if so the results are unlikely to be as dramatic as in Lithuania. These two republics are not united around a single national religion, and they have a higher proportion of Russian settlers.

In Armenia national and religious traditions are intertwined, as in Lithuania, but memories of the Turkish massacres appear to have acted as something of a brake on the growth of the national movement. The latter seems to have developed at the end of the 1960s. Major arrests and trials of dissenters occurred in 1968-70[30] and 1973-4.

In Georgia documentary *samizdat* evidence of national dissent began to appear only in 1973.[31] One catalyst appears to have been the removal in 1972 of First Party Secretary Mzhavanadze and the drive of his successor, Shevardnadze, against corruption. Another catalyst was a revolt by laymen and priests against profound corruption in the hierarchy of the Georgian Orthodox Church. But although the Armenian example might prove infectious, the contribution of the church revolt to the national stirrings is likely to be limited, as the church is in general much weaker in Georgia than in Armenia, let alone than in Lithuania or the western Ukraine.

In Moldavia national stirrings favour, as might be expected, the return of the republic to the Rumanian motherland, which, with its militant nationalism, has not refrained from hinting that it would favour the same thing.

Belorussia and, even more, Azerbaijan, it should be noted, show little sign even of stirrings. The Central Asian republics are a more complex phenomenon, but it must suffice to say here that they have not yet produced any *samizdat* documents except those by the exiled minorities to be discussed below. Anti-Russian nationalism and pan-Islamicism clearly exist, but they have not yet progressed, apparently, beyond moods and attitudes and what dissenting scholars can convey between the lines of their writings.

THE DISSENT OF NATIONAL MINORITIES WITHOUT THEIR OWN REPUBLICS

Attention will now be turned to a different source of national dissent, those peoples who wish, in large numbers, to emigrate from the USSR or to return from their places of internal exile to their homelands inside the USSR.

The Jews

The best known of these peoples are the Jews, whose national movement has received wide publicity since 1969-70. The movement's development is of special interest and importance, as the Jews are not tucked away in some corner of the Soviet Union like all the peoples described above except the Ukrainians. They are, on the contrary, scattered in many parts of the country, especially in its large cities, where some of them occupy important positions in the economy, the arts, higher education, research and the professions.

In the late 1960s the still extant traces of the Russian

Zionism of forty years earlier received a boost from, first, the Israeli victory in the Six-Day War, and second, the emerging human rights movement, in which many Jews were participating. The result, especially as the KGB pressed down increasingly on the human rights movement, was the rapid development of a movement to emigrate to Israel. The movement spread quickly from Kiev, Moscow and the Baltic to Georgia, Leningrad, Kharkov, Novosibirsk, Sverdlovsk and Central Asia. Imitating the methods of the mainstream dissenters, it produced a *samizdat* journal, *Exodus,* adopted the juridical approach in appeals to the authorities, staged demonstrations and sit-ins, and passed its news and other materials to foreign journalists and tourists. They also pioneered a new method, soon imitated by the dissenters, of communicating regularly with the West by international telephone, dictating whole documents on to tape recorders in London, Paris, New York and San Francisco.[32]

At first the authorities resisted. But in 1970, as the Jewish lobby in the West began to operate, and as the thwarted would-be emigrants resorted to increasingly militant methods, including the planned hijack of a plane, the KGB had little choice but to yield. The other options were presumably unacceptable. To put thousands of Jews in camps was impossible for reasons of foreign policy, and was anyway no longer, for a fully bureaucratised KGB, an easy task. But to tolerate the *status quo,* in which the Jews were with virtual impunity providing an example of militancy to many other oppressed groups in various cities, and in which publicity was building up abroad, was also impossible.

So the gates were unlocked and by 1974 the 100,000th Jew had pushed through them. A radical change in emigration policy had been forced on the regime, a change which the 'Jackson Amendment' had capitalised on, but in no way initiated, and which may prove to be little affected by the Soviet renunciation in January 1975 of the USA-USSR Trade Agreement of 1972. The major limiting factor in future, as regards the volume of Jewish emigration, may prove to be the capacity of Israel and the West to absorb it. At the same time the regime can be expected to detain various Jewish scientists and other economically valuable people for considerable periods before letting them go. Meanwhile, some of them will probably continue to give support of various kinds to the mainstream dissenters, especially in Moscow.

The Soviet Germans

The Soviet Germans, at present almost 2 million in number, were deported by Stalin after the Nazi invasion of 1941 and simultaneously lost their Autonomous Republic on the Volga. In 1955 the punitive exile regime imposed on them was lifted, but not until 1964 were they legally exculpated of their alleged crime of having helped the Nazi invaders *en masse.* These easings of their position were closely connected with the evolution of Soviet-West German relations. But their long campaign for permission to return to their Soviet homelands and to have their Autonomous Republic restored had still, in 1974, been unsuccessful. Indeed, from the early 1970s a growing number of them decided that the struggle was hopeless and that in any case the Jewish movement had been setting a very persuasive example.

Thus a German emigration movement emerged, using the same militant tactics as the Jews. In 1974 close links were established with the mainstream dissenters, demonstrations were staged in Moscow and Tallin, and a *samizdat* journal, *Re Patria,* began to appear.[33]

Again, militancy, helped by the conjuncture of Brandt's *Ostpolitik,* appears to have paid off. In the years 1971-4 some 15,000 Germans reached West Germany, and the rate rose steadily to over 6000 per year in 1974. Few Germans appear to have gone to East Germany. As with the Jews, though, Soviet policy has been two-pronged: some forty Zionist Jews were, in late 1974, in labour camps, along with about twenty-five activists of the German movement. Although the Soviet Germans are about a million less numerous than the Jews, their movement seems likely to become a strong one and to figure increasingly prominently in negotiations between the Soviet and West German governments.

The Meskhetians
The Meskhetians are a small Turkic people, of probably less than 200,000, from the south Georgian border with Turkey.

In November 1944 they were deported by Stalin to Central Asia, evidently to clear possible opposition from the path of a planned Soviet advance into Turkey. No charges were preferred against them, and in the mid-1950s the punitive regime imposed on those who survived the deportation was lifted. At once they began a campaign to be allowed to return home, organising 'congresses of the people' at which, in the mid-1960s, 6000 delegates elected campaign committees. They also sent emissaries to Moscow to lobby both officials and, to greater effect, the circles which produced the *Chronicle.*[34]

In 1974, however, success on the key issue had still eluded them, even though from 1970 they had begun demanding that if the authorities would not let them return home they should allow them to emigrate to their brothers and fellow Muslims in Turkey. So far the Turkish government has shown no public readiness to accept them, and apparently none of them have received exit permits. As the regime apparently forbids their return home for strategic reasons, the problem they pose will presumably fester until such time as emigration is allowed.

The Crimean Tartars

The recent history of the Crimean Tartars has certain similarities to that of the Meskhetians. Their deportation in 1944 was, however, punishment for their alleged wholesale collaboration with the Germans, and not until 1967 did they win the removal of this charge from the record. Earlier, nearly half of them had died as a result of the deportation to Central Asia and elsewhere, and the survivors had undergone a punitive exile regime until 1956. From that point on a powerful and democratically organised campaign to return home was launched, with similar features to that of the Meskhetians. The Moscow dissenters, led by Kosterin and Grigorenko, took up the Tartars' cause with vigour, but to no avail. Between 1956 and 1974 over 200 members of their movement were imprisoned, and thousands who returned to the Crimea without permission were expelled.[35]

Presumably, again, strategic reasons inhibit the regime from allowing them home. And presumably the problems of this notably united people of nearly 500,000 will continue to generate dissent until the authorities relent. If they continue not to relent, the Tartars, too, may be driven to demand emigration to Turkey, their traditional haven for nearly two centuries when times have been bad in Russia. But the mere demand, as noted about the Meskhetians, may not change anything.

Nor have the numerous Crimean Tartar appeals to the UN and other bodies abroad helped them much as yet. World opinion has been indifferent to their situation, as to the Meskhetians', in contrast to its response to the Jews.

RUSSIAN NATIONALIST DISSENT

Russian nationalist dissent of the variety less liberal than Solzhenitsyn's or Osipov's is an important, but still little studied sector in the spectrum of dissent. To put it in perspective a brief review of the full range of semi-legitimate and extra-system Russian nationalism since the early 1960s may be useful. Its emergence at that time was probably provoked in part by Khrushchev's orthodox Marxist-Leninist position on the nationalities and religious questions as embodied, for example, in the new party programme of 1961. This position tended to injure those Russian as well as Ukrainian (and other) national feelings which had been developing during the gradual de-atomisation of society in the 1950s. Hence the emergence in 1964 of both the officially approved 'Motherland' [*Rodina*] clubs and the liberal nationalist underground group of Leningrad Social-Christians,[36] and in 1965 of the All-Russian Society for the Preservation of Historical and Cultural Monuments. The blossoming of this society, whose membership reached 3 million in a year and 7 million by 1972, suggested that the new party leadership hoped to gain popular support by making concessions to national feelings. Further evidence of benevolent tolerance, or even support, in high places were the thinly disguised neo-Slavophile writings which appeared in a leading Komsomol organ, *Molodaya gvardiya,* in 1967-70, discreetly propagating disapproval of industrialism and pro-letarian internationalism, and approval of various traditions and qualities associated with the Orthodox Church and the Russian nation.

But official tolerance declined in 1970. In November *Molodaya gvardiya's* chief editor, Anatoly Nikonov, was dismissed and replaced by a Central Committee apparatchik, and a few months later one of his neo-Slavophile contributors, Yury D. Ivanov, was sacked from his post at Moscow University. The main response to this came within two months of Nikonov's removal, when Osipov and others founded the *samizdat* journal *Veche* for Russian patriots loyal but not subservient to the regime. Almost at once, from the summer of 1971, the KGB reacted by threatening Osipov with arrest and harrassing him and his wife.[37] But soon the 1972 campaign against the *Chronicle* and the *Ukrainian Herald* took precedence, and only in 1973 did the KGB go beyond harassment of *Veche*. This was when it sponsored efforts to 'co-opt' the journal to a position more acceptable to the regime, in which *Veche* would disown Orthodoxy and anti-industrialism in favour of neo-paganism, virulent anti-semitism and recognition of the party as the preserver of national unity and stability against the many threats of disintegration which faced the country.[38] When this attempt foundered on the Orthodoxy which apparently united the producers of *Veche* the KGB opened a criminal investigation against *Veche* and its numerous supporters, and in this way forced Osipov at last, in March 1974, to close it down after nine book-length issues. Soon, though, a different *Veche* faction, accused by Osipov and his supporters of unsavoury collaboration with the authorities, revived it. The new group put out a tenth issue, denounced Osipov for alleged personal misdemeanours, and, while showing some signs of a shift 'to the right', asserted its intention to continue the established line. But in July this group, too, closed *Veche* down under pressure of the KGB's investigation. When Osipov, who described himself in 1974 as 'a liberal patriot', then started *Zemlya (The Earth)*, his arrest, as noted above, swiftly followed.[39]

All this suggests that in late 1974 the regime was trying, by neutralising the most independent figures, to bring the dissenting Russian nationalists as closely into line as possible, but, by largely avoiding arrests, to keep their alienation to a minimum. However, as a number of *Veche* collaborators, including several of the Leningrad Social-Christians, had remained unbroken by their camp-terms, and as one of these, Leonid Borodin, started another new publication, *Moscow Almanach [Moskovskiy sbornik]* in September 1974, it seemed doubtful whether the KGB would achieve any easy *Gleichschaltung*. At the same time the patrons of the *Molodaya gvardiya* line of 1967-70, whoever they may have been, had clearly retained some power since 1970. The first detailed, high-level rebuttal of this line had reportedly been barred by them from publication for nearly a year, prior to its appearance in late 1972,[40] and shortly thereafter its author, A. Yakovlev, acting-head of the Propaganda department of the Central Committee, was removed from his post and 'exiled' to Canada as ambassador. The notably defensive tone of his article made this development less surprising than it would otherwise have been.

Veche was concerned primarily with: the thought of Slavophils, nationalists and neo-Slavophils; the Orthodox Church and religious thought; Alexander Solzhenitsyn; problems of ecology and the preservation of old Russian architecture; literary and musical themes; and the collapse of moral standards, genuine culture and self-respect in the Russian nation. Broadly speaking, *Veche* may be said to have represented all the main Christian tendencies — liberal, centrist and rightist — within dissenting Russian nationalism, with its editorial position more on the liberal side. The word 'liberal' implies, in this context, not a commitment to classical political liberalism and a multi-party system, but rather a desire for a liberalised, benevolently authoritarian regime incorporating the best traditions of the Russian nation, and also a liberal attitude on issues such as political censorship, anti-semitism, the right of minority republics to secession, and the permissibility of publicly criticising the Orthodox Patriarch and the hierarchy. In these terms, Solzhenitsyn and Osipov are liberal nationalists and can be distinguished from centrist and right-wing tendencies. This said, though, it is worth noting the view (however debatable) of A. M. Ivanov, writing under his pen-name 'A. Skuratov' in *Veche* no. 10, that *Veche's* supporters completely share the basic position of Solzhenitsyn as expressed in his 'Open Letter to the Soviet Leaders'.

In any case, the right-wing fascistic tendency is relatively weakly expressed in *Veche*. This tendency is more often atheistic or pagan, it glorifies strong leaders like Stalin and even (for his Jewish policy) Hitler, and it has a world-view permeated by belief in a world Jewish conspiracy as set forth in 'The Protocols of the Elders of Zion'. By late 1974 only a few documents of this tendency were as yet available, although some had, in disguised form, achieved official publication.[41] It was still impossible to gauge the strength of the support in regime circles for either this tendency or the *Veche* tendencies. Even more unclear was how much this support was based on any belief in the ideas themselves, and how much on the view that they might prove a useful instrument in intra-party stuggles, in the way that anti-semitism was used in the Polish leadership struggles of the late 1960s.

RELIGIOUS DISSENT

Religious dissent has a somewhat marginal political element to it, as most religious dissenters − of whom there are many varieties − simply want greater freedom for religion and are not concerned much about politics (except where religion is intertwined with it, as in Lithuania, the western Ukraine, Armenia, Georgia, and, incipiently, Russia itself). But their persecution naturally tends to alienate them from the regime. Also, their causes have often been taken up by mainstream dissenters, and some of the latter belong to a church or faith and act as link men. However, as these questions are discussed in another chapter they will not be developed here.

WORKING-CLASS DISSENT

It is clear that discontent is quite widespread among workers and peasants, but except for frequent 'go-slows' and rather rare strikes, and the mass participation in certain national and religious dissent movements, it is not yet organised. It may well become more so in the future, and focus on wages and conditions − a development which would please the mainstream dissenters. In due course it may grow and link up in certain ways with the mainstream. The regime clearly fears this, partly because a link-up of that sort was a critical factor in the growth of opposition in the period 1900-17, and so it has tried hard over the last decade to raise steadily the real incomes of the working class. It must also fear the latter as a potentially destructive force in the long tradition of elemental Russian revolt 'from below'. However, the evidence easily available on the whole subject is as yet of low quality, and so only very tentative speculations can be advanced.[42]

THE PATTERN OF THE DECADE

Let us now pull the different threads of the discussion together and see what pattern emerges from the decade since Khrushchev's fall. For nearly a year after October 1964 no clear line on dissent was visible. The trend appeared, in fact, to be somewhat liberal, as certain authors and editors took advantage of the general uncertainty to get 'liberal' writings into print, and as young, mostly bohemian writers and artists in Moscow became more active. In late August 1965, however, the arrests began in the Ukraine, and two weeks later extended to Sinyavsky and Daniel in Moscow: this was a clear signal to the 'creative intelligentsia' as a whole. The latter, however, reacted by developing over the next two years the new techniques of collecting signatures on mass appeals and gaining publicity for them through *samizdat* and the foreign news media. To combat *samizdat* and unauthorised demonstrations, articles 190-1 and 190-3 were added to the Criminal Code in 1966, along with new laws to suppress religious dissent. 1967, it is true, saw the concession of legal exculpation (for their alleged wartime crimes) granted to the Crimean Tartars, who had recently begun sending regular delegations to Moscow and also establishing links there with dissenting intellectuals. But 1967-8 also saw, in response to the Galanskov-Ginzburg case, an acceleration of *podpisantstvo* [the signing of collective protests] and the natural extension of this into the human rights movement and the production of the *Chronicle*.

In spring 1968 the KGB moved against this trend rather cautiously, limiting itself largely to expelling key figures from the party and getting others dismissed from their jobs. But the invasion of Czechoslovakia on 21 August 1968 changed the situation, especially when the Red Square demonstrators had been arrested four days later and sentenced. Political arrests now became a regular occurrence. The KGB had presumably received — from a Politbureau shocked by how rapidly liberalism had burgeoned in Czechoslovakia — new guidelines aimed at preventing the growth of the human rights movement and cutting its links with the Crimean Tartars. In 1969 the KGB set up a new chief directorate to co-ordinate and direct all activities dealing with the types of dissent discussed in this chapter. As there are in fact only two other chief directorates, this move reflected clearly the KGB's growing concern. By the end of 1969, with people like General Grigorenko and Anatoly Marchenko, a good proportion of the Initiative Group for the Defence of Human Rights, ten Crimean Tartar leaders, and a dozen Armenian nationalists all either arrested or sentenced; with Solzhenitsyn expelled from the Writers' Union; with Shelest having reached a viable *modus vivendi* with the Ukrainian dissenters; and with western opinion passive — the situation had apparently been brought more or less under control.

Now it was important to weed out heterodoxy in the 'thick journals'. First came *Novy mir* under Tvardovsky and his revisionist lieutenants, a journal with which the dissenters had many links. In February 1970, after a six-month rearguard action, it succumbed to a forcible takeover by literary officials and hacks.[43] Then later in the year, as noted above, a similar takeover brought the excessively nationalist *Molodaya gvardiya* into line.[44]

But 1970 also witnessed the rapid aggravation of a new problem, the Jewish emigration movement. This force was powerful enough that it had to be met by concessions as well as repression. By mid-1971 the guidelines were established: jail those Jews who form underground groups or plan hijacks, but create a safety valve by allowing emigration on a significant (and, we should note, unprecedented) scale.

In 1971 the groundwork was laid for the policy of '*détente*' with the USA, and plans made for President Nixon to visit Moscow the next year. It was now important, therefore, to impress on the western-oriented dissenters from the start that *détente* would mean a tightening, not a loosening of political controls. So the *Chronicle,* which had obstinately survived the KGB's salami tactics for nearly four years, became from January 1972 the object of an intensive investigation, to which, by the end of the year, it had succumbed. The simultaneous assault on the Ukrainian dissenters probably resulted from a KGB assessment that Shelest's *modus vivendi* with them had, in view of the vigorous development of the *Ukrainian Herald* over the last two years, broken down in a way that was too dangerous to tolerate any longer.

The drive against the *Chronicle's* creators continued in 1973, but, with the *Chronicle* silent, Sakharov and Solzhenitsyn virtually replaced it by their increasingly frequent public statements and interviews. Hence the decision in August to settle accounts with Sakharov, and then, when he was immediately and aggressively defended by Solzhenitsyn, with him too. However, by late October the unprecedented foreign campaign in their defence had forced the KGB on to the retreat. It was only the publication in Paris of *The Gulag Archipelago* two months later — the timing being partly fortuitous — which caused a new press campaign against its author to flare up. This led to his deportation in February 1974 and the persecution of some of his friends, especially in Leningrad.[45]

Meanwhile, the pressure on Sakharov and the *Chronicle* circles had eased somewhat, and the KGB had turned some of its attention to the organising of sudden waves of searches, interrogations and arrests in Lithuania (19-21 November 1973) and also in Armenia (19 November). The sequels to these operations continued in 1974, those in Lithuania showing no signs of ending, and a new, if much smaller operation was also launched in Georgia.[46] Other drives, as noted earlier, were aimed at the Russian nationalists and the Germans.

CONCLUSION

Dissent in its many different forms is, we may conclude, deeper rooted in the USSR than most westerners realise, and carries a much stronger emotional charge to it than the majority of western dissent. This is especially true of minority nationalism, which has continued to advance in many parts of the world for over a century, but has received repeated setbacks in Russia and the USSR. Thus, in a political system as potentially brittle as the Soviet one, where the ideological vacuum in public life seems likely to produce increasing tensions, the regime could easily in the future mishandle dissenting groups and provoke sudden crises. At present these groups have reached a stage at which they represent dissent rather than political opposition. But the process of the pluralisation and re-politicisation of society is likely to continue, and possibly accelerate, whatever the KGB does, just as the authority of the Communist Party is likely to decline.

In 1965 no organised dissent existed on any significant scale, except among the Crimean Tartars, Meskhetians, Germans and Baptists. But even in these cases it was (apart from a few successful Baptist efforts) completely unpublicised. Nine years later the situation is radically different. The *de facto* freedom of expression of a steadily increasing number of groups has increased from virtually nil to a very significant level. The media involved — *samizdat* and foreign publications and radio stations — have been either semi-legitimate or illegitimate: the regime has not, even occasionally, allowed access to its own media. But it has also not been willing, or able, to practise oppression severe enough to curtail the newly won freedom.

The exact degree of oppression of any particular group or individual has depended on many factors, including: the amount of support it (or he) has in the USSR and, often more importantly, abroad; the relevance of its (or his) foreign support to the Soviet economy; the importance of it (or him) to the economy; and how vigorously it (or he) is likely to practise self-defence. These sort of considerations have, taken together, meant that Solzhenitsyn can be dealt with at least cost by deportation, as adverse foreign literary opinion does not affect the economy; whereas similar treatment of Sakharov might seriously affect Soviet-American scientific and even trade agreements, and must therefore be eschewed. Also, of course, Jews need to be granted concessions, but not Meskhetians or Crimean Tartars: these peoples have no foreign lobby at all, let alone one in a position to influence matters affecting the Soviet economy.

But for dissenting groups to win some *de facto* freedom of

expression, and thus be able to articulate their demands loudly, is one thing. To have the demands satisfied is another. Here the record of the last decade is very different. Only the Jews and the Germans have received much satisfaction, and that has been over emigration, not any reform of internal Soviet structures. The mainstream dissenters have scored some marginal, but usually reversible gains, such as an apparent reduction in the use of police psychiatry against dissent, and, especially in Moscow, a slight reduction in the arbitrariness of legal procedures in political cases. But most of their human rights proposals and demands have failed to produce even a tacit dialogue with the authorities, let alone any satisfaction. Even more has this been true of the broader political, economic and social reforms for which various dissenters have pressed.

Perhaps, in the decade to come, the regime will discover in itself a hidden capacity for change, renewal and constructive dialogue with dissenting groups. If not, however, Andrei Amalrik's assessment, written in 1969, will presumably have been proved right:

> The regime . . . has no wish to change its ways either of its own free will or, still less, by making concessions to anyone or anything. The current process of 'widening the area of freedom' could be more aptly described as the growing decrepitude of the regime. The regime is simply growing old and can no longer suppress everyone and everything with the same strength and vigour as before.[47]

NOTES

1 This chapter is a much revised version of a paper written for the Commission on Critical Choices for Americans, but the conclusions are my own. I am grateful to the Commission for permission to print the paper in its revised form.

2 i.e. if one views the nature of politics as does Bernard Crick in his *In Defence of Politics* (London, 1962).

3 A party, we may note, which claims to know the full truth about the past, the present and the future, and proclaims in its 1961 Programme the goals of rearing citizens 'who will harmoniously combine spiritual wealth, moral purity and a perfect physique' and of producing a society in which observance of the rules of Communism 'will become an organic need and habit with everyone'.

4 e.g. the Leningrad 'Social-Christians', a group of anti-Soviet revolutionaries, or 'The Democrats', a Moscow-Leningrad-Baltic group. On the former see P. Reddaway, *Uncensored Russia* (London, 1972) pp. 376-80; also a forthcoming study by John Dunlop, *The New Russian Revolutionaries*, Nordland Press, Mass. On the latter see the trials of Davydov, Petrov, Bolonkin and Balakirev in *A Chronicle of Current Events*, no. 29, 30, Amnesty International Publications (London, 1975).

5 Naturally, the nature of this intellectual opposition varies greatly, being coloured in particular by each author's temperament and view of his own role. Medvedev is above all a political animal; Sakharov a humanitarian and truth-seeker. Solzhenitsyn, a writer-teacher and prophet in the manner of Tolstoy (but with a different message), in some ways comes into this category too.

6 See e.g. R. Conquest, *Power and Policy in the USSR* (London, 1961), and Carl Linden, *Khrushchev and the Soviet Leadership, 1957-64* (Baltimore, 1966).

7 The most penetrating discussion of most of the issues raised in this section is to be found in Valery Chalidze, *To Defend These Rights: Human Rights and the Soviet Union* (New York, 1974; London, 1975).

8 On the Khrushchev period see especially the documentary collections of Hugh McLean and Walter Vickery (eds), *The Year of Protest, 1956* (New York, 1961), and Priscilla Johnson, *Khrushchev and the Arts: The Politics of Soviet Culture, 1962-64* (Cambridge, Mass., 1965).

9 The most useful books on the mainstream in the second half of the 1960s are: the collection edited by Max Hayward and Leopold Labedz on the Sinyavsky-Daniel trial, *On Trial* (London, 1967); the two collections edited by Pavel Litvinov, *The Demonstration in Pushkin Square* (London, 1969), and *The Trial of the Four* (London, 1972); the collection edited by Natalya Gorbanevskaya, *Red Square at Noon* (London, 1972); A. Amalrik, *Will the Soviet Union Survive Until 1984?* (London, 1970); and A. Brumberg's anthology, *In Quest of Justice* (London, 1970).

10 The first eleven issues of the *Chronicle* appear in full in P. Reddaway, *Uncensored Russia: the Human Rights Movement in the Soviet Union* (London, 1972). Issues 16-27 have been published as individual booklets by Amnesty International Publications, 53 Theobald's Road, London, WC1, 1971-3, and issues 28-32 are due in 1975, as two books, from the same publishers. When the *Chronicle* was silenced in late 1972, the journal *A Chronicle of Human Rights in the USSR*, ed. V. Chalidze, P. Litvinov, E. Kline and P. Reddaway began to be published in early 1973 by Khronika Press, 505 Eighth Avenue, New York, NY 10018, operating on lines very similar to those of the Moscow *Chronicle*. It appears six times a year in separate but identical Russian and English editions.

11 This was the area of activity of the Human Rights Committee, founded in 1970 by Dr A. Sakharov, V. Chalidze, and A.

Tverdokhlebov. See *Dokumenty Komiteta prav cheloveka: Proceedings of the Moscow Human Rights Committee*, International League for the Rights of Man, 777 UN Plaza, New York, NY 10017, 1972; also *A Chronicle of Human Rights in the USSR*, no. 5-6 (1973) pp. 51-4.

12 Apart from the *Chronicle's* extensive materials, the most important sources on the contemporary forced labour camps are A. Marchenko, *My Testimony* (London, 1969), and Edward Kuznetsov, *Prison Diaries* (London, 1975). On the mental hospitals see United States Senate Committee on the Judiciary, *Abuse of Psychiatry for Political Repression in the Soviet Union* (New York, 1973), and R. and Zh. Medvedev, *A Question of Madness* (London, 1971).

13 The most useful book on this subject is M. Dewhirst and R. Farrell (eds), *The Soviet Censorship* (Metuchen, New Jersey, 1973).

14 This very rough estimate is made up of about a thousand such people named in *Chronicle*, no.1-32, plus several hundred more who appear in P. Litvinov, *The Trial of the Four*, but not in the *Chronicles*, plus the balance who do not appear in either of these sources but in the hundreds of other available *samizdat* documents and books which concern 'mainstream' dissent. Less rough estimates than this would, incidentally, involve not only great labour but also severe problems in defining the precise criteria for distinguishing a 'mainstream' dissenter from other categories of dissent, and in obtaining enough information about certain people to be able to apply the criteria to them with confidence.

15 Two useful collections of their writings and documents are George Saunders (ed.), *Samizdat: Voices of the Soviet Opposition* (New York, 1974) and *Samizdat I* (Paris, 1969). Both books should be used with caution as regards their editorial interpretations, which wrongly suggest that Trotsky and Trotskyism are popular among dissenters and also give an exaggerated impression of the level of organised working class dissent in the USSR.

16 See e.g. the groups of Saratov and Ryazan students and the Leningrad group of Yury I. Fyodorov, all of whose cases are described in *A Chronicle of Current Events*, no. 12; *Possev: 4-yy spetsialnyy vypusk*, Frankfurt (June 1970).

17 See Grigorenko's collection of writings, *Mysli sumasshedshego (Thoughts of a Madman)*, Herzen Foundation, Amsterdam, 1973, due for publication in English in 1975.

18 See his books *On Socialist Democracy* (London, 1975), and *Let History Judge* (London, 1972). It should be noted that a much expanded version of *Let History Judge*, dated March 1973 and 1136 pages long, was published in Russian in 1974 by Knopf, New York, under the title *K sudu istorii: genezis i posledstviya stalinizma*.

19 *Politicheskiy dnevnik*, Herzen Foundation, Amsterdam. The first volume appeared in 1972 and the second, with a foreword by one of its compilers, Zhores Medvedev, in 1975. The two volumes total some 1700 pages.

20 See the latter's *Sakharov Speaks* (London, 1974), an important collection of writings and documents with an autobiographical essay. See also Daniel Weissbort (ed.), *Selected Poems by Natalya Gorbanevskaya with a Transcript of her Trial and Papers Relating to her Detention in a Prison Psychiatric Hospital* (South Hinksey, Oxford, 1972).

21 The most useful collection of materials on the relation of Solzhenitsyn to literary and human rights dissenters is Leopold Labedz (ed.), *Solzhenitsyn: A Documentary Record* (London, 1972). See also Solzhenitsyn's interview and essay in *Index*, London, no. 3 (1974).

22 See *Sakharov Speaks*, pp. 204-5.

23 See note 10. For extensive detail on the cases against the *Chronicle* and the *Ukrainian Herald* see *Chronicle*, no. 24-30.

24 Other important source books on Ukrainian dissent in the 1960s are Michael Browne (ed.), *Ferment in the Ukraine* (London, 1971), and Ivan Dzyuba, *Internationalism or Russification?* 1st ed. (London, 1968) and 2nd rev. ed. (London, 1970).

25 Two useful and similar collections have appeared in English: J. Kolasky (ed.), *Report from the Beria Reserve* (Toronto, 1974), and Y. Bihun (ed.), *Boomerang: The Works of Valentyn Moroz*, Smoloskyp, PO Box 6066, Patterson Station, Baltimore, Md 20231 (Baltimore, 1974).

26 Issues 1-4, 6-8 have been published in Ukrainian as five books by Smoloskyp (see previous note) and PIUF (3 rue du Sabot, Paris 6). No. 5 has so far reached the West only in a few extracts. No. 7 and 8 are edited in a markedly more militant and underground style than no. 1-6, whose style is similar to the *Chronicle's*.

27 See *A Chronicle of Current Events*, no. 21-3. The *Chronicle* began to report regularly on Lithuanian developments from late 1970 onwards.

28 See ibid., no. 26, 27.

29 Issues 4-7 have appeared in English as booklets, published by the Lithuanian Roman Catholic Priests' League, 64-14 56th Road, Maspeth, Long Island, New York 11378, and further booklets are due. Extracts in English are in *Religion in Communist Lands*, Keston College, Heathfield Road, Chislehurst, Kent, no. 4-5 (1973) and no. 4-5 (1974). No. 1-7 have appeared as a book in the original Lithuanian, *Lietuvos Kataliku Bažnycios Kronika*, LKRSR, 6825 So. Talman Avenue, Chicago, Illinois 60629.

30 See *Chronicle*, no. 16.

31 See several items in ibid., no. 32.

32 The most useful book on the Jewish movement up to 1973 is Leonard Schroeter, *The Last Exodus* (New York, 1974). Also the *Chronicle* has reported on it extensively from no. 8 onwards. Since 1972 a weekly bulletin of documents and information has been published, *Jews in the USSR*, Contemporary Jewish Library, 31 Percy Street, London W1.

33 No. 1, dated January 1974 and 110 pages long, has been published

as document AS 1776 in Radio Liberty's Samizdat Archive series, which had registered by late 1974 nearly 2000 items. For a useful account of the Germans' history since 1941 see Ann Sheehy's study, *The Crimean Tatars, the Meskhetians and the Volga Germans*, Minority Rights Group, 36 Craven Street, London WC2 (London, 1973). On the 1974 developments see *Chronicle*, no. 32, and *A Chronicle of Human Rights*, no. 7, 10 (1974), and for an important document of 1965 see *Politicheskiy dnevnik* (Amsterdam, 1972) pp. 92-6.

34 See no. 7, 9, 19-22; also Sheehy, op. cit.

35 On the Crimean Tartars see Sheehy, op. cit., *Chronicle*, no. 31; P. Reddaway, *Uncensored Russia*, ch. 12; and *Tashkentskiy protsess*, Herzen Foundation, Amsterdam, due in 1975, the first large collection of documents on the subject. Nearly 100 such documents have been published in Radio Liberty's Samizdat Archive series.

36 See note 4. For several points in this section I am indebted to John Dunlop's forthcoming article in *Frontier*, London, vol. 18, no. 1 (1975), and to the article on the press debate about neo-Slavophilism by Vladimir Pavloff in *Grani*, Frankfurt, no. 82 (1971).

37 See *Chronicle* 22, p. 43 of the Amnesty edition, no. 24, p. 139, and no. 26, p. 257; also, for the text of one of Osipov's sharpest statements, concerning the confiscation of *Veche*, no. 7, from his typist, *A Chronicle of Human Rights in the USSR*, no. 3 (1973) p. 48. *Veche*, no. 1-10 have been published in the Samizdat Archive series of Radio Liberty, and an abbreviated text of no. 5 in *Volnoe slovo: Samizdat: Izbrannoe*, Frankfurt, no. 9-10 (1973).

38 See M. Agursky's *samizdat* article, 'The Increase in the Neo-Nazi Danger in the Soviet Union' and the attached anonymous document, 'Critical Notes of a Russian about the Russian Patriotic Journal *Veche*', published as documents 1858 and 1858*b* in the Samizdat Archive series.

39 On these episodes see *Chronicle*, no. 32; also documents 1705, 1706, 1787, 1790-3 and 1845 in the Samizdat Archive series. *Zemlya* is no. 1909 in the series.

40 See *Literaturnaya gazeta*, 15 Nov 1972, where the article occupied two whole pages. Yakovlev also attacked nationalist deviations in Georgia and Armenia.

41 See M. Agursky's essay on Yury S. Ivanov's book, *Caution, Zionism!*, in *New York Review of Books*, 16 Nov 1972; also his article and its two attachments referred to in note 38, and *Chronicle*, no. 7's material on the Fetisov group in Reddaway, *Uncensored Russia*, pp. 431-33. The 'Russian Patriots' document of 1970, 'Message to the Nation', is strongly Christian and Orthodox but still belongs to this fascistic genre. See excerpts in *Survey*, London, no. 80 (1971) pp. 191-9, complete text in the Samizdat Archive, no. 590. See also the as yet unpublished work by V. Kapshitser, *The Trojan Horse of Fascism*.

42   It would now be possible, however, systematically to interview working-class Jewish and German emigrants of recent years and to compare the results with what can be gleaned from the Soviet press.
43   See Zhores Medvedev, *Ten Years after Ivan Denisovich* (London, 1973) ch. 19, for a vivid account.
44   It should be noted, though, that *Nash sovremennik* soon began to act as a forum for rather similar views and writers.
45   On the episodes in this paragraph see *Chronicle*, 30, 32.
46   See *Chronicle*, 32, especially the items concerning V. Pailodze, L. Alimonaki, Yu. Gastev and M. Kostava.
47   *Will the Soviet Union Survive Until 1984?* (New York, 1970) p. 30.

7 Religion

MICHAEL BOURDEAUX

BACKGROUND

The study of religion in the Soviet Union over the last decade begins from a premise not only different from, but contradictory to, the broad lines of the recent development of Soviet society as a whole. Even in the academic community, not to mention the popular mind, Khrushchev is almost universally regarded as a liberaliser. This was the tenor of the somewhat enthusiastic obituaries published by both *The Times* and the *Daily Telegraph* when he died in 1971.[1] The fact is passed over in silence that Khrushchev, who undoubtedly brought new ideas to many areas of government, was one of the greatest persecutors of the church that Christian history has known. The present-day psychology of Russian believers can be explained in this light alone. For the main body of the Russian Church, the years of liberalisation were from the end of the Second World War up to the time when Khrushchev was firmly in the seat of power (some time between 1959 and 1960).

The renaissance of the church under Stalin had included the reopening of theological seminaries for the first time since the revolution, the establishment of a regular church administration, both central and diocesan, the reopening of thousands of churches, and the beginning of a monthly publication, *The Journal of the Moscow Patriarchate*. Despite serious persecutions in the areas which fell under Soviet rule at the end of the Second World War, believers elsewhere began to experience if not well-being, then at least the feeling that the worst of the persecution was over and that penalties for religious adherence were far less crippling than they had been.

The years immediately after Stalin stimulated these feelings even more, and many of the *de facto* restrictions were lifted. New congregations sprang up in many places with scant regard to the existing laws on registration,[2] while local Communist agencies ignored the religious question altogether. In 1956 the state permitted publication of the Bible, in a limited edition, for the first time since 1917 and the Moscow Patriarchate produced a book proclaiming its own freedom from restraint.[3]

No sooner was Khrushchev established in his position as sole leader than the *status quo* was shattered. The extent of the new persecution and the force with which it erased the guidelines of the existing accommodation between church and state have been extensively documented both in Soviet and western sources.[4]

Between 1959 and the fall of Khrushchev in 1964 churches of all denominations were closed in their thousands, theological education and publications were restricted, thousands of Christian leaders found themselves in courts of law for propagating their faith among the younger generation and for resisting the new measures being imposed.

The sudden removal of liberties which had not only been promised, but actively enjoyed, for more than a decade struck the religious community at an unexpected time. Their reaction was forthright. Millions of people who had been known for decades as 'the Church of Silence' found a collective voice. Many strands of what has subsequently become known as the Human Rights or Democratic Movement in the Soviet Union originated within the sphere of the church's influence five years before the timetable which is commonly adopted by commentators.[5]

This article will not, of course, be dealing primarily with the reaction of the church to the new spate of persecution, because its perspective is that of official party and state policy towards the phenomenon of religion. Nevertheless, for a full understanding of the present religious situation in the Soviet Union as a whole, the reader should acquaint himself with some of the basic texts emanating from religious circles within recent years, many of which delineate the present religious situation with the greatest force and clarity.[6] After discussing the main policy guidelines, we shall consider some of the principal ways in which these have affected the life of the major Christian denominations and other religions.

TOWARDS A NEW *STATUS QUO*

The fall of Khrushchev forms a landmark in recent Soviet atheist policy. Of course, a few missiles which had been launched before October 1964 continued to strike the edifice of the church, but as soon as the noise of their impact had died into the distance it became immediately clear that there was a basic reconsideration of anti-religious policies. In a perceptive article Andrew Blane has called 1965 'a year of drift'.[7] It was also a year in which public discussion was permitted of what the new atheist policy should be. At no time before or since has the Soviet press reflected quite such a debate on the permissibility or otherwise of physical reprisals against the religious communities. Even during this year, however, there was no public discussion of whether or not Soviet Communism was right to continue the basic hostile stance towards religion which Lenin had evolved.[8]

The continued acts of physical persecution at the end of 1964 and 1965 were quite clearly haphazard or resulting from decisions previously taken. For example, the Russian Orthodox theological seminary at Lutsk closed in 1965,[9] thus sharing the fate of four other seminaries which had closed under Khrushchev. Now only three survived and they continue to do so up to the time of writing. No less than a month after the fall of Khrushchev there was a serious attack on the Pochaev monastery, an attack renewed only eight months later in the summer of 1965 when 'militiamen beat up Christians who were taking overnight refuge in the cemetery'.[10] Peace was not restored until the autumn. The campaign, against the children of religious families continued strongly in some places and it was still likely that young people who were outstandingly zealous in the propagation of their faith would come face to face with severe difficulties. Perhaps the best known example of this is Aida Skripnikova of Leningrad, whose years of suffering began in 1965.[11]

The 1965 debate in the Soviet press and elsewhere brought out attacks which were not only totally divergent from existing practice, but roundly stated that the Khrushchev policy was responsible for bringing about the opposite of what had been intended. In March 1965 came the first indication of a public debate. The main publicistic tool of the anti-religious organs had been the journal *Nauka i religiya [Science and religion]*, founded to spearhead the attack in 1959, the pages of which had been full of the most virulent criticism of all aspects of religion. Now a 'letter from the editors'[12] attacked Alla Trubnikova, who had been associated with some of the more grotesque excesses. She had depicted believers as scoundrels or vagrants, as mental or moral cripples, and she considered the practice of the faith to be a manifestation of criminal behaviour. The editors contradicted such attacks by saying that the only way to convert people misguided into the ways of religion was to engage them in a patient dialogue. Trubnikova was picked out for a special ridicule because she had gone to the lengths of disguising herself as a pilgrim in order to insinuate herself into a Russian Orthodox convent and gathered notes for her exposé of what occurred there. This article called forth a voluminous correspondence from the journal's readers — not perhaps surprising in itself, but in this unique instance it was actually printed over a period of months.[13] The deputy editor of *Nauka i religiya,* V. G. Grigoryan, further showed his open-mindedness by participating in a free-ranging debate with the eminent Orthodox publicist, Anatoli Levitin, on 21 May 1965.[14]

While some central newspapers such as *Izvestiya* continued the pre-existing policies, others opened up the debate before the public as never before. Perhaps the most remarkable article was that published by an atheist lecturer, G. Kelt, in the youth newspaper, *Komsomol'skaya pravda:*

> And today we are again lulling ourselves by the thought that many believers in our country have left the church and religion. This is self-deception. It is true that in the greater part of the territory of the Soviet Union there are no churches and no servants of the cult. But believers there are; if not Orthodox, then all shades of sectarians . . . The closing of a parish does not make atheists out of believers. On the contrary, it attracts people all the more to religion and in addition embitters their hearts . . . Insults, violence and the forcible closing down of churches not only fail to reduce the number of believers, but they actually tend to increase their

number, to make clandestine religious groups more widespread and to antagonise believers against the state.[15]

The indictment of Khrushchev's policies was clear-cut and specific. It has been a monumental miscalculation. Where there had been a church threatened by the general drift of the twentieth century towards secularism, there were now thousands of believers wearing an aureole of martyrdom, ready to lead the church into an era where ideological gains would be made from within the very fastnesses of atheism. Religious communities who had been out in the open had been forced to revert to a clandestine activity more reminiscent of the 1930s, so the state found itself far less able to chart and control what was happening than it had been previously. Finally, loyal citizens, wanting nothing more than to work hard and pray hard, proving themselves always ready to make positive contributions to the society in which they lived, now had seriously to question their basic attitudes to a state which had demonstrated itself to be basically unwilling to allow the amount of ideological divergence which their faith entailed. All this is contained in the arguments which Kelt adduces. She had no original, new solutions, propounding the rather tired formula that the answers lay in a new ritual 'that would replace the liturgy of the church'.[16] The stabilisation of a new leadership in 1966 led to a closure of this debate before it was able to develop and express the facets of opinion which undoubtedly would have been revealed if the 'mini-thaw' of 1965 had not been followed by a further ideological freeze.

Khrushchev himself had made certain changes in the law in order to facilitate the work of his anti-religious brigade.[17] Now the Brezhnev-Kosygin leadership, as soon as it was in firm control, also indicated its intentions by passing further restrictive legislation. While at no time reverting to the crudest excesses of the Khrushchev era, the present leaders have gradually tightened the controls and evolved a new *status quo* considerably less favourable to the religious communities than that before 1960, but at the same time nowhere near as catastrophic as the situation would have been had the Khrushchev policies been carried to their logical conclusion. Except in isolated instances, no further churches were closed. The mass imprisonments were replaced by a much more selective judicial campaign. The official church leadership was naturally cowed through its sufferings and the removal of some of its outstanding members during the Khrushchev period; but gradually it acquired some bargaining power, not least under the stimulus of the outstanding moral thrust provided by the emergent religious section of the democratic movement. The nature of the concessions gained will be set out under the individual denominations discussed in the latter part of this chapter.

The religious counterpart of the emergent campaign against the intellectuals and dissidents, designated most notably by the arrest and trial of the writers Andrei Sinyavsky and Yuli Daniel, was the passing of new legislation in March 1966.[18] Since this date not only have the laws on religion themselves remained in force, although they have not subsequently been imposed as severely as one might have expected at the time when they were passed, but also their implementation in the courts has shown a limited degree of consistency. The harshest provisions of Khrushchev's legislation remain theoretically available to the courts. As many 'social activities' coincide with church services, the very presence of people in church could, on the severest interpretation, be taken as an incitement by religious leaders of people 'to refuse to participate in social activity or fulfil their civic obligations'. The direct consequences of such legislation have never been enforced. The same might be said of the new version of Article 142 of the Penal Code passed in 1966. The aim was apparently to clarify what constituted an offence. Some of these provisions are not unexpected, such as those concerning the refusal to register congregations with the state authority (despite the constitutional requirement of the separation of church and state), the laws forbidding religious education for young people, and the printing and distribution of literature 'calling for an infringement of the laws'. But if clarity was the expressed aim, there is one clause which introduces an element of total confusion; it deals with 'the performance of deceitful acts with the aim of arousing religious superstitions among the public'. Though this has never happened in practice, there is now a law on the Soviet statute book which could be used to bring to court a priest who celebrated the liturgy in a registered church. The framework has clearly been established for a renewed, more violent persecution of the church at any time convenient to the Soviet government.

Only one subsequent piece of legislation has affected religion — and that somewhat obliquely. The new marriage and family law of October 1968 insists that parents must 'bring up their children in the spirit of the moral code of the builder of communism'; 'exerting a harmful influence' on them may result in a court case and a deprivation of the parental rights (Articles 18 and 19). In other words, the family may be broken up by law if parents attempt to being up their children according to their religious beliefs (a guarantee in the Universal Declaration of Human Rights).

Perhaps the main weapon besides strict legal controls employed by the present political leadership to secure reduction of religious activity has been the attempt to elevate a docile leadership and to remove or bar men with an independent cast of mind. There are no Cardinal Wyszynskis in office in the Soviet Union. Nevertheless, the attempt has only partially succeeded, due both to the pressure put on the church leadership by reforming opinion from within its constituency and the encouragement and educative effect of growing foreign contacts which the recognised leaders have been able to develop in the last decade. The Soviet government undoubtedly had its own reasons for making a major concession and allowing Russian church leaders to circulate more freely than heretofore within such circles as the World Council of Churches, the Baptist World Alliance and the Vatican.[19] Obviously, the Soviet regime hoped that these tactics would secure silence or passivity within the western churches. At first this seemed to be succeeding, but there are ever-stronger indications that the limits of this policy may now have been reached and that tougher reactions from the West to Soviet persecution can be expected.[20]

The Khrushchev persecution swept away many elements in the church leadership which were unready to compromise,[21] although there were others still to be removed under Brezhnev and Kosygin. Examples of this will be given in our discussion of the situation of individual churches and religions. In return for political docility (which is by no means the same as capitulation on the basics of the faith) the new regime was prepared eventually to permit some limited concessions to the churches in their efforts to undertake activities considered normal elsewhere. Clearly, a situation has emerged where the regime can, if it wishes to, once again step up the physical persecution of religion. Despite certain disquieting signs, the indications are that, except in isolated areas, the situation is not now as threatening for the churches as it was in Khrushchev's time.

THE ORTHODOX CHURCH

As one would expect, the main lines of tension between a strong church and an anti-religious state are drawn particularly clearly within the sphere of the Russian Orthodox Church. Remaining a large religious body (some estimate 30 or even 50 million strong, though there are problems of definition here), it has attracted a major effort from the atheist agencies to reduce its influence.

One does not have to look below the surface at all, however, to discover that an apparently conformist leadership under Patriarch Pimen and the Moscow patriarchate is not representative of major trends of thought within the Orthodox community. Even at the level of the humble individual and the local congregation, whose apparent conformism and devotion are so often remarked upon by visitors to the liturgy, there are a number of believers who are prepared to demand that the measure of state control affecting their religious lives should be lessened.[22] Over the last decade there have been several notable instances of the determination of whole religious communities to establish their constitutional right to freedom of worship and to establish a registered church in their area. This happened in the towns of Gorky[23] and Naro-fominsk.[24] This is the organic culture from which has grown an intellectual demand for religious liberty, expressed at its most challenging by Alexander Solzhenitsyn. But he has drawn the attention of the world to what had already been expressed a decade earlier by a group of Orthodox intellectuals.

Their first spokesmen were the Moscow priests, Fathers Nikolai Eshliman and Gleb Yakunin; but from the outset they were closely associated with Archbishop Yermogen, one of the most forthright leaders the Russian church has seen this century. The group included the lay writers Anatoli Levitin and Boris Talantov, as well as the Moscow parish priests Fathers Vsevolod Shpiller and Dmitri Dudko. Among these men, who were too loosely knit to be called a circle, there was a wide variety of theological viewpoints, but they were united by a common desire to secure the freedom of their church from state interference.[25]

The thinking of these men began to make an impact abroad, where a view of the church as being free was being assiduously propagated by the officials of the Moscow patriarchate, whilst at home for the first time the persecuted believers in the parishes began to feel that there was someone who would speak out clearly and effectively for them.

For more than a quarter of a century after 1945 the Soviet regime prevented the Russian Orthodox Church from coming together to discuss its internal situation. The longevity of Patriarch Alexis for long held off the one event which would make a meeting unavoidable: on the death of a patriarch a *Sobor* [Council] must convene to elect a successor. Then in 1970 Alexis died, aged 92, and a *Sobor* was held the next year.

For five years the regime had been systematically attempting to hush the emergent Orthodox opposition, while being unwilling to revert to the extremes of physical persecution practised under Khrushchev. Archbishop Yermogen was forcibly retired to a monastry in 1965,[26] while Fathers Eshliman and Yakunin were barred from service as priests.[27] The fact that Patriarch Alexis himself signed the letters authorising these acts demonstrates the very interference which the archbishop and the priests were criticising. Yet the relative lightness of the administrative punishments against them illustrates the state's change of method in its fight against the church since Khrushchev (not to mention the purges of the 1930s).

The only way the state could have avoided the test of the *Sobor* would have been to prevent or postpone the election of a new patriarch. Such action was not compatible with the other policy being consistently followed: the development of foreign relations through the office of the Moscow patriarchate. Naturally, therefore, in the thirteen months between the death of the patriarch and the *Sobor* the state intensified its efforts to throttle dissident voices. Anatoli Levitin, perhaps the most outspoken and determined critic of the Moscow Patriarchate's accommodation with the regime, was arrested, held without trial, released, arrested again, sentenced, released and finally — in an abrupt change in policy in 1974 — allowed to leave the Soviet Union.

The state was successful in its efforts to suppress discussion of sensitive issues at the 1971 *Sobor*. Despite determined efforts of the 'reformers' beforehand to secure consideration of the contentious issue of the removal of the priest in 1961 from any administrative function in his own parish (thus making state interference easier), the state managed to keep such sensitive matters off the agenda, either through the careful screening of delegates or through the tightest control over the agenda and choice of speakers. Probably both factors operated.[28]

The state authorities, from their side, allowed some concessions, for example a small printing of the Bible,[29] the continuation of the *Journal of the Moscow Patriarchate* (now with an English-language version and a parallel publication in the Ukraine), the maintenance of theological education in the reduced number of seminaries, a very limited amount of monasticism, and a vigorous worship in perhaps 7500 parishes (the figure is questionable and there is no certain evidence as to whether or not the total number of parishes is now more than it was in 1965).

THE CATHOLICS

With the Catholic Church (both eastern and western rites), the Soviet state has been somewhat less successful than with the Orthodox in its efforts to prevent ferment from insinuating into the basic fabric of church life.

Perhaps Lithuania (where the main concentration of western-rite Catholics is to be found) suffered less under Khrushchev than some other places. If this was so, it was because of the fear of stoking nationalist fires in an area which had more reason than some others to resent the imposition of the Soviet yoke. Then towards the end of the 1960s there emerged a movement of Christian dissent which rivalled that among the Baptists in providing the most organised challenge ever to the illegal Soviet control of church life.[30]

Beginning with a letter of protest in January 1968 from sixty-three priests of the Telsiai diocese to Kosygin on the arbitrary restrictions on training for the priesthood, it rapidly grew to a mass movement in which over 17,000 people signed a petition to Brezhnev in December 1972 and January 1973.[31] An addendum to the document stated, 'only an insignificant portion of religious believers in Lithuania' were able to sign the memorandum, 'since the organs of the militia and the KGB have used all kinds of means to interrupt the collection of signatures' — including arrest of those doing the collecting.[32]

Rapidly, events moved further beyond the control of the KGB. The first issue of a clandestine publication, the *Chronicle of the Lithuanian Catholic Church,* appeared in March 1972. Although it is not known how many copies of this and the regular (roughly quarterly) issues have been circulating, the *Chronicle* appears to have had a remarkable effect in uniting Lithuanian opinion (political as well as Christian) and an ability to gather and sift information from all corners of the republic.

The state response was in line with its policy towards other denominations: some concessions but a rigorous repression of those who could not be pacified thereby or terrorised into silence by threats. As with the Orthodox Church, the state's influence had been so direct as to secure the elevation of men to the episcopate who were ready to yield to pressure and condemn the dissidents. The KGB used its methods of persuasion to force such condemnation, while the state allowed some concessions to the church, such as the consecration of two new bishops in 1969, the printing of 10,000 copies of the New Testament in 1972, and the removal from office of Justas Rugienis, the ruthless head of the Lithuanian branch of the government's Council for Religious Affairs.[33]

Meanwhile the attempt to suppress dissent was continued and made more sophisticated. Early in 1973 the authorities forced all institutions, including Catholic parishes, to send in samples of print from all their typewriters and of the type of paper used.[34] This was clearly a prelude to an intensified campaign against the new activities in the Catholic Church. It was immediately followed by a republic-wide attempt to confiscate petitions with lists of signatures and then house searches, detention and interrogation of many of the signatories. The main aim was to identify those who were the prime movers in the *Lithuanian Chronicle* exercise, suppress it, and destroy whatever printing and distribution facilities the organisers were using.[35] The KGB did find a home-made press and printing materials soon afterwards, but so far this and the subsequent arrests of those responsible have failed to stop the *Chronicle,* the tenth issue of which reached the West in the summer of 1974.[36] Five of those being held received prison sentences in January 1975.[37]

There is no space here to consider the separate problem of the Eastern-rite Catholic (Uniate) Church of the Ukraine, which since 1946 has had no legal existence whatsoever. The evidence for its continued underground activity is, however, decisive. This was already happening under Khrushchev and it has continued under Brezhnev and Kosygin, with the KGB apparently equally powerless to suppress it in either period, though keen to do so during both. The tendency seems to be in line with what is happening in other denominations: greater determination than ever before by a growing number of people to establish the rights of the believer in Soviet society.[38]

THE BAPTISTS AND EVANGELICALS

In the Soviet era, the Baptists and Evangelical Christians have advanced from being a relatively minor group to a Union-wide organisation, the existence of which is a major factor in Soviet policy-making on religion.[39] The Pentecostals are a totally post-revolutionary phenomenon. Nowhere is the current policy of 'encourage malleable leadership, suppress dissent' more clearly etched than with the Evangelicals.

Because the independent leadership under Georgi Vins and Gennadi Kryuchkov has been so totally single-minded in pressing for reforms since 1960, the persecution of them and their followers has been persistently savage, both under Khrushchev and since.[40] In contrast, there has been a significant change in policy towards the official leadership and the registered churches, consistent with the main lines laid down. The effect of its implementation has been to cement a schism between the registered and unregistered churches, with the leadership of the former criticising the latter for allegedly prejudicing the whole Evangelical situation by 'not accepting Soviet legislation', while the latter have stated that the alleged compromises of the former are not consistent with Gospel principles.

Under Khrushchev registered and unregistered suffered alike. Then concessions were offered by the state, in return for docility on the part of the leadership, who were to keep a strict rein on all evangelistic initiatives and the desire of Baptists to petition the Soviet government for a new deal.

The concessions began even under Khrushchev himself, with the permission given to hold in 1963 the first congress since the Union of the Baptists and Evangelicals nearly twenty years previously (the probable purpose of which from the state's point of view was to strengthen the official leadership against that of Vins and Kryuchkov, who were not informed that the congress was to take place.[41] The 1963 congress took place in an atmosphere of mounting physical brutality towards those who had raised their voices against the persecution.[42] Further congresses followed in 1966, 1969 and 1974, and other concessions to the official church have also been cautiously, though increasingly, permitted. There have been printings of the hymnbook, the Bible, and the New Testament on its own. The state has registered some new churches. The All-Union Council of Evangelical Christians and Baptists in Moscow has instituted a correspondence course for pastors, the members of which are permitted to convene in Moscow twice a year — presumably for some common instruction as well as examinations — even though no seminary as such has been permitted since 1927. At the 1974 congress several foreign guests were invited and they observed the whole proceedings, except for the elections to positions of authority in the Council. While what occurred there could scarcely be called freedom of speech, there were at least spontaneous reactions from the floor which indicated that the mood was a complex one, with by no means a universal willingness to accept whatever the current line of church-state accommodation was supposed to be.[43]

As usual, however, the congress represented the registered congregations only, while the followers of Vins and Kryuchkov have consistently stated that such an occasion should represent all Evangelical Christians and Baptists, and then there could be a true debate about major issues facing believers.

Significantly, and almost slavishly in line with the main features of current policy, Georgi Vins was being held for trial at the time of the congress in December 1974. He had been in custody since March of that year and apparently subjected to inhumane conditions, so that his relatives had expressed fear for his life.[44] His earlier sentence had been in 1966, the year of the previous congress.[45]

Neither the all-out violence of the state nor the growing willingness to allow concessions to the registered churches seems to have lessened the determination of the leaders of the unregistered churches to continue the struggle for their rights. Any apparent silencing of voices is only temporary and is explicable by the imprisonment of the leaders.

Soviet policy towards the Pentecostals is consistent with what we have outlined above, though it may be even more severe. Congregations have been able to achieve registration only by uniting with Baptists and thus losing their identity, while those determined to secure the recognition of an independent Pentecostal Church have been consistently persecuted. As an example of this, the case of I. P. Fedotov is particularly well documented.[46] Released from prison in 1970 after serving a ten-year sentence in full, he was once again arrested in 1974. There have been rumours very recently of the independent registration of a very small number of Pentecostal congregations, but so far the information is too fragmentary to assess the significance of this.

The high degree of organisation and determination among Evangelicals, as among Lithuanian Catholics, continues to make them a major barrier to the implementation of Soviet atheist policies.

MUSLIMS

With the major non-Christian religions — Islam, Judaism and Buddhism — the same guidelines of policy apply as have been indicated above, though they are less easy to document, and, at least with the Jews, they have been less successfully applied. They all have some form of complaisant leadership, below which — and increasingly on the surface — there are counter-currents which flow very fast indeed.

It is more difficult to gauge reaction to Soviet atheist policies among Muslims than any other major religious group (and with perhaps some 40-5 million people belonging to the Central Asian nationalities and the number rapidly growing, they may already surpass the Russian Orthodox Church numerically and therefore be the largest of all).

Stalin's policy towards Muslim leaders was crushing and went so far as to attempt the genocide of some nationalities. The deportation of the Crimean Tartars and the death of many of them is the best documented and most serious example of this.[47] It has been claimed that there was a strong Muslim leadership in the revolt in the labour camps after Stalin's death.

It is difficult to determine whether there was an increase in pressure on Soviet Muslims under Khrushchev and, if so, whether this was later eased. It seems probable that since the death of Stalin the situation has remained more or less constant because of the Kremlin's fear that to dig in too deeply the goad of the anti-religious campaign might have the effect of stimulating disaffection in a huge area where there may well be less love for the Russians than there was for the British in India or Africa.

Somehow (and there is research waiting to be done on this) the regime succeeded in their encouragement of the evolution of a docile Muslim leadership.[48] Their scope for legal activity is limited. The leaders are encouraged to promote the Soviet 'peace campaign' in the Middle East. They administer about 500 registered mosques, under the care of perhaps twice that number of mullahs. There are two *medressehs* [theological schools] with no more than about eighty students in all. This limited phenomenon which the regime permits probably represents less than 1 per cent of the total Islamic life of the Soviet Union. There is no religion which is expressed more fully or persists more tenaciously through family and social activity. Domestic structures remain almost dogmatically Muslim throughout the relevant areas.

Although there is no known *samizdat* criticising the complaisant leadership and describing non-official activities, the existence of the 'hidden' 99 per cent is still extensively documented through the anti-religious campaign which has been conducted in the press. As this seems to have been mainly a paper war in the last fifteen years, the details which have surfaced are perhaps more precise than with many Christian denominations.

For example, in Azerbaijan only sixteen registered mosques were left by 1969, but the number of clandestine ones probably exceeded 1000, in addition to which there were 300 places of pilgrimage. One district had only one official mosque, but no less than seven unregistered ones were built (note, *built*) in 1970 alone, 'at the expense of the local *kolkhoz* and *sovkhoz*'.[49]

There are secret Muslim brotherhoods [*tariqa*] which run an extensive network. Admission to them is by an initiation ceremony. The most active of these is the Naqshebandiya *tariqa* which is represented in all Muslim areas. Founded in the late eighteenth century, it has always been the militant core of anti-Russian resistance.[50]

The Soviet press accounts stop short, of course, of expounding the ideology of the resistance. They rather criticise the extensive, almost universal, continuation of traditional Muslim customs: bride purchase, sex segregation, polygamy, excessive respect for the elders, and so on. The patriarchal nature of the Muslim family constitutes a barrier to the Sovietisation of Central Asia, a barrier which the regime has so far devised no successful strategy to remove. Russian-Muslim marriages remain rare. Alexandre Bennigsen's description of the core of the resistance is revealing:

> The Soufi *tariqa* with their iron discipline based on initiation and their old tradition of underground action provide the Muslim communities with learned Arabists who can and do replace the rare 'registered' clerics, perform the religious rites: marriage, circumcision,

burials; run the clandestine Koranic schools and oppose an efficient oral propaganda to the clumsy bureaucratic atheism. They are dangerous rivals of the Communist Party and represent a serious obstacle to the 'Marxist-Communist education of the popular masses'.[51]

At the moment, there are no signs that the Soviet regime is evolving any more effective strategy for combatting Islam than it has in the recent past.

JEWS

The case of the Soviet Jews is considerably different from that of any other religion. The international element plays a much greater role: this is the one instance where major international opinion has been brought to bear on an aspect of Soviet policy, with the effect, which would never have seemed within the realm of possibility a decade ago, of basically changing Soviet practice and leading to the current wave of emigration to Israel.

In the world-wide publicity which has clad these events the religious aspect of the Jewish question has gone almost unremarked, though that is not to say that it is unimportant. It may, indeed, be confidently stated that international Zionism has paid less attention than might have been expected to the ongoing situation of those Jews remaining in the Soviet Union. For example, one recalls no petition from the outside to the Soviet authorities asking them to open synagogues.

In fact, the total number of these open in the Soviet Union is less adequate, comparatively, than churches for some of the major Christian denominations. In 1960 Moscow Radio gave the total number of synagogues as being 150.[52] It is impossible to verify this figure, but it is certain that even this very small number was unevenly distributed according to Jewish population, and it was further reduced during the Khrushchev period. During the time of the new religious purges the Soviet press published numerous instances of the closure of synagogues for alleged infractions of the Soviet laws.[53] By the time Khrushchev fell the number had further dropped to about sixty, though there has not been any publicity about this in the Soviet press since Khrushchev — undoubtedly because of the unfavourable impression this would have made with world public opinion.

The docility of the official Soviet Jewish leadership (there is no central Jewish organisation comparable to the Moscow patriarchate) has been far less successful than its counterparts in the other faiths in instilling a feeling among co-religionists abroad that there is no persecution in the Soviet Union, or that if there is it would be wiser to do nothing about it. In fact, such attempts from the Soviet side have failed with some margin to spare.

When the Rabbi of Moscow, Yehuda Leib Levin, died in 1971, he was replaced by Yaakov Fishman, who was at once stated to be a totally compromised figure by Jewish organisations world-wide.[54] He has been able to make no impact on religious circles abroad which is in any way comparable to that of, say, Metropolitan Nikodim in the Russian Orthodox Church or Pastor Mikhail Zhidkov of the All-Union Council of Evangelical Christians and Baptists. Nor has he been able to build up anything like the store of religious credibility which the two latter are considered to have by many western church leaders.

Soviet controls over the remaining synagogues are undoubtedly severe, though this has not prevented many of them from becoming a rallying point for the renaissance of Jewish sentiment.[55]

The difference of the Jewish case, over against other religions, is most marked in the nature of the Soviet concessions. Nationality policies and the nature of the Soviet involvement in the Middle East and other aspects of international affairs (including, for example, trade relations with the USA) come into play here more than the specifically anti-religious policies of the Soviet regime. The important and well-known Soviet concession on emigration is quite different from those made to any other religious group. The only comparable one has been to the Soviet Germans, numbers of whom have been permitted to emigrate to West Germany in the last few years. Though many of these are strongly religious people (Baptists, Mennonites, Lutherans), the factor of nationality plays the predominant part, just as it does with the Jews.

The future of Jewish institutions in the Soviet Union, principally the synagogue but also more purely cultural ones as well, is one of the most difficult aspects of Soviet religious policy to calculate. Owing to the failure to bring forward the necessary docile leadership, one might almost say that there is no recognisable policy on this at present. It is difficult, furthermore, to see where one will come from while the regime continues to refuse to allow the training of rabbis on Soviet soil. (The nominally-existing *yeshivah* in Moscow is not known to have graduated a single one, though students have been expelled from it.)

BUDDHISTS

Buddhism is among the most severely persecuted of all religions in the Soviet Union, for while it has the standard passive, tolerated leadership, the concessions to Buddhists have been virtually non-existent and this religious group has become the object of a more violent campaign than was being waged under Khrushchev.

At the time of the revolution, the Buddhists were one of the most highly organised religious groups to come under Soviet rule. Furthermore, their leader, Avgan Dordzhiev, a man of outstanding calibre, believed that Buddhist teachings were compatible with the building of a socialist society on the Leninist model.[56] But Stalin was always liable to be more severe to his friends than to his enemies, and he used the full weight of the state apparatus to crush the whole fabric of Soviet Buddhism. By the outbreak of the Second World War it looked as though this was the end of it.

As with the Christian faith, however, it was only the superstructure which had been destroyed. Popular belief, in the Buryat-Mongol Republic and elsewhere, soon came out in the open again, accompanied by the establishment of an officially-permitted Buddhist Central Council at Ivolginsk, near Ulan-Ude in Buryatiya. As with the Russian Orthodox Church, one of the main purposes of this concession was to provide a mouthpiece for the Soviet cause when this was required in dealings with the Buddhist peoples of Asia. In 1970 the Moscow correspondent *of The Times* was able to visit Buryatiya, and the Bandido Hambo (chief) Lama claimed that 'practically every village in Buryatiya has its own lama'.[57] He was almost certainly not referring to registered ones for the popular revival has been considerable and Soviet sources admit this in even more pointed language: 'Pilgrims constantly come to the datsan (monastery) at Ivolginsk, arriving on horseback, in cars and by aeroplane;'[58] 'active religious propaganda in post-war years has succeeded in attracting a considerable number of young people into the religious communities;'[59] 'when it was decided to send to the Mongolian Buddhist School for Monks a party of ten youths who had had secondary education, numbers of volunteers promptly appeared.'[60]

Soviet atheism has recently sounded a sterner note about Buddhist activities, which has broken out into one of the most violent aspects of the present anti-religious campaign. If the threats contained in this warning have been carried out (and this is not certain), then there is the same kind of legal repression being brought against the leaders of popular Buddhism as against the leaders of the unregistered Baptists:

> Lamas and those acting as such are infringing the legisla-tion on religious cults; they carry out religious rites even in believers' houses and some practise traditional medicine. The lamas are resurrecting old customs, such as giving minors in marriage, collecting bride-money, and so on.[61]

As with the Baptists, reprisals against the unofficial leadership, particularly its intellectual spearhead, have recently been brutal. Soviet Buddhism is no longer just a popular practice confined to certain remote areas of European Russia. This new factor is no doubt the reason why Soviet atheism has acted so violently against Buddhism recently.

To date, the focal point of this new campaign has been the person of Bidiya Dandaron, whose case is fully documented in *samizdat*[62] and through the evidence of his friend Alexander Pyatigorsky, now in the West. Dandaron was the outstanding Buddhist scholar to have emerged in the Soviet period and enjoyed world renown as an expert on the Tibetan language. He was arrested in August 1972, tried that December, and sentenced to five years on the charge of having founded a Buddhist sect. The *samizdat* documents about his case allege deliberate falsification of evidence about the nature of his activities. Several others in his circle have also been arrested and some are now incarcerated in a mental hospital. Pyatigorsky states: 'The objective evidently is to liquidate all study of Buddhism . . . This trial is patently the first act leading to much worse deeds. Times are worse than they have ever been since 1953.'[63]

These words rapidly proved to be only too true. In November 1974 news reached the West that Dandaron had died in the prison camp where he was held.[64]

There are other religious groups being as badly treated today as the Buddhists, but it may be doubted whether there is any other whose fortunes have declined as sharply since the fall of Khrushchev.

CONCLUSION

The nationwide phenomenon of a religion which continues to flourish and even attract the young in so many places ten years after Khrushchev's campaign, the complexity of its social bases, the infinite variety of its denominational expression, render generalisations about current trends impossible. There are foreign observers in Moscow with a developed specialised interest in the subject who say that church-state tensions have recently eased considerably. At the same time, Academician Andrei Sakharov, who is in close touch with many of the individuals now being persecuted for religious reasons, says: 'These persecutions have been heavily intensified, and a very great number of people have been arrested in the Baltic States.'

Probably regional and ethnic policies are so varied that neither generalisation is entirely accurate. What may be true for the Baptist leadership who assembled for their congress in Moscow in December 1974 was untrue for Dandaron, the Buddhist who had died in prison just previously.

Is there any centralised policy towards religion at all at the moment? Under Stalin in the 1930s and again in a quite different sense in the late 1940s, one could say yes, while still listing exceptions. The same may be said for the Khrushchev period — and further evidence about Muslim and Buddhist areas may yet prove the exceptions to be less notable than this study suggests. The 'mini-thaw' of 1965 was a fact, though it may well have lasted too short a time for its effects to have been experienced throughout the Soviet Union. 'Encourage docile leadership; repress dissent' is the only possible generalisation about the trends of the Brezhnev-Kosygin years. Given these policy aims, one will naturally find most repression where intellectual thought is keenest — particularly when it shows signs of attracting the young towards religion.

But all this having been said, another essay could be written on the exceptions. They are so numerous, and some so important, that some authorities in some places have clearly had sufficient autonomy to be more or less severe than the general line of the time.

If there is a debate taking place in inner party circles on this issue, there is no evidence of it. Yet one may hazard the guess that some group somewhere must be holding it — if only for one incontrovertible reason: Soviet atheist policies, whether in their severe form under Khrushchev or their more subtle expression since, have signally failed to go any way towards the eradication of religion from society. Perhaps the opposite has happened.

NOTES

1   *The Times,* and *Daily Telegraph* 13 Sep 1971.
2   See Michael Bourdeaux, *Religious Ferment in Russia,* henceforth *RFR* (London, 1968) pp. 3-6.
3   *The Russian Orthodox Church, Organization, Situation, Activity* (Moscow, 1958).
4   See e.g. Bourdeaux, *RFR;* Bourdeaux, *Patriarch and Prophets: Persecution of the Russian Orthodox Church today,* henceforth *P & P* (London, 1970); William C. Fletcher and Donald A. Lowrie, 'Khrushchev's Religious Policy, 1959-64', in *Aspects of Religion in the Soviet Union 1917-67,* ed. Richard H. Marshall (Chicago, 1971) pp. 131-55.
5   See Anatoli Levitin, *Dialog s tserkovnoi Rossiei* (Paris, 1967).
6   See e.g. the documents and bibliography sections in the bi-monthly journal, *Religion in Communist Lands,* henceforth *RCL*, Keston College, Keston, Kent (1973-00).
7   See *RCL*, vol. 2, no. 3 (May-June 1974) pp. 9-15.
8   The best discussion of Lenin's anti-religious policy is contained in the chapter by Bohdan R. Bociurciw, 'Lenin and Religion', in *Lenin, the Man, the Theorist, the Leader,* ed. Peter Reddaway and Leonard Schapiro (London, 1967), pp. 107-34.

9 See Gerhard Simon, *Church, State and Opposition in the USSR* (London, 1974) p. 78.

10 See Bourdeaux, *P & P*, pp. 113-16.

11 See Michael Bourdeaux and Xenia Howard-Johnston, *Aida of Leningrad* (Reading, 1972).

12 Discussion in *RCL*, vol. 2, no. 3 (May-June 1974) pp. 11-12.

13 See Bourdeaux, *P & P*, pp. 264-70.

14 See Bourdeaux, *P & P*, pp. 265-9.

15 *Komsomol'skaya pravda*, 15 Aug 1965.

16 For a discussion of new traditions see *RCL*, vol. 1, no. 3 (May-June 1973) pp. 18-19.

17 See *Religious Minorities in the Soviet Union (1960-70)*, ed. Bourdeaux, for Minority Rights Group, Benjamin Franklin House, 36 Craven Street, London WC2N 5NG, rev. ed. (London, 1973) pp. 4-5.

18 See *Vestnik verkhovnogo soveta*, no. 12 (1966) pp. 219-20.

19 For an examination of some of the basic relations between the Russian churches and the outside world and their political rationale see W. C. Fletcher, *Religion and Soviet Foreign Policy, 1945-70* (London, 1973).

20 See particularly the report written by Trevor Beeson for the British Council of Churches, *Discretion and Valour: Religious Conditions in Russia and Eastern Europe* (London, 1974).

21 See W. C. Fletcher, *Nikolai* (New York, 1968).

22 Evidence for this in the mid-1960s is contained in the chapter, 'The Ordinary Believer', in Bourdeaux, *P & P*, pp. 156-88.

23 See *A Chronicle of Current Events*, Amnesty International Publications, 20 Sep 1971, pp. 246-8.

24 Ibid. See also Valeri Chalidze's letter in support of Naro-Fominsk believers, written 28 Feb 1971, *Posev*, no. 5 (1971) p. 8.

25 Some of their major writings are translated in Bourdeaux *P & P*. See also the quarterly *Vestnik russkogo studencheskogo dvizheniya*, Paris, *passim*.

26 See Bourdeaux, *P & P*, pp. 239-44.

27 See Bourdeaux, *P & P*, pp. 226-7.

28 For a full discussion of the *sobor*, see Bourdeaux, 'How Soviet State kept control of Church Council', *Church Times*, London, 17 Mar 1972, p. 11 (concluded on p. 8).

29 See Walter Sawatsky, 'Bible Work in Europe Since 1945: A Country by Country Analysis', footnote 12, available from Keston College.

30 For a full account of the Lithuanian Catholic Situation, see Bohdan R. Bociurkiw, 'Religious Dissent in the USSR: the Lithuanian Catholics', paper presented on 5 Sep 1974 at the Banff (Canada) 1974 International Conference on Slavic Studies.

31 Ibid., pp. 4-9.

32 Ibid., p. 9.

33 Ibid., pp. 18-19.

34 *Chronicle of the Lithuanian Catholic Church*, no. 6 (1973) pp. 21-2.

35   Ibid. Quoted in *Elta Information Service*, no. 3 (182) (May-June 1974) p. 1.

36   *Elta*, no. 4 (183) (July-Aug 1974) summarises the contents.

37   See *Guardian*, 31 Dec 1974, based on article in *Sovetskaya Litva*, 29 Dec 1974, p. 3.

38   For a recent account of the main lines of this revival, see Bociurciw, 'Religious Situation in the Soviet Ukraine', paper delivered at a symposium to mark the 30th anniversary of the *Ukrainian Quarterly*, New York City, 7 Dec 1974, to be published in *Ukrainian Quarterly* in 1975.

39   For an account of its effect on Soviet policy, see Bourdeaux, *RFR*.

40   See Bourdeaux, *Faith on Trial in Russia* (London, 1971).

41   See Bourdeaux, *RFR*, p. 75.

42   See Bourdeaux, *RFR*, pp. 50-65.

43   See Ronald Goulding, 'USSR Baptist Congress: A Breath of Air and a Cold Wind', press release of the European Baptist Federation, 4 Southampton Row, London WC1B 4AB, 24 Dec 1974.

44   See Bourdeaux, 'Three Generations of Suffering', *Church Times*, 31 May 1974, p. 9.

45   For a partial transcript of his trial, see Bourdeaux, *Faith on Trial in Russia*, pp. 110-30.

46   See Bourdeaux, 'The Harassment of a Soviet Christian', *Church Times*, 13 Dec 1974, p. 3.

47   See *The Crimean Tartars, Volga Germans and Meskhetians: Soviet treatment of some national minorities*, Minority Rights Group (London, 1971).

48   I am heavily indebred to Professor Alexandre Benningsen for the substance of this section. It is taken from a paper delivered at the Banff (Canada) 1974 International Conference on Slavic Studies, 5 Sep 1974.

49   Ibid., p. 3.

50   Ibid., p. 4.

51   Ibid., p. 6.

52   *Religious Minorities in the Soviet Union (1960-70)*, ed. Bourdeaux, rev. ed. (London, 1973) p. 22.

53   Ibid., p. 23.

54   See *Jewish Chronicle*, 19 Nov 1971, p. 1.

55   The most notable description of this is in Eli Wiesel, *The Jews of Silence* (New York, 1967) pp. 58-97.

56   See Walter Kolarz, *Religion in the Soviet Union*, pp. 454-62.

57   *The Times*, 6 Oct 1970.

58   *Nauka i religiya*, no. 7 (Moscow, 1961) p. 7.

59   *Spravochnik propagandista i ateista* (Moscow, 1966) p. 150.

60   *Uchitel'skaya gazeta*, 12 Dec 1972.

61   A. N. Kochetov, *Buddizm* (Moscow, 1968) p. 156.

62   *RCL*, vol. 1, no. 4-5 1973, pp. 43-7.

63   To be published in Keston College's *White Book*, International Committee for the Defence of Human Rights in the USSR, Place Flagey 28, B-1050, Brussels.

64   *Observer*, 1 Dec 1974.

8 Soviet Russian Literature and Literary Policy

MARTIN DEWHIRST

The high point and the turning point in Soviet post-Stalin literary and literary-political developments came at the end of 1962. On 20 November the eleventh issue for that year of the journal *Novy mir[New World]* was put on sale (it had been passed for printing on 3 November), and those lucky enough to obtain one of the 121,900 copies were able to read Alexander Solzhenitsyn's long story, *Odin den' Ivana Denisovicha [One Day of Ivan Denisovich]*, with an introduction by the chief editor of the magazine, the poet Alexander Tvardovsky, and also the first part of Viktor Nekrasov's travel notes, *Po obe storony okeana [On Both Sides of the Ocean]*. It must be admitted, however, that they could also read, if they wanted to, Yury Zhukov's essay, *Zhizn' i smert' Patrisa Lumumby [The Life and Death of Patrice Lumumba]*. Who would have guessed then that ten years after Khrushchev's exit from the political scene the entire editorial board of *Novy mir,* apart from K. Fedin, would have been changed and the journal run for the last five years, after Tvardovsky's dismissal and death, by a journalist (V. Kosolapov); that Solzhenitsyn would be living in Switzerland; that Nekrasov would be staying with Abram Terts (Andrey Sinyavsky) in Paris; and that Yury Zhukov would still be writing about Patrice Lumumba?[1] The next ten years may bring similar surprises.

If November 1962 was the high point, then December 1962 was the turning point. On 1 December Khrushchev visited an art exhibition in the centre of Moscow, and his reactions, if not as violent as those displayed so forcibly on 15 September 1974 by some 'ordinary Soviet people' at another art exhibition on the outskirts of Moscow, were none the less of much greater importance for the future development — or lack of it — of the arts and literature in the USSR. Fortunately, there is no need to detail here the gradual reimposition of tight control over 'official' literary life between the end of 1962 and the fall from power of Khrushchev. Priscilla Johnson and Leopold Labedz have taken the story up to the spring of 1964,[2] and Mihajlo Mihajlov has published a lively and graphic description of the mood and literary climate in and around the Soviet capital in the summer of that year.[3] We can therefore justifiably examine the Soviet literary-political scene only from October 1964 onwards, stressing, however, that in this field the new leaders largely continued a policy line which had already been in operation for nearly two years when the man whose bark was by now worse than his bite was replaced by people who valued peace and quiet, probably wanted neither to bark nor to bite, and desired above all to reduce to the minimum the chances of something — anything — getting out of hand.

What this meant in literature amounted to (a) an attempt to prevent the large-scale circulation of works which would, or even might, induce a large section of the population to contest the value of the Soviet socialist system, while (b) trying at the same time to mollify people with a political mind of their own by permitting the small-scale, legal publication of excellent books and articles on specialised subjects.

This overall policy, which may be regarded as having been well thought out and executed, and thus highly successful, has, like any policy, had some consequences which are probably regarded by the present Soviet authorities as on balance undesirable. Thus, the steady trickle abroad of *samizdat* proper, which the present writer is inclined to date from the three documents circulated in December 1962 once the results of Khrushchev's visit to the art exhibition became clear,[4] may well be regarded by most Central Committee officials as 'dysfunctional', despite its very useful function in making some people in the West think that the Soviet regime is in some important ways becoming both weaker and safer to have '*détente*' with.

Let us now look at some of the results of this general policy of striving for tranquillity and stability on the literary 'front'. First and foremost, this policy has meant that nothing has been officially published under the Brezhnev-Kosygin leadership that has caused as much excitement and admiration as did Solzhenitsyn's first work in 1962. Indeed, only one article (significantly, though, it was about the sorry state of the Russian language in the contemporary USSR)[5] and one short story, 'Zakhar Kalita' (characteristically, again, it was about the lack of a sense of history, the absence of an understanding of traditional Russian cultural values, on the part of the Soviet authorities),[6] by Solzhenitsyn have been published in his homeland since the fall of Khrushchev.

Nearly all the most striking new Soviet prose works printed there during the last decade are, however, similar in inspiration to the story by Solzhenitsyn just mentioned, and one imagines they have appeared in print because of the pressure (mainly by writers) and the desire (sometimes of officials) to let at least *some* good (if not very good) writing see the light of day in official publications. The works we have in mind are by the *derevenshchiki,* writers who lived (and in many cases still live) in the Russian provinces and generally write on life in rural areas. In an interview published in August 1973 in *Le monde,* Solzhenitsyn commended the writing of Abramov, Astaf'ev, Belov, Shukshin (1929-74), Mozhaev, Evgeny Nosov, Soloukhin, Tendryakov, Trifonov, Kazakov, Zalygin, Voynovich, Bykov, Vladimov, Maksimov and Okudzhava, the first eleven of whom can certainly be regarded as *derevenshchiki,* whose main forum is *Nash sovremennik [Our Contemporary],* the best Soviet literary journal since Tvardovsky had to leave *Novy mir* in 1970. The most striking feature of these writers is their 'Russianness' — they are not particularly 'Soviet', 'pro-Soviet' or 'anti-Soviet' — and so, for better or worse, they have not aroused much interest or enthusiasm in the West. There may not be a Leskov among them, but they often write better than, say, Gleb Uspensky. And like Leskov (and Solzhenitsyn) they have a real feel for the Russian language; helped by their residence outside the large towns, they are undoubtedly bringing their native language back into literature and intellectual life again after several decades of almost unrelieved Sovietese (i.e. bureaucratese or officialese).[7]

In contrast to prose, all other genres have apparently been stagnating or degenerating. Poetry, some of which was so 'public' and demonstrative in the late fifties and early sixties, has gone almost entirely 'private', and however much one might welcome this, one hesitates to credit it to the pressures of the Soviet authorities. Evtushenko may simply have had little left to say, Voznesensky could well have preferred to address a smaller and more select audience, Akhmadulina always regarded mass 'Poetry Days' with apprehension. There are now hundreds, probably thousands, of people in the USSR who can turn out technically accomplished verse, and some of them, like the elderly philosophical Moscow poet Arseny Tarkovsky and the much younger Leningrad poets Viktor Sosnora and Aleksandre Kushner, nearly always make rewarding reading. From the political point of view both we and (it is to be hoped) the Soviet authorities can safely overlook them.

For those in search of new playwrights, memoirists and essayists, Soviet publishers have little to offer. The only promising dramatist, Alexander Vampilov, was drowned in 1972 at the age of 35. None of the recent autobiographical works can compare with the reminiscences of Erenburg (1891-1967) and Paustovsky (1892-1968),[8] not to speak of Nadezhda Mandel'shtam's. The *ocherkisty* (essayists, mainly on rural life) who were so popular under Khrushchev — Dorosh (1908-1972), Ovechkin (1904-68) and others — have been largely superseded by the *derevenshchiki*.

One might at this point mention that the literary scene has been much less colourful, animated and hopeful during the last ten years than in the decade between the second congress of Soviet writers and the fall of Khrushchev because so many of the most talented Soviet writers left the scene, became more quiet and cautious, or in some way compromised themselves in the eyes of their erstwhile admirers and/or the Soviet authorities.

We have already noted the deaths of Tvardovsky, Shukshin, Vampilov, Erenburg and Paustovsky. Akhmatova died in 1966, and Chukovsky in 1969. One of the best younger prose writers, Anatoly Kuznetsov, defected in 1969. An older writer, Valery Tarsis, was allowed to emigrate in 1966; perhaps the best young Russian poet, Iosif Brodsky, was virtually forced to emigrate in 1972, and Solzhenitsyn was flown out of his country against his will in 1974. Viktor Nekrasov and Vladimir Maksimov left in 1974 and went to France, where Andrey Sinyavsky had been living since the previous year. One of the most popular Soviet poets and singers, Alexander Galich, left Russia shortly after the excellent poet Naum Korzhavin. Most of them had been expelled from the Writers' Union months or years before their departure (Solzhenitsyn was expelled in 1969). Other expellees, such as Voynovich and Chukovskaya, are still in the USSR but cannot publish anything. The Soviet Union is again becoming a paradise for hacks.

But even some of the most prominent writers who remained in Russia also faced difficulties, and many of them decided or were forced to discredit themselves. Two of the very few remaining writers with a pre-Soviet education, Valentin Kataev (b. 1897) and Veniamin Kaverin (b. 1902), wrote letters attacking Solzhenitsyn and Mrs Mandel'shtam respectively. Mikhail Sholokhov (b. 1905), the author of one of the greatest modern Russian novels, *The Quiet Don,* failed to produce anything new and continued to lambast other writers. Several of the best officially tolerated prose writers were obliged to publish letters in the weekly *Literaturnaya gazeta* disassociating themselves from editions of their works published in the West. Such writers included Galina Serebryakova (52/1967), Tvardovsky (7/1970), Vladimir Voynovich (42/1970), Varlam Shalamov (8/1972), Bulat Okudzhava (48/1972), Anatoly Gladilin (48/1972), and Boris and Arkady Strugatsky, the leading Soviet SF (scientific fantasy) writers (50/1972). Relatively unimportant though such letters may be, they are hardly edifying or signs of a healthy literary situation.

Signs of health are to be found in two other areas, literary criticism (*literaturovedenie,* not the more superficial *literaturnaya kritika*), and the publication or republication of original works by, and archival material on, authors now dead. Soviet work in both these fields is amply documented in English elsewhere,[9] and here it is perhaps necessary only to give a few examples of recent publications and stress one particular aspect of present publishing policies and research activities.

The most 'dangerous' pre-revolutionary Russian author is surely Dostoevsky, and research on his works has never been so intense anywhere in the world as in the Soviet Union during the last ten years. In 1971, the 150th anniversary of Dostoevsky's birth, a new thirty-volume edition of his works was announced, each of the eleven volumes which have so far appeared being printed in 200,000 copies. The superb *Literaturnoe nasledstvo [Literary Heritage]* series has now reached volume 86, and three of the fifteen issues (some in two parts) published since 1965 have been devoted to Dostoevsky. Perhaps the best-known Soviet specialist on Dostoevsky was Mikhail Bakhtin, whose *Problemy poetiki Dostoevskogo* (second edition 1963, third edition 1972) is now available in English.[10]

Bakhtin has recently been honoured by festschrifts published by the universities of Tartu in Estonia and of Saransk in Mordoviya, which reminds us of the large number of interesting works of literary criticism which have appeared during the last ten years in the more outlying parts of the Soviet Union. The University of Tartu is undoubtedly the place where the most stimulating and original teaching and research is being undertaken, but valuable work on Russian literature has been published in many other towns, such as Kaluga, Tula, Voronezh, Saratov, Alma-Ata and Samarkand. True, these collections usually have to be printed in a very small number of copies (for example, the festschrift for Yury Lotman, the head of the Russian literature department at the University of Tartu, came out in only 500 copies), but this does at least mean that people who can get hold of them are able to read them without the risk they run when harbouring *samizdat*. Another welcome sign is that it is becoming much easier for Soviet scholars to contribute to western periodicals, such as the *International Journal of Slavic Linguistics and Poetics* and *Russian Literature* (both published in the Netherlands).

There is probably something odd about a situation in which serious literary criticism and research are thriving (naturally, *most* Soviet literary criticism is extremely poor)[11] but literature itself is not. The USSR is not the only country, however, in which few first-rate original works have been published in the last ten years, and people with access to *samizdat* will have read recent works by Solzhenitsyn, Sinyavsky, Voynovich, Brodsky and others which are undoubtedly up to 'world standard'. Moreover, one of the most striking features of recent years is the extent to which older works unknown to all or most Soviet readers have been printed or reprinted by Soviet publishing houses. One thinks immediately of the 1973 editions of the novels by Mikhail Bulgakov (1891-1940) and poems of Osip Mandel'shtam (1891-1938). But these books had been preceded by excellent editions of poems by such little-known (until their republication) writers as Konstantin Bal'mont (1867-1942) and Andrey Bely (1880-1934); of nearly all the fiction by the first Russian Nobel prize-winner for literature, Ivan Bunin (1870-1953); and of foreign writers until recently regarded as highly undesirable, like Franz Kafka and Samuel Beckett.[12]

The overall picture is, then, a far from simple one, with a huge amount of extraordinarily mediocre writing being published for the masses, but a good deal of first-rate literature and works on literature also made available, if usually only for the few.[13]

How satisfied Soviet readers are with the present publishing policy of the CPSU is, of course, impossible to say. The major clues are given by the periodical *Problemy sotsiologii pechati [Problems of the Sociology of the Press]* (Novosibirsk) and the two issues entitled *Chitatel' i gazeta [The Reader and the Newspaper]*, published as Information Bulletins 35 and 36 (1969) by three groups of Soviet sociologists.[14] Further details of a survey in 1968 of readers of *Literaturnaya gazeta* are given in issue number 63 of the *samizdat* journal *Politichesky dnevnik 1964-1970 [Political Diary 1964-1970]* (Amsterdam, Fond imeni Gertsena, 1972), from which we take the following details. The survey found that *Literaturnaya gazeta* readers were most of all dissatisfied with the literary section of this weekly newspaper (rather more than half of whose space is normally devoted to literature). Of its subscribers, 30 per cent regularly also read *Yunost' [Youth]*, 29 per cent — *Novy mir,* and only 5 per cent — *Oktyabr' [October]*, an anti-liberal magazine. *Novy mir* was least popular among workers, to judge from replies to the questionnaire. The most popular journal among party employees was *Oktyabr',* whereas *Inostrannaya literatura*

[Foreign Literature] was the least popular publication in the eyes of this group. *Oktyabr'* was least popular among people of the 'free professions' (only 1 per cent of them read it).

The authors whose works the subscribers to *Literaturnaya gazeta* would most have liked to read in the paper were, in descending order of popularity, Paustovsky, Solzhenitsyn, Simonov, Aksenov, Sholokhov, Kazakov, Soloukhin and Nagibin. The list of *recent* literature which had most appealed to *Literaturnaya gazeta* readers was headed by works by Simonov, then Bulgakov, Solzhenitsyn, Erenburg, Kataev, German, Aytmatov and Paustovsky. 69 per cent of the works named had been first published in *Novy mir.*

Only 35 per cent of those polled answered the (possibly risky) question, 'Which works by Soviet writers did you very much dislike?' The most unpopular author by far was Kochetov, a 'poor' second was Kozhevnikov, and then came Babaevsky, Polevoy, Pilyar, Alekseev, Gonchar, Andreev, Leonov, Grekova, Fedin, Sofronov, Soloukhin and Shevtsov. The list of poets whom readers specifically disliked was headed by Voznesensky, with Rozhdestvensky very closely behind and Evtushenko not a 'bad' third. Only then came Asadov, Prokof'ev, Gribachev, Sofronov, Akhmadulina, S. Vasil'ev, Kobzev, Markov and Firsov. The three most disliked poets were, however, also the three most popular Soviet poets.[15] The winner here was easily Evtushenko, followed by Rozhdestvensky and Voznesensky, some names were Esenin, Simonov, Gamzatov, Svetlov, Pasternak, Drunina, Martynov, Matveeva, Okudzhava, Akhmatova, Vinokurov, Akhmadulina, Asadov, Smelyakov, Berggol'ts, Tsvetaeva, Slutsky and Mandel'shtam. Unlike Evtushenko, Rozhdestvensky and Voznesensky, some poets were mentioned almost exclusively in the context of *un*popular poets; they were Prokof'ev, Sofronov, Gribachev, S. Vasil'ev, Markov and Firsov.

Literaturnaya gazeta subscribers were also asked to name authors who had written works between 1920 and 1950 which had withstood the test of time. Sholokhov came first, followed by A. N. Tolstoy, Il'f and Petrov, Ostrovsky, Fadeev, Paustovsky, Babel', Mayakovsky, Bulgakov and, only in tenth place, Gorky. The most popular Soviet literary critics were Andronikov, Lakshin, Chukovsky and Shklovsky.

The very short list of specifically unpopular critics was headed by Dymshits, followed by Kryachko, Ermilov, Nazarenko, Idashkin and Starikov.[16]

Whereas the weekly *Literaturnaya gazeta* is read by a wide section of the so-called 'intelligentsia', *Trud [Labour]* is a daily newspaper intended mainly for workers and engineers. Asked about recent literature on contemporary themes, subscribers to *Trud* expressed a marked preference for Yu. German (an easy winner with his novel, *Dorogoy moy chelovek*), Shamyakin, Fedoseev, Polevoy, Iskander, Erenburg and Chakovsky. Solzhenitsyn only just beat Kochetov, but it is interesting to note that *Oktyabr'* (of which Kochetov was then chief editor) was the least popular Soviet journal mentioned in the survey.[17] With the exception of Iskander, *Trud* readers evidently preferred somewhat stodgy, army-type fare to the rather more sophisticated and varied civilian diet that best suited the taste of *Literaturnaya gazeta* subscribers.

The 'literary process' in the USSR, as Sinyavsky has called it,[18] is not, of course, allowed to take place in a 'spontaneous' or 'elemental' (i.e. natural) way. The authorities attempt to control everything that happens, through such agencies as the censorship *[Glavlit]*,[19] the State Committee for Publishing, Polygraphy and the Book Trade (until October 1973 this was the State Committee for the Press), the Department of Culture of the Central Committee, the Department of Progaganda (until May 1966 the Department of Progaganda and Agitation) of the Central Committee, the Ministry of Culture, and the KGB. This is not the place to write about these bureaucratic organisations, because very little has changed in their activities during the past ten, or indeed forty, years. It should, however, be noted that the employees of these official bodies are now much more sophisticated and better educated than before — they are smoother characters and the departments they serve in work more smoothly. In the opinion of some observers,[20] all these organisations put together are less responsible for the present state of Soviet literature than are the writers themselves, or rather, than is the Union of Writers of the USSR, which *has* changed somewhat in the last few years and so deserves some attention here.

In order to be a full-time professional writer in the Soviet Union one has to join the Union. The highest body of the Union is its Congress, which has met only five times so far, in 1934, 1954, 1959, 1967 and 1971. At these congresses, 591, 738, 497, 537, and 527 delegates represented 1500, 3695, 4801, 6608 and 7270 members of the Union, respectively. These last figures show that there has been a good steady increase in the output of 'engineers of human souls', as writers are sometimes called in the USSR. At the last congress 432 of the 527 delegates (i.e. over 80 per cent) were party members, whereas in 1967 'only' 76.8 per cent of the delegates were in the party.[21]

Only 51 delegates in 1971 were under forty-one years of age, 155 were aged between forty-one and fifty, 162 between fifty-one and sixty, 125 between sixty-one and seventy, and 34 were over seventy. At the fourth congress in 1967 A. Keshokov had said that 26 of the delegates were over seventy, 'but they are sitting in the "literary saddle" with enviable dignity, gladdening us and all the friends of Soviet literature', [22] Four years later, as noted above, septuagenarians turned out in greater force. Over 40 per cent of the delegates in 1971 joined the union before the end of the war; 86 of them had been founder members of the union in 1934.

These delegates in 1971 represented 6271 male and 999 female union members; only 494 of the 7270 had begun to publish *[po nachalu literaturnoy raboty]* after 1958 (of these, only four began to publish after 1966). Only 90 members were under thirty, whereas 546 were over seventy.

The delegates to an All-Union Congress elect a board *[pravlenie],* [23] which is the highest organ of the union between congresses. The board then elects its chairman (in 1971 Konstantin Fedin) and its first secretary (Georgy Markov), and also, from out of its own members, a secretariat, which 'guides' *[rukovodit]* the work of the union between plenums of the board.[24] However, partly because only about half the members of the secretariat reside in Moscow, it was decided in 1971 to formalise the existing unofficial arrangement and further centralise literary life by creating *[obrazovat']* an official bureau of the secretariat, made up of some of the secretariat members, which would be responsible for Soviet literary life between sessions of the full secretariat. This, then, is where the power resides and the action is — the bureau of the secretariat of the board elected by the delegates to the All-Union Congress of the Union of Writers of the USSR. The chairman of the bureau set up in 1971 is G. Markov (b. 1911); his deputies are Yu. Verchenko,[25] V. Ozerov (b. 1917) and S. Sartakov (b. 1908); and the other members are A. Keshokov (b. 1914), V. Kozhevnikov (b. 1909), M. Lukonin (b. 1918), S. Mikhalkov (b. 1913), S. Narovchatov (b. 1919),[26] K. Simonov (b. 1915), N. Tikhonov (b. 1896), N. Fedorenko (b. 1912) and A. Chakovsky (b. 1913). All of them are Russians, except for Keshokov, and only Simonov is known to entertain from time to time what are occasionally referred to in the West as 'liberal' views. Ten of the thirteen were born before the October 1917 revolution.

Other changes made in 1971 to the 1967 statutes *[ustav]* of the Writers' Union mainly involve changes in terminology. For example, *zashchita* and *zashchishchat'* [defence, to defend] were replaced by the good old terms *okhrana* and *okhranyat'* [protection, to protect] , and writers were told to strive to affirm the ideas of Soviet patriotism and socialist internationalism instead of the earlier socialist patriotism and proletarian internationalism. Many of the changes in the mumbo-jumbo may not be very significant, but one is struck by the fact that the main tasks of the Writers' Union have been increased from ten to twelve[27] and some of the old ones made more onerous. Thus, in 1967 Union members had to engage in 'an ideational struggle for the principles of socialist realism', whereas in 1971 they were told to wage 'an offensive *[nastupatel'ny]* ideational struggle' on behalf of this curious doctrine. Moreover, one of the two new tasks Soviet writers were given was to 'struggle for the affirmation in art of the lofty principles of socialist humanism, Soviet patriotism and proletarian internationalism'. Perhaps the most important change to the statutes, however, is the arrangement to hold All-Union Congresses of the Writers' Union every five, not four, years. As the 1971 congress took place just after the congress of the CPSU, which is also scheduled to take place once every five years, it is evidently intended to make it as difficult as possible for the writers to initiate any new line of development at their congress. They will be expected to follow the guidelines set down just before by the party's congress.

In the light of the foregoing details (many more could have been provided) it hardly seems surprising that the Writers' Union has not been and is unlikely to become a force for change in the Soviet Union.[28] Most members of the secretariat (and of the other bodies concerned with the artistic and ideological 'front' in the USSR) probably have nothing in principle against first-rate literature, but it is not their job to further the creation (or at any rate the present publication) of masterpieces if these might have an unsettling effect on the stability of the country and the regime. Since the fall of Khrushchev they have made a few miscalculations (particularly by mishandling or underestimating the impact of the trial of Andrey Sinyavsky and Yuly Daniel' in February 1966),[29] but on the whole they can be well satisfied with their contribution to the ever-increasing strength of the Soviet Union.[30]

NOTES

1 See his article, 'Otraviteli' [The Poisoners], *Znamya [The Banner]*, no. 10 (1974).

2 See their *Khrushchev and the Arts. The Politics of Soviet Culture, 1962-1964* (Cambridge, Mass., 1965).

3 See his *Moscow Summer* (London, 1966). For a useful survey of the period 1953-63 see Klaus-Dieter Seeman, 'Die sowjetische Literaturpolitik seit Stalins Tod in historischer Sicht', *Jahrbücher für Geschichte Osteuropas* (Apr 1965). For a detailed chronicle of literary and literary-political life in the Soviet Union from 1966 see the Moscow annual *Literatura i sovremennost'* from issue no. 7 onwards. Peter Hübner describes Soviet literary policy from 1917 to 1971 in *Kulturpolitik der Sowjetunion*, ed. Oskar Anweiler and Karl-Heinz Ruffmann (Stuttgart, 1973). Zhores Medvedev's *Ten Years After Ivan Denisovich* (London, 1974) also gives an authentic account of the literary scene in the 1960s.

4 See Johnson and Labedz, op. cit., pp. 9-10. These documents were, characteristically, a reaction also to an 'anti-liberal' letter circulated in November by 'a large group of artists' who complained about increasing 'formalist trends' in art and literature and asked the Party to intervene.

5 *Literaturnaya gazeta [Literary Gazette]*, 4 Nov 1965.

6 *Novy mir*, 1 (1966). English translation: 'Zakhar the Pouch', in *For Freedom: Theirs and Ours*, ed. R. G. Davis-Poynter (London, 1968).

7 For a good introduction to the *derevenshchiki*, see the article by Geoffrey Hosking, 'The Russian Peasant Rediscovered: "Village Prose" of the 1960s', *Slavic Review* (Dec 1973), and his 'Selected Bibliography of Recent Village Prose in the Soviet Union', *ABSEES*, University of Glasgow (Oct 1973).

8 See Ilya Ehrenburg, *Men, Years – Life* (London, 1962-6), and Konstantin Paustovsky, *Story of a Life* (London, 1964-74).

9 See e.g. my article, 'Soviet Literary Criticism: A Survey' (covering the years 1963-8), *Studies on the Soviet Union*, no. 3 (1969), and the contributions on Russian (and Ukrainian) literature in each issue of the annual, *Year's Work in Modern Language Studies.*

10 *Problems of Dostoevsky's Poetics* (Ann Arbor, Michigan, 1973). He is also the author of *Rabelais and his World* (Cambridge, Mass. and London, 1968).

11 The basic reference work, the *Kratkaya literaturnaya entsiklopediya [Short Literary Encyclopaedia]*, which began to appear in 1962 and has now reached volume 7 (of 9), is showing clear signs of being under gradually increasing pressure to distort the picture.

12 e.g. F. Kafka, *Roman. Novelly. Pritchi [The Trial, Stories and Parables]* (Moscow, 1965) and S. Beckett, *V ozhidanii Godo [Waiting for Godot]*, *Inostrannaya literatura [Foreign Literature]*, 10 (1966).

13 It is obvious that the authorities deliberately make it difficult even for most of 'the few' to gain access to many such works. Without time, determination and 'contacts', even a Moscow member of the Writers' Union may have to wait months before he can borrow a copy of such a book or journal. The present writer met an editor of the monthly *Yunost' [Youth]* just after the *tirage* had been increased during 1965 from 1 million to 2 million copies. The editor was extremely depressed by this, as it would, he said, make it virtually impossible to publish any more good works. He was right. The editorial board of *Yunost'* (like the editorial board of *Sel'skaya molodezh' [Rural Youth]* in 1966) was later purged, presumably to make it easier to publish mediocre works. In general (but by no means always) the higher the *tirage*, the worse the book or journal, but the reasons for this are not the same in the Soviet Union as in the West.

14 Nauchny sovet AN SSSR po problemam konkretnykh sotsial'nykh issledovaniy; Sovetskaya sotsiologicheskaya assotsiatsiya; Institut konkretnykh sotsial'nykh issledovaniy AN SSSR. *Informatsionny byulleten'*, 35, 36. Seriya: Materialy i soobshcheniya. *Chitatel' i gazeta. Itogi izucheniya chitatel'skoy auditorii tsentral'nykh gazet* (Moscow, 1969). For more details see note 17.

15 The two-part question giving rise to this polarisation was: Nazovite, pozhaluysta, sovetskikh poetov, stikhi kotorykh Vam ochen' nravyatsya. Ne nravyatsya [Please name the Soviet poets whose poems you very much like. Don't like]. For this and most of the other questions on literature see *Problemy sotsiologii pechati*, 2

(Novosibirsk, 1970) p. 105, or pages 116-17 of issue 36 of the *Informatsionny byulleten,* (see previous note). This section of the questionnaire is referred to in Il'ya Fonyakov's article in *Literaturnaya gazeta,* no. 43 (1968) p. 11. Evtushenko, Voznesensky and Rozhdestvensky were probably the three most published, read and listened to poets in the USSR in the first half of the 1960s.

16 Dymshits was rewarded for his well-deserved unpopularity by being sent to Canada in September 1974 to represent Soviet letters at the international conference of Slavists. He died shortly afterwards.

17 See pages 76-7 of issue 35 of the *Informatsionny byulleten'* referred to in note 14 above. The main survey of *Trud* readers was carried out in February and March 1967, that of *Literaturnaya gazeta* readers in February and March 1968. *Izvestiya* readers were polled in November and December 1966, and *Pravda* readers in July and August 1968. For data on *Trud* see issue 35; for *Literaturnaya gazeta* and *Izvestiya* see issue 36. All the *Trud* respondents were interviewed, whereas two-thirds of the *Izvestiya* questionnaires were returned by post. It is not clear exactly how many people were polled or whether they felt they could be guaranteed anonymity. The representativeness of the sample and the techniques used for the *Literaturnaya gazeta* survey appear to be better than for the *Trud* and *Izvestiya* polls. No information on the survey of *Pravda* readers is available except in section two of the article 'Chetyre tysyachi i odno interv'yu, *Zhurnalist,* no. 10 (1969) pp. 34-7. For further information on the Soviet press see Mark Hopkins, *Mass Media in the Soviet Union* (New York, 1970), and *Notes et Études Documentaires,* Secrétariat Général du Gouvernement, Paris, no. 3679-80, 16 Apr 1970.

18 See his article in the journal *Kontinent,* no. 1 (1974).

19 See Martin Dewhirst and Robert Farrell (eds), *The Soviet Censorship* (Metuchen, New Jersey, 1973).

20 e.g. Arkady Belinkov, in ibid.

21 Fifty years after the October 1917 revolution, almost two thirds of the delegates were people who had been born before that event. (Delegates to the All-Union Congress are elected at Congresses of the Writers' Unions of the fifteen Union Republics.)

22 *Chetverty sezd pisateley SSSR. Stenograficheskii otchet* (Moscow 1968) p. 85. The data for this section of my article are taken from this volume and its companion, *Pyaty sezd . . .* (1972).

23 It had 192 members in 1967 and 225 in 1971.

24 The secretariat had 42 members in 1967 and 45 in 1971 (not counting Markov or Fedin).

25 This ex-Komsomol and Party official has been in charge of organisational matters at the Writers' Union since November 1970. He is not a writer in the normal sense of that word.

26 Narovchatov was appointed Chief Editor of *Novy mir* in the autumn of 1974.

27 Only one of these was and is to help in the creation of ideationally and artistically (note the word order: the first is regarded as more important) high-level works.

28 A number of years ago articles appeared in the West about a struggle said to be taking place between 'liberals' and 'conservatives' in the Soviet literary world. However, only about 1 per cent of the members of the Writers' Union can be clearly identified with one or the other group. The overwhelming majority of Soviet writers have a vested interest in the security provided by the *status quo*.

29 This trial was the subject of a 'White Book' compiled by A. Ginzburg and dedicated to the memory of F. Vigdorova, who had collected materials on the no less disgraceful trial of the poet Iosif Brodsky for parasitism in February 1964 (i.e. under Khrushchev).

30 Since this chapter was written, an incisive and extremely revealing study on Soviet literary life in the 1960s has appeared: A. Solzhenitsyn, *Bodalsya telenok s dubom* (Paris, 1975). It is essential reading for anyone interested in this subject.

9 The Economy: a General Assessment

MICHAEL KASER

If this chapter were devoted to a period 100 times as long — to the millenium of recorded Russian economic history instead of the last decade — one could offer the general proposition that economic life has been over-regulated but under-managed. The seven years during which Khrushchev was effectively in control of the Soviet economy, 1957-64, notably exhibited that characteristic. Institutions of control were created, reorganised or abolished with astonishing speed, leaving those in charge of them scarcely time to adjust to novel practices, let alone accumulate and apply experience in decision-making which is at the heart of good management. The one institution which had, under Stalin, lubricated the stiff cogs of a hierarchical state structure — the regional and Union-republican party apparatus — was itself thrown into the same turmoil by the 'bifurcation' into industrial and rural sectors. While party life, as Peter Reddaway noted in an earlier chapter, was depoliticised under Stalin, one major economic function remained. Local appeals by the *obkom* for interventions above the heads of the departmental authorities and trans-ministerial arrangements through the departments of the Central Committee not only served to mitigate the rigidities of the later-Stalin structure, but gave party agencies a purpose and a scope for initiative which would not, normally at least, rebound to the discredit of the initiator.

Malenkov made his week-long tenure of the party secretaryship on Stalin's death one of administrative re-organisation, grouping industrial ministries under supervising ministers on the 'overlord' principle, adopted just over a year earlier by a British Conservative government when it took over a multiplicity of departments from a Labour administration. But his successor as Chairman of the Council of Ministers, Bulganin, turned the emphasis towards the industrial manager, who regained many powers lost under Stalin at the July 1955 Plenum of the Central Committee. The first effect of the plenum, the decree on the rights of the enterprise director of August 1955, was virtually the last, because the further proposals formulated by Pervukhin at the December 1956 plenum were swamped by the investment crisis which undermined the Sixth Five-Year Plan at the end of its initial year. Khrushchev's seizure of the initiative in economic reorganisation, in his 'Theses' of February 1957, and the enactments of May that year, swung industrial management into the hands of local party secretaries. A shorthand version of the events leading to October 1964 might say that the local secretaries came to reject such responsibilities, and with them Khrushchev himself, for Kosygin reinstated the enterprise director immediately after Brezhnev's creation of a corresponding manager in the *kolkhoz.* The parallel is worth drawing that neither 'taut planning' in industry nor the arbitrary exactions of Stalin's farm procurement permitted responsible managerial practice. The lack of micro-economic stability was most deleterious on the collective farms. In liquidating the MTS's (Machine Tractor Stations) in 1958, Khrushchev had intended to eliminate the duplication of control — the two *khozyain,* as he called the MTS director and the farm chairman — but, at least in the short term, he reduced management potential by demoting the former and by frequent replacements of the latter in favour of industrially experienced cadres.

The plenums of the party Central Committee in March and September 1965 respectively endowed both farm and factory with a stable environment for management. In agriculture sales and purchases by collective farms were made more secure. Procurement quotas for delivery of produce to the state and their prices were to be fixed for five years at a time, while, since the MTS no longer controlled equipment, farms could buy (in principle without constraint) what industrial inputs they needed from a single state agency, *Soyuzsel'khoztekhnika.* Having applied what they purchased to their land and labour, anything above the output quota was for disposal at their discretion. In order to encourage some of that surplus output to be sold to the state, a 50 per cent premium was added to the state procurement price. In practice, administrative pressures soon re-emerged to obtain above-quota deliveries (as Alec Nove observes in the opening pages of this book), and the fact that a target was included in the 1971-5 plan for such procurement enshrined the persistence of such pressures.

In industry the withdrawal of 'administrative methods' — and hence the limitation of arbitrary intrusions into a stable managerial frame — was twofold. First the number of indicators to which the enterprise must conform was codified and reduced and the weight accorded specific indicators shifted in favour of so-called 'economic levers', which by their nature embodied managerial incentives to choose wisely, and away from quantitative targets which merely required a manager's compliance. The establishment, or development, of such 'levers' as sales, profits, a capital charge, and payments into incentive funds was linked with a reform of wholesale price ratios (with both supply and demand conditions in the minds, though not always the acts, of the price-setting authorities). That reform took place on 1 July 1967,[1] but a complement to the strengthening of managerial choice — the opportunity to buy at those prices — was not undertaken. According to an article by the chairman of the State Planning Committee in late 1966, that complementary second phase should have taken place in the then current five-year plan. The check to reform of late 1968 and 1969 — between the invasion of Czechoslovakia and the December plenum — delayed it, and the promise (more weakly expressed) by Kosygin's report to the XXIV Party Congress in 1971 to do so during the Ninth Five-Year Plan has not been fulfilled.

The allowance to managers of state enterprises to use as they pleased the incentive funds with which the 1965 reform credited them remained therefore limited by the rationing of industrial inputs, both current and capital, just as their choice of outputs remained constrained by central price-fixing and compulsion to meet targets for aggregate sales or for individual products. But the freedom within those limits helped to reduce the incidence of waste implicit in *shturmovshchina* [mobilisation of resources to reach a target on time within a cycle of under- and over-utilisation of capital and manpower] and in resistance to innovation. Stability of production flow and openness to technical progress were thereby encouraged.[2]

A corresponding stability was not, however, accorded to the authorities immediately above the enterprise. It was unfortunate that the industrial ministries had to be formally re-established simultaneously with the micro-economic reform. Had they not been substituted for Khrushchev's regional economic councils [*sovnarkhozy*], they might there and then have been reorganised. As it was, they were brought back roughly as they were in 1957, or, more precisely, in the forms in which they reappeared (usually in the guise of 'State Committees') in tandem with the *sovnarkhozy* in 1962 and after. The 'three-level' structure of control thus re-established — from ministry, via product-specialised administration [*glavk*] to enterprise — either cancelled or reduced the local groupings which *sovnarkhozy* had been setting up since 1961. The example of the two Lvov 'firms' of that year (one for leather, the other shoemaking) had been copied by 590 others by the time of the 1965 reform.[3] Typically comprising an advanced or 'head enterprise' with less developed affiliates, the *firma* disseminated technology appropriate to local conditions, rationalised its members' output, and undertook some vertical integration. But in the first four years of the ministries' re-establishment (1965-9), 240 of them were liquidated and only 180 new ones authorised. Because of their redivision into *glavki,* ministries would allocate the constituents of a 'firm' between a number of *glavki,* which imposed a variety of constraints on their operation. Local governments, reasserting their modest economic and fiscal powers after the dissolution of the *sovnarkhozy,* were the allies of the *glavki* in resisting the spread of *firmy,* because of fears for their tax base and scope for local procurement.[4]

A change was signified by both Kosygin and Brezhnev at the XXIV Congress in expressing encouragement for firms[5] and in two years it was the *glavki* which had been abolished. The reorganisation of April 1973 was, however, not *de facto* quite as sweeping. Certainly a much wider scope was allowed 'two-tier management', whereby the *glavk* disappeared from the hierarchy, leaving the enterprise or enterprise group (*firma, kombinat*[6] or — a novel entity — the 'production association'). Yet three-tier management remained, with the *glavk* converted to an 'industrial association', and in a very few cases four tiers (where a central Union-republican ministry was divided into 'republican associations').

The enterprise manager has lost authority by the creation of associations, but in the long run he may gain from being handed down more feasible orders. One factor lies in the transfer of the former *glavki* on to *khozraschet* [a 'break-even' or 'positive-profit' constraint on their financial operation] when they became an association, but the other lies, more broadly, in the second of the two major changes in economic organisation since 1964.

The review of central planning practice is not as precisely attached to dates as the phases of policy at the level of execution, but Kosygin's appeal at the September 1965 plenum for scientists to participate in the reassessment is an evident starting point.

His call was part of a new reliance on scientists and technicians in general, but in this context was especially to economists and mathematicians to engage in a search for new planning methods. Some modification was essential if the central constraints just described were to be maintained, but it was also necessary in the political sphere. If the party was to be reinvigorated after Khrushchev's 'bifurcation' into farm and non-farm sections (1962-4), it had to be shown to fulfill its promise of implementing a 'scientifically-based Marxism-Leninism'. That 'scientific base' could not be sapped by accusations that it ignored or rejected the technical achievements of the capitalist camp. The ideological grounds on which certain concepts had previously been rejected had to be seriously questioned. Thus 'management science' itself became admissible, and in 1965 a management school of sorts was established in each of four Soviet university towns.[7] Their directors came to London, Manchester and Oxford in 1967 as part of a tour of centres of UK management education. Mathematical methods could freely be applied to economic problems even if procedures of marginal equilibrium or optimisation seemed to be treasonable to the treatment of the mean by Marx and Stalin. And practices consigned by Stalin to the infernal circles of capitalism — capital profitability and product marketing — and which had begun to be edged into socialism by Khrushchev, were squarely adopted in the 1965 reform.

Kosygin adopted the standard Soviet practice of announcing the change of policy by criticising those who had implemented that superseded. 'It must be said,' he observed to the plenum of September 1965, 'that our economists have not greatly concerned themselves with analysis of the effectiveness of social production and the elaboration of proposals for increasing it.' Khrushchev, at the XX Congress, at which he denounced Stalin, had castigated the Statistical Office for not publishing the data it had been prohibited to reveal.

Two further ideological obstacles which were swept away may be mentioned in particular. The quiet shelving of the slogan 'communism in our generation' in the 1961 party programme allowed planners to work in terms of relative scarcities. Khrushchev might be said to have been trying to abolish economics, in the sense of the study of the allocation of scarce means to limitless ends. Secondly, the assumption was withdrawn that a labour theory of value precluded payments with respect to natural resources, whence, if labour is the sole source of value, no compensation need be paid for non-labour endowments. Agricultural rent had already penetrated practice through Ricardian differential rent, since the variant returns to land only arose when the same volume of labour was applied to alternative land, but a pure rental charge for resources remained excluded. The issue was actively debated in the second half of the 1960s — particularly in the academic journal *Voprosy ekonomiki* — but the protagonists of a charge were little satisfied with a water resources law of December 1970. Despite arguments by some of the leading economists of the country (including Khachaturov, Fedorenko and Loiter) for a purposive water charge, the Law 'emerged as a limp document devoid of meaningful provisions'.[8] A similar, and so far fruitless, campaign for conservation charges on other resources seems after that date even to have been repressed. Fedorenko complained in 1972 that a paper of his on the issue had remained unpublished by the organ of Gosplan for two years. Losses, low extraction rates and waste persist.

Although charges on natural resources are not yet levied, those on replaceable assets have been refined. Gosplan published in 1972 a set of 'uniform and interrelated indicators' for measuring the macro-economic efficiency (national income and consumption per capita, per rouble of capital, and per rouble of wages) to guide the planners in each of the fifteen Union-republics and f ⁀ the Union as a whole. Republican national accounting had been started in the late 1950s, but has been much developed with the elaboration of regional input-output tables. Although these macro-economic criteria were intended for use in drafting the 1976-80 plan, the current plan was said by the Gosplan chairman to have been elaborated with a much wider range and variety of efficiency criteria than any previously.[9] A new Standard Methodology for Calculating the Efficiency of Capital Investment was promulgated in 1969, revising and making mandatory a methodology introduced in 1959. Unlike the latter, it introduces a macro-economic incremental output to capital ratio for aggregate and sectoral planning and unifies the latter's use of coefficients for choice between projects. Whereas project recoupment periods had varied under the 1959 regulations between industries, a standard relative coefficient of 0.12 is used, or a discount rate of 8 per cent.

Finally, and in an area which has received much publicity, mathematical methods and computer processing of data for planning and management information were actively promoted. Two all-Union conferences (in 1968 and in 1972) discussed the issues and techniques involved, Gosplan set up its own Department for the Introduction of Mathematical Methods into Planning, and the State Committee for Science and Technology (a much reinforced version of Khrushchev's *Gostekhnika*) launched OGAS (a National Automated System for Collecting and Processing Information for Planning and Administration) to service various planning systems — ASPR for plan calculations, ASN for technological coefficients, ASGS for statistical flow, and ASOI Tsen for price computation. The first of these, ASPR, was outlined in 1966, approved in 1969, made formally operative within Gosplan in 1972, and should be fully functioning by 1979 (against an intended 1977) when some 300 sectoral and supporting sub-systems would replace the 'manual balance-planning procedures' inherited from the 1930s.

Computerised data-processing and control systems have been introduced in production and service units — in such major complexes as the State Bank and the State Standards Office and, as Table 9.1 shows, in over 500 individual enterprises by the end of 1973. At this level, however, some conflict of interest can arise between them and the 'central' demand for full information and compliance with directives based thereon. Managers (and local party officials whose patronage partly lies in mediating between the managers and Moscow) do not necessarily wish their 'reserves' to be exposed, nor their 'easy plans' to be revised: the terms are the standard critiques of central authorities. It may be that the renewed concern with 'economic reform' in the 1965 sense, discernible from early 1975, reflects some disenchantment by enterprise directors with the centralised automation of management.

TABLE 9.1: Installation of Automated Management Systems (ASU)

	1966-70	*1971-3*
Enterprises on ASU	151	353
Production processes on ASU	170	216
Regional agencies on ASU	61	197
Ministries and departments on ASU	19	46
Automated systems of information processing (ASOI)	13	31

Source: SSSR v tsifrakh v 1973 godu (Moscow, 1974) p. 77.

Four versions of economic management have been tried in successive periods since the death of Stalin. The first, employed during the remainder of the 1950s, could best be termed 'normalisation'. The parallel to clothing the state factory manager with the modest authority already mentioned was permission for intra-party discussion; the acceptance of foreign travel — mostly inward, but a little outward — and of East-West trade was a concomitant. All were seen as providing a limited environment in which new ideas could, cautiously, be put forward. Some of them might improve technology or productivity and here the July plenum of 1955 was also a peak. Normalisation, especially in response to the Polish and Hungarian protests of October-

November 1956, was also proffered to other Comecon members, but in the negative sense of withdrawing disabilities rather than positively promoting rational economic relations.

The second period ran from 1959 until late 1962. Khrushchev, in the afterglow of the first sputnik (1957) and hearing American complaints of their own weakness during the 'missile gap', was confident in the prowess of Soviet science. He was concerned with mobilising Soviet technology, as Hanson's chapter shows, and put up to Comecon the 1962 proposals for supranational planning to mobilise their resources. His demobilisation of some of the armed forces — which Holloway's chapter notes — in favour of aerospace strategic development required reliance on the manpower of Eastern Europe.[10] Both Comecon and the Warsaw Pact had to be revitalised, but the emphasis was on collecting their resources rather than improving their utilisation. Indeed, the very lack of new economic techniques was the downfall of Khrushchev's plan to mobilise Comecon and led directly to the movement for economic reform.

In his last twenty months as first secretaryship, Khrushchev had to concede failure to reorganise Comecon and to return to heavier defence spending at home. Signs emerged of the reforms that were to come under his successor, notably Liberman's article in September 1962, the reduction of the number of *sovnarkhozy* and the re-establishment of quasi-ministries in November, the *Bolshevichka-Mayak* experiments in consumer-goods supply. But the third period properly begins with the acceptance by Brezhnev and Kosygin of some devolution of the control over industrial transactions. As indicated above, the reform was aimed at improving economic efficiency, but it may have emerged that capital demands of the newly liberalised managers, exhibited in their pressure for ploughing back profits, threatened military spending. At the time, the defence establishment could show a political strength which it had not possessed since the dismissal of Zhukov in 1957. Both demands could be the more readily satisfied, the more purchase of western technical innovation was substituted for domestic spending. The evidence is that this was Brezhnev's view: Kosygin may have been in agreement, but his silence at the crucial December 1969 plenum suggests that his position was at least uncertain at the time.

Thereafter, as Hanson has shown earlier in this book, the West was seen as the supplier of research and technology which would obviate excessive 'managerialism' within the Soviet frontiers. The technology was above all to be bought on credit and Soviet indebtedness grew to a proportion which in mid-1973 threatened to reach danger-point if its further growth were not checked.[11] Parallel with the organisational measures taken at home in the creation of industrial associations in April 1973, was the inclusion of the USSR in a network of transnational associations within Comecon. Their number rose from six to twenty-three in 1973 and 1974: they are not commercial cartels, but they do permit international rationalisation of particular industries.

But chance came to save centralism and fend off managerialism. The quintupling of the price both of gold and of oil in the latter part of 1973 placed very considerable purchasing power in Soviet hands. With either the sale of the current output of gold or the gain in the terms of trade on commodities, the USSR could buy all the western equipment it was buying in the late 1960s. Table 2.1 shows that such imports averaged $937 million (current prices) in 1969-72. Against this one may report gold sales in 1973 at $855 million and in 1974 at $600 million; the improvement in the prices of exports as compared with those of imports converted a 1973 deficit of $1140 million on visible trade with the developed West into a surplus of at least $150 million in 1974.[12]

Price changes in the West, from which the gain in the terms of trade has arisen, must be contrasted with price stability in Soviet trade with Comecon. Members of that organisation respected until 1975 the *de facto* practice since 1957 to determine prices of their sales to members at five-year intervals. Annual negotiations have some influence on manufactures — since the composition of trade by individual products changes — and it is clear that the USSR managed to check the upward trend in the prices of goods it predominantly imports (manufactures) in 1970 while a little later (1972) obtaining higher prices for those it chiefly exports to the rest of Comecon (primary commodities).[13]

Until these price changes, the share of trade with Comecon members was stable under the administration of Brezhnev and Kosygin: it represented 59.3 per cent of turnover in 1964 and 59.6 per cent in 1972, but it sank to 54 per cent in 1973 and to barely above 50 per cent in the first half of 1974. From 1975 onward the Comecon share is certain to rise, both because of a penetration of western inflation into inter-member pricing (by the use of five-year rolling averages of world prices, as agreed by Comecon on January 1975) and because of a real reconcentration of trade within Comecon, as forecast by Brezhnev in his speech to the Hungarian party congress on 18 March 1975. Khrushchev had abandoned Comecon integration when forced to buy grain from the West in 1963; Brezhnev has overcome any political difficulties associated with the still heavier grain purchases of 1972 and defended his pressure for Comecon integration (in the Budapest speech just referred to) on the grounds of group protection from world inflation and crisis.

The home economy reflected the crop failures which necessitated the 1972 imports. Table 1.1 shows that gross farm output in 1972 was reduced to little more than the 1966-70 average and the grain harvest precisely to that average. But, Nove goes on to comment, with weather in 1972 at least as bad as in 1963, the grain crop was some 60 per cent higher and, although livestock had to be slaughtered as feed diminished, the mass losses of 1963 (when pig numbers dropped from 70 to 41 million) were avoided.

The official index Nove uses puts 1972 gross agricultural output at 26 per cent above the three-year average of 67,000 million roubles in 1965 prices for 1963-5. This is precisely the increment computed by United States government officials for the Congressional Joint Economic Committee on the basis of outputs of 41 crop and animal products weighed at 1968 prices, but they complement Soviet published statistics by computing an index of agricultural inputs, viz. net increment in the value of land, productive livestock, capital assets, and current supplies of labour and materials.[14] With that input index for the three years around 1972, 17 per cent over the three-year average around 1964, total factor productivity had increased 8 per cent. The much more favourable weather of 1973 certainly allowed productivity to be higher, for the grain harvest was a record at 222.5 million tons, but it declined in 1974 when, against a plan of 205 million tons, 195.5 million tons was harvested (at least well above the previous record of 186.8 million in 1970). The grant of internal passports over the period 1976-81 to collective farmers should enhance productivity as the remaining underemployed agricultural workers leave for other employment.

A corresponding estimate by United States officials of factor productivity in industry shows an annual increment over 1966-70 of 1.5 per cent in man-hour terms (the working week having been reduced, it grew by 1.7 per cent in numbers employed). That rate compared with a productivity growth of 0.8 per cent in 1961-5 (man-hour terms), but it comprised only a 1.6 per cent decline in capital productivity, whereas the last five years under Khrushchev's influence had seen capital productivity fall by 3.6 per cent, again annually.[15] The same calculation for 1971-2 nevertheless shows capital productivity declining by 3.0 per cent over the two years, almost offsetting the entire improvement in productivity per man-hour, to put the rate of productivity growth of the two factors together at 0.8 per cent.[16] It is tempting to associate the favourable performance of 1966-70 with the release of managerial talents during that period and the reversal of 1971-2 with the check to that devolution.

If the 1971-5 plan is to be precisely fulfilled, capital productivity on the American estimates[17] could only be allowed to drop 0.4 per cent annually and manpower productivity would have to gain 6.7 per cent, again per annum. Annual rates of industrial growth consequently fell behind the 7.3 to 7.9 per cent laid down in the five-year plan — 7.7 per cent in 1971, 6.5 per cent in 1972, 7.4 per cent in 1973, and 6.8 per cent planned for 1974 — but the reorganisation of industrial management and the selective increases in imports of technology may already be showing an effect: the rise in 1974 was 8.0 per cent.

The calculations of productivity just made conform to the type of production function most commonly applied to the Soviet economy. There is of course a substantial critical literature on the production function and its inherent validity even in a market system, and in application to the Soviet economy many more conceptual difficulties arise, one of which is the determination of production from the supply side rather than (as under a market) from aggregate demand. Production functions similar to that cited above have been used by Bergson, Brubaker, Diamond and Kruger, Greenslade and Robertson, Moorsteen and Powell, and Noren and Whitehouse, and they assume a constant capital share and seek explanation of growth movements in the rate of technical progress. The two principal weaknesses of this approach are, firstly, that the constant capital share is chosen in an essentially arbitrary manner and, secondly, that it has failed to offer any quantitative estimate of the factors which are listed by its authors to be potential contributors to changes in the growth rate of technical progress. Another line by Weitzman, followed by Desai, assumes that the productivity residual (in the Hicks sense) is constant, and finds the elasticity of substitution sub-unitary; hence it relates growth to change in the (imputed) share of capital. Other studies are by Gomulka, Hocke, Kýn and Wagener, Green, and Toda. These studies follow Weitzman in applying direct estimation techniques to find the parameters of the Soviet production function, but they differ in the data used and in the production functions tested. Gomulka's finding on the productivity shown as a residual after increments in man-hours and capital have been allowed for is that in the Khrushchev period it was declining very slightly but remaining at a high level (7.2 per cent productivity gain in 1956, 6.6 per cent in 1961), but that it began to fall sharply to around a mere 2 per cent. Between 1966 and 1969, however, the rate rose to around 4.6 per cent.[18] Again, this confirms that an improvement in efficiency followed the 1965 economic reform, and it is worth considering the evidence that its motivations for efficiency were sapped after 1969.

The extent to which Liberman's proposal for the use of profit as a 'synthetic' indicator of enterprise performance fell into disfavour after the December 1969 plenum may be judged from a criticism the following year. Allakhverdyan, a prominent economist of the later Stalin period (when he specialised in national accounting), was also taking issue with the advocates of 'market socialism' in Czechoslovakia, Hungary and Yugoslavia.

A number of economists consider that the most acceptable criterion of economic efficiency is profit maximization. But, as practical experience shows, under the new conditions, the maximization of profit is not the best local criterion of optimalization. ... To make profits an absolute yardstick — the basis of market equilibrium — is the fruit of an exaggerated idea of the role of market relations under socialism.[19]

His use of the phrase 'under the new conditions' indicated that a policy change had recently taken place, and it is of considerable relevance to a study of the Kosygin-Brezhnev period to note when that change began. The proceedings of the All-Union Conference on the Improvement of Planning and of Economic Work, published in the Gosplan journal in August 1968, and an article of the Gosplan chairman of October 1968[20] were the last statements at that level that a further substantive phase of the reform was still being envisaged. An article by Allakhverdyan in the organ of the Institute of Economics of the Academy of Sciences published in November[21] was the first signal of retraction on reform itself. The cognate issue that the economic reforms of Comecon members should be more closely aligned, was raised in an article in the same journal the next month by the director of the Institute for the Study of the World Socialist Economy, himself a close colleague of Stalin's penultimate Head of Gosplan. Sorokin's article was, however, footnoted 'for discussion' and could well have represented only a tentative view of the need for institutional convergence within 'socialist economic integration'. If a political fore-runner of that view is to be sought, it may be dated from Kovalev's concept of the 'socialist commonwealth' presented in late September.[22]

Between the first check to further development of the reforms around late October 1968 and the plenum of December 1969, one important measure of devolution was enacted, the decree of 28 April 1969 on the transfer of certain enterprises to so-called 'non-allocational supply'.[23] Not only were such producers to be allowed to sell their products at wholesale, i.e. without requiring a client to have a quota authorisation, but a 'Decree on Wholesale Trade in Producers and Capital Goods' was to be drafted. The one was only partially, the other never, executed.

The first phase, under the title 'The New System of Planning and Economic Stimulation', proceeded at least until the end of that five-year plan. By the end of 1970, when statistical reporting on this topic ceased, 41,041 industrial enterprises or 83 per cent of the total (and earning 95 per cent of the sector's profits) had been transferred to the 'New System'.[24] This was slower than the schedule of 1965, which set completion by the end of 1968, but Kosygin at the XXIV Party Congress promised to complete the transfer during the 1971-5 plan. It is an open question whether the cessation of statistical reporting concealed a postponement even of this, but it is relevant that the new series which began to be published was of 'the creation of automated Management Systems' (see Table 9.1).

Even at the peak of the reform, it must be stressed, the Soviet government maintained in its own hands the dynamic planning of the economy, that is in selecting projects to add to productive capacity. The decree of 10 July 1967 'On Rules for Planning Capital Investments and Approving Title Lists of Construction Projects' required all new investment schemes valued at 2.5 million roubles or more to be specifically approved by the Council of Ministers on the recommendation of the USSR Gosplan; those valued at between 1 and 2.5 million had to be endorsed by all-Union ministries if within their area of responsibility. Yet in 1968, the first year of devolution for smaller projects, more than half of total investment went to projects valued at 10 million roubles or more.[25]

The gross outputs of agriculture and of industry, of which statistics have just been cited, respectively contributed 15.7 and 63.7 per cent of gross social product (Soviet official measure, at current prices) in 1973, against 16.4 and 64.1 per cent in 1964. The decline in the share of both is accounted for by increases in those of construction (9.4 to 10.5 per cent) and trade (5.8 to 6.0 per cent), while transport remained at 4.1 (1973) or 4.2 (1964). The enlargement of the share of building and installation work reflects the faster increase of gross capital-formation, 81 per cent, over 1964-73 against the 86 per cent for gross social product and 85 per cent for net material product.[26]

The somewhat larger share of resources allocated to

investment (29.0 per cent, against 26.3 per cent in 1965) somewhat reduced the share of personal consumption, which fell from 65.6 per cent of net material product utilised to 62.1 between 1965 and 1973.[27] The annual percentage increments in real income were nevertheless rather larger in the past ten years than in the seven years under Khrushchev's administration, as the following figures show:

Khrushchev		Brezhnev-Kosygin	
1958	5.9	1965	6.8
1959	1.8	1966	5.9
1960	6.4	1967	6.7
1961	1.6	1968	6.0
1962	3.2	1969	5.5
1963	1.4	1970	5.6
1964	4.8	1971	4.5
		1972	3.9
		1973	5.0
		1974	4.2

Source: Nar. khoz., issues for relevant years; *Pravda*, 25 Jan 1975.

The real income increments aggregate the wages of state employees with the dividends of collective farmers,[28] both adjusted for changes in the cost of living. Nove has shown that collective farm dividends per labour day have risen greatly (a 63.4 per cent rise between 1965 and 1973) and that many collective farms were transformed into state enterprises, at which rates of pay were higher. Although he cannot quantify the overall improvement, he concludes that, despite the constancy of the private sector, collective farmers' incomes must have come up quite close to those of non-farm workers.

As Table 9.2 shows, this is by no means equality in institutional income, for collective farmers' receipts from their farms were in 1973 one-tenth of the aggregate wage bill (excluding the military and students, who are not counted as 'wage earners'), whereas they represented double that proportion of persons gainfully occupied. The ratio was higher under Khrushchev, but the factor not demonstrable in Soviet published statistics is the transfer of wage income to collective farmers by sales on collective farm markets.

Personal incomes and expenditure 1

		1958	*1959*	*1960*	*1961*	*1962*	*1963*	*1964*
Average wage[a]	(1)	77.8[c]	79.0[c]	80.6	83.9	86.7	88.2	90.8
Wage earners[b]	(2)	56.0	57.9	62.0	65.9	68.3	70.5	73.3
Total wage bill	(3)	52.6	95.0	60.0	66.4	71.0	74.5	79.9
Income of collective farmers	(4)	(7.3)	(7.6)	7.4	(7.5)	(8.4)	(9.3)	(10.4)
Social security transfer incomes	(5)	8.7	9.3	9.8	10.9	11.6	12.0	12.6
Aggregate specified income	(6)	68.6	71.9	77.2	84.8	91.0	95.8	102.9
Direct taxes	(7)	5.2	5.5	5.6	5.8	6.0	6.3	6.8
State and co-operative retail sales	(8)	67.7	71.9	78.6	81.1	87.3	91.7	96.4
Sales of personal services	(9)	(0.8)	(0.9	1.0	(1.1)	(1.3)	(1.5)	(1.7
Savings Bank deposits								
end-year total	(10)	8.7	10.1	10.9	11.7	12.7	14.0	15.7
annual increment	(11)	0.6	1.4	0.8	0.8	1.0	1.3	1.7
Direct purchase of state bonds	(12)	0.7	0.2	0.1	0.0	0.1	0.1	0.1
Aggregate disbursements	(13)	75.0	79.9	86.1	88.8	95.7	100.9	106.7
Excess of disbursements over reported incomes	(14)	6.4	8.0	8.9	4.0	4.7	5.1	3.8

Notes:

Row (3) is the product of rows (1) and (2), and row (6) is the sum of rows (3), (4) and (5).

Row (4) has only recently appeared in published statistics and is intrapolated for missing years (figures in brackets) on basis of money incomes of collective farms. These rose 49 per cent between 1960 and 1965, while farmers' incomes ro 55 per cent.

In row (8) figures in brackets are estimated: by extra- and intrapolation for 1958-9 and 1961-4, respectively, and from da on constant prices, spliced at 1965, for 1966-7.

Row (11) is the annual increment of row (10).

Row (12) excludes purchases of state bonds by the Savings Bank (included in row (10)).

Row (13) is the sum of rows (7), (8), (9), (11) and (12).

1965-74 in thousand million roubles

1965	1966	1967	1968	1969	1970	1971	1972	1973	1974
96.5	100.2	104.7	112.7	116.9	122.0	125.9	130.2	134.9	140.7
76.9	79.7	82.3	85.1	87.9	90.9	92.8	95.2	97.5	99.6
98.1	95.9	103.3	115.1	123.2	132.0	140.2	148.8	158.0	168.2
11.5	12.8	13.7	14.3	14.1	15.0	15.3	15.6	16.6	17.4
13.6	15.0	16.0	18.3	20.0	21.8	23.5	25.5	27.0	(28.5)
113.9	123.7	133.0	147.7	157.3	168.8	179.0	189.9	201.5	214.1
7.7	8.4	9.3	10.5	11.6	12.7	13.7	14.8	15.8	16.8
104.8	113.0	123.6	134.2	144.4	155.2	165.6	176.4	185.7	195.0
1.9	(2.2)	(2.6)	3.0	3.6	4.0	4.5	5.0	5.5	6.0
18.7	22.9	26.9	32.4	38.4	46.6	53.2	60.7	68.7	78.9
3.0	4.2	4.0	5.5	6.0	8.2	6.6	7.5	8.0	10.2
0.2	0.2	0.1	0.3	0.4	0.5	0.3	0.3	0.4	(0.4)
117.6	128.0	139.6	153.5	166.0	180.6	190.7	204.0	215.4	228.4
3.7	4.3	6.6	5.8	8.7	11.8	11.7	14.1	13.9	⁄14.3

Row (14) is row (13) less row (6).

Roubles per month.

Millions at mid-year.

These unrevised figures are not precisely aligned with later figures restrospectively published (e.g. the unrevised figure for 1960 is 80.1). Information on the availability of Soviet wage data is from G. E. Schroeder in V. G. Treml and J. P. ardt (eds), *Soviet Economic Statistics* (Durham, N.C., 1972) p. 290.

ources:

ar. khoz. v 1960 godu, pp. 681, 844, 854; v 1962 godu, pp. 492, 635; v 1963 godu, pp. 509, 654; v 1965 godu, pp. 566,)0, 631, 781; v 1967 godu, pp. 397, 585, 660, 769; 1922-1972 gg, pp. 263, 346, 391, 481; v 1972 godu, p. 724; v 1973 du, pp. 574, 586, 634, 652, 695, 778, 779; 1974 Plan fulfilment report in Pravda, 25 Jan 1975.

The diminishing of the income gap between farmers and urban workers on a rising trend of money wages taken with a policy of retail price stability has raised for the Brezhnev administration issues of repressed inflation which Khrushchev avoided.

Table 9.2 brings together all the main published components of personal income and expenditure for the years of each administration. The wage bill is calculated from average wage and employment data and a few years of the collective farmers' income series have had to be interpolated, but on the income side only student stipends and military pay are omitted for lack of published returns. The use to which that aggregate income is put comprises in the public data direct taxes, retail sales of goods and services (which include indirect taxes), and savings (through the Savings Bank or purchase of state bonds). Money is also spent on housing and associated outlays, social insurance premia, and party and trade union dues, to name the main heads of outlay. Table 9.2 shows these reported disbursements as exceeding reported incomes, a situation which does not reflect the actual balance in the USSR, where net financial assets are increasing and not, as would be implied, being drawn down. Rather, the apparent excess of expenditure over income arises mainly from the inclusion in retail sales of purchases by state institutions and collective farms, whose finance does not figure among personal incomes. If the retail sales unrequited by personal income have not undergone much change relative to the main items, these latter indicate trends in the Soviet prices and wages policy.

The first conclusion to be drawn from Table 9.2 is that the overhang of savings in relation to income has risen greatly — from one-eighth in 1958 to 37 per cent in 1974 (viz. column 10 as a proportion of column 6). The second is the remarkable rise especially since 1970 of the difference in unreported incomes and inadequately reported expenditures. Whereas under Khrushchev this margin had been declining, it has quadrupled under the Kosygin-Brezhnev administration. This partly represents spending on housing, travel and other goods and services not entered in the standard two retail heads, but must be offset by incomes not recorded under wages, farm dividends and social security. Thirdly, in the Khrushchev period very little was provided by way of personal services, expenditure on which rose 3.5 times between 1965 and 1974. Fourthly, social transfer payments have more than doubled. That part which is a consequence of the extension to collective farmers of a state-supported pension scheme is attributable to a decision taken by Khrushchev in his last year of authority. Whereas in its first full year (1965) the government subsidy to collective farms' own pension funds was only 437 million roubles, it was 2400 million in 1973. But a major extension of the child allowance scheme was announced in November 1974 for low-income families and will take 1800 million roubles in 1975. Khrushchev decreed in 1957 a moratorium on the servicing and repayment of state bonds, to which subscription had previously been virtually compulsory, but amortisation has now begun and will require 1000 million roubles under the 1975 Budget.

The vast bulk of purchasing power is nevertheless still paid over through wages. The average money wage in the state sector of the economy was 140.70 roubles a month in 1974, compared to 96.50 in 1965; the 46 per cent rise must be set against a retail price index officially held constant (though increases hidden by changes in types available have been affected). But within the wage structure a particularly significant change took place. In 1973 engineers and technicians in industry earned only 27 per cent above the average for manual workers in that branch, whereas their margin had been 46 per cent in 1965. Under Khrushchev their relative position had been even better (51 per cent above manual in 1960). Staff in scientific research institutions had earned, on average in 1965, 15 per cent more than manual workers in industry, but they earned virtually the same amounts in 1973 (147.30 against 145.60 roubles). The sharp decline in the earning power of intellectual and technical work says much for the absence of trade union pressure for maintaining relativities, but it offers a key to Brezhnev's claims to the support of the man in the street, the *prostoi narod,* and indeed to his leadership of what was founded as a workers' and peasants' state.

NOTES

1 Followed in 1969 by a new method of pricing new products so as to balance productivity increases, asset life and installation and operating costs to the consumer within the new price (see M. J. Lavelle, 'The Soviet "New Method" Pricing Formulae', *Soviet Studies* (Jan 1974) pp. 81-97).

2 See the section, 'The new stability', in the present writer's *Soviet Economics* (London, 1970) pp. 226-30.

3 This summary is drawn from A. C. Gorlin, 'The Soviet Economic Associations', *Soviet Studies*, loc. cit., pp. 3-27.

4 See Gorlin, loc. cit., p. 9.

5 Kosygin reported on a review of industrial administration just completed and on the consequential abolition of trusts (*tresty*) between enterprise and combine (*kombinat*) in the coal, oil and chemical industries and advocated the two or three-tier system.

6 A vertical integration of plants with a high degree of centralisation which had first developed in the 'thirties.

7 But not in universities themselves: they were established within the Moscow Institute for Engineering and Economics, the Leningrad Institute for Engineering and Economics, the Urals Polytechnical Institute and the Engineering Economics Institute at Kharkhov from which Liberman launched his famous article, 'Plan, Profit and Premium', in *Pravda*, 9 Sep 1962. An Institute for Problems and Organisation and Management, devoted solely to management studies, was opened by Kosygin personally, in Moscow in February 1972. His son-in-law, D. Gvishiani, the deputy chairman of the State Committee for Science and Technology, published the major Soviet work on management, *Organizatsiya i upravlenie* (Moscow, 1970).

8 This quotation and the summary in this paragraph is from M. I. Goldman, 'Pollution Comes to the USSR', in United States Congress, Joint Economic Committee, *Soviet Economic Prospects for the Seventies* (Washington, D.C., 1973) pp. 56-70.

9 N. Baybakov, in N. Baybakov (ed.), *Gosudarstvenny pyatiletny plan razvitiya narodnogo khozyaistva SSSR na 1971-1975 godakh* (Moscow 1972) p. 13, as cited in G. E. Schroeder, 'Recent Developments in Soviet Planning and Incentives', in US Congress, loc. cit., pp. 11-38.

10 See J. Hardt, 'Choices Facing the Soviet Planner', in M. Kaser (ed.), *St. Antony's Papers 19* (Oxford, 1966) pp. 20-44.

11 The present writer, 'The Soviet Balance of Payments', *International Currency Review* (July-Aug 1973) pp. 88-93, suggested that debt servicing might absorb half Soviet export earnings by 1980, but some of the underlying components were over-estimated (see ibid., (May-June 1974) pp. 60-2).

12 In loc. cit., the present writer estimated the gain in the terms of trade to be around $1000 million in a full year. The actual year figures are from his 'Russia Pays Its Way — Just', *Financial Times*, 25 Apr 1975.

13 See the present writer, 'Impact of Western Inflation in Eastern Europe', *International Currency Review* (Sep-Oct 1974) pp. 27-9.

14 D. B. Diamond and C. B. Krueger, 'Recent Developments in Output and Productivity in Soviet Agriculture', United States Congress, op. cit., pp. 316-39. Of the factor weightings they provide, the above uses one which accords land 21 per cent of inputs.

15 J. H. Noren and F. D. Whitehouse, 'Soviet Industry in the 1971-75 Plan', ibid., pp. 206-45. Inputs of labour and capital were weighted respectively at 58.4 and 41.6 per cent, the latter including a 12 per cent charge on assets against the official Soviet maximum of 6 per cent.

16 R. V. Greenslade and W. E. Robertson, 'Industrial Production in the USSR', ibid., pp. 270-82.

17 Noren and Whitehouse, loc cit.

18 S. Gomulka, 'The slowdown in Soviet post-war industrial growth: an alternative explanation', in *Proceedings of the Banff Congress on Slavic and East European Studies*, Z. Fallenbuchl (ed.), to be published by Praeger, New York.

19 D. Allakhverdyan, 'On Financial Problems of the Economic Reform', *Voprosy ekonomiki*, no. 11 (1970) p. 64.

20 Respectively, *Planovoe khozyaistvo*, no. 8 (1968) pp. 71-96 and N. Baybakov, 'The Plan and Production under New Conditions', *Pravda* (1 Oct 1968) p.2.

21 *Voprosy ekonomiki*, no. 11 (1968) pp. 3-15.

22 Respectively, G. Sorokin, ibid., no. 12 (1968) pp. 77-86 and S. Kovalev, *Pravda* (26 Sep 1968).

23 *Bezfondovoe snabzhenie;* the decree appears in full in *Resheniya Partii i pravitel'stva po khozyaistvennym voprosam*, vol. 7 (Moscow, 1970) p. 397.

24 *Nar. khoz. v 1970 godu* (Moscow, 1971) p. 132.

25 M. Sidorov, *Planovoe khozyaistvo*, no. 11 (1968) p. 89.

26 That is, the Soviet concept of net national income which falls short of the western net national product by the value of 'non-productive' services (the military, the civil service, health, education and personal services).

27 Certain comparisons have to be made with 1965 because of the absence of Soviet statistics for 1964 on appropriate bases.

28 Income from private plots was 27.1 per cent of a collective farm household income in 1972 against 36.5 per cent in 1965, but the relative fall was only partly due to a rise in collective earnings (40.0 to 43.4), and rather to the pension scheme which Khrushchev introduced in 1964.

10 Political Developments: Some Conclusions and an Interpretation

ARCHIE BROWN

When the political decisions and achievements of the post-Khrushchev Soviet leadership are considered as a whole, it is not immediately obvious that there is any pattern to them. It may, nevertheless, be useful to begin by devoting attention to some of the major policy tendencies and outcomes of the past decade, most of which have already been considered in greater detail by other contributors, before going on to enquire if any broad strategy underlying them may be discerned and to attempt to place the various changes in a broader political context.

The first part of this chapter will, therefore, be concerned with outlining the developments that have occurred in the following areas of policy and of political activity: (i) the major institutional changes; (ii) economic changes of political significance; (iii) foreign policy; (iv) intellectual freedom and censorship; (v) changes in the official attitude to Stalin; and (vi) dissent: political, national and religious.[1]

INSTITUTIONAL CHANGES

One of the major criticisms levelled at Khrushchev by his successors was that he had a mania for reorganisation and that many of the institutional reforms which he pushed through were hasty and ill-considered. Not surprisingly, therefore, much of the institutional change in the period following Khrushchev's removal has been concerned with restoring to institutions and offices the functions of which they had been deprived during the period between Khrushchev's victory over the 'anti-party group' in 1957 and the October plenum of the Central Committee in 1964. Some of these changes will be discussed briefly in this section, but two of the earliest institutional reforms were of such importance that special attention will be paid to their significance later in the chapter. The first of these was the separation of the first secretaryship[2] of the Central Committee of the party from the chairmanship of the Council of Ministers on the day of Khrushchev's removal (14 October 1964) and the decision at the same plenary session of the Central Committee 'not to permit the concentration of excessive power in the hands of one person'.[3] The second was the reunification as early as the plenary session of the Central Committee in November 1964 of the regional party organs (and regional soviets) which had been divided in 1962 into organs for industry and organs for agriculture.

In the framework of the economic reform announced by Kosygin at the September plenary session of the Central Committee in 1965, the *sovnarkhozy* (regional economic councils) set up by Khrushchev in 1957 were replaced by state committees and resuscitated ministries. Before the end of the year another Khrushchevian innovation, the Committee of Party-State Control[4] (set up in November 1962 with the avowed aim of preventing maladministration and ensuring that party and state directives were carried out) was replaced by a Committee of People's Control which, unlike its predecessor, was concerned only with checking up on state organs and not upon party organs as well. The new Committee of People's Control, like the Committee of Party-State Control, exists at all levels of the administrative structure down to the district, but it appears to have more limited powers of investigation than the body set up by Khrushchev. Among the likeliest reasons for the reduction in scope of the committee's functions (two of which help to explain the significance of the change of name) are, firstly, that its powers as laid down by Khrushchev made for even more overlap between party and state functions than many party and government leaders deemed desirable; secondly, that it involved checking up on party officials as well as state officials (which party secretaries did not like); and, thirdly, that the chairman of the Committee of Party-State Control at the time when it became the Committee of People's Control was the already over-powerful and ambitious Alexander Shelepin. Shelepin lost that particular power base when the

Committee changed its name and functions, and in 1967 he was eased out of the secretariat of the Central Committee as well (on his appointment as chairman of the trade union movement), though he remained until April 1975 a member of the Politburo.

The bureau of the Central Committee for the Russian republic (RSFSR) which was set up under Khrushchev at the XX Party Congress was abolished ten years later (and only eighteen months after Khrushchev's fall) at the XXIII Congress in 1966. One of the reasons for its abolition was doubtless the official one that the Russian republic is so large and important that anything of real political consequence affecting it had to be considered also by the all-Union party organs. In the words of one party commentator, it had been found that 'all the most important problems of the work of territorial and regional party organisations of the Russian federal republic were examined by the Praesidium and Secretariat of the Central Committee of the CPSU' and so the RSFSR bureau became a 'parallel organ'.[5] Khrushchev's creation of the bureau had, however, been partly a measure of party decentralisation and the abolition of the bureau may also, therefore, be seen as a victory for the secretariat of the Central Committee over a body which, in view of the size and importance of the Russian republic and the fact that the bureau was led *de facto* by such significant party figures as G. I. Voronov and A. P. Kirilenko, could not simply be brushed aside in the event of a conflict of opinion.

Another policy of Khrushchev's to be abandoned by his successors was that of a compulsorily high percentage turnover in the membership of party committees. The 1961 party rules stated that at each regular election not less than a quarter of the membership of the Central Committee *and of its Praesidium*, not less than one-third of the Union-republican Central Committees and of the regional party committees, and not less than one-half of members of town and district party committees and of primary party organisation committees or bureaux, had to be renewed. The long article which incorporated these points in the 1961 rules (Article 25) was dropped from the rules at the XXIII Party Congress in 1966 when a more general sentence on systematic renewal was added to Article 24. This made no mention either of the

Politburo or of fixed percentage turnover in committee membership and it was reproduced verbatim in the rules as amended at the XXIV Congress in 1971. The new formulation simply reads: 'At elections of all party organs — from primary organisations to the Central Committee of the CPSU — the principle of the systematic renewal of their composition and of continuity of leadership will be observed.'[6] It was widely held that Khrushchev had introduced the compulsory percentage turnover in order to be able to move people from party office at will, while maintaining himself and his supporters in positions of authority by invoking the escape clause in the rules which safeguarded the position of people of particular prestige and ability. The 1966 change accordingly strengthened the security of tenure of the various members of the collective leadership.

So far as state, as distinct from party, bodies are concerned, in addition to the creation of new (and the revival of some old) ministries, there has been an expansion of the committee system of the Supreme Soviet since 1966[7] and attempts to enhance the role and powers of local soviets. In the first comprehensive legislation on the local soviets since 1957, the Supreme Soviet in March 1971 'responded to [a] long-standing request by setting down in one authoritative place all the major rights and responsibilities of city governments'.[8] As William Taubman has noted, the new legislation introduced a 'somewhat greater specificity about what sorts of facilities should be transferred to city soviets, when they should be turned over, and what new resources and powers the cities' governments would require to carry out enlarged responsibilities'.[9]

ECONOMIC CHANGES

There have been significant improvements in production and productivity in both industry and agriculture, real incomes have risen substantially, and the quality (as well as the quantity) of consumer goods has improved. This general picture of progress obscures many specific problems and most notably the differences between the favoured large cities, on the one hand, and provincial towns and rural districts, on the other. Even here, however, there has been a definite levelling-up as a result of the disproportionate rise in agricultural incomes as compared with industrial wages and professional salaries. Increased savings in rural banks partly reflect this, though they are also a reflection of the scarcity of durable goods (and sometimes of such essential foodstuffs as meat) in rural shops.[10] As Alec Nove observed in the conclusion to Chapter 1, it also has to be remembered that the undoubted progress in agriculture which has been made in the past decade has been an advance from very low levels. Putting this in a comparative perspective, Roy Medvedev notes that productivity of labour in Soviet agriculture is six times less than that in the United States and three to four times less than that obtaining in the majority of western European countries.[11]

The increase in the rate of the rise in real incomes and the levelling-up of previously under-privileged groups is, as Michael Kaser has shown in the previous chapter, one of the most politically interesting and significant developments in the Soviet economy during the past decade. So far as the intelligentsia are concerned, certain groups such as engineers and technicians and teachers in higher education have begun to suffer from relative deprivation. Notable improvements were, however, made to the incomes of some of the least well paid sectors of the intelligentsia in September 1972. School-teachers and doctors received an average rise of 20 per cent in money incomes and students in higher educational institutions an average 25 per cent increase in their grants.[12] Pensions have been improved substantially, even if they are still low. In July 1971 the minimum old-age pension for retired manual workers and white collar workers went up from 30 to 45 roubles a month, and the pensions of retired collective farm workers (who are assumed to have some income in kind) were increased to 20 roubles.[13] Among the working population agricultural workers in particular but also industrial workers have done better than the intelligentsia and white collar workers, and the Soviet Union has become markedly more egalitarian than it was under Khrushchev (and still more so in comparison with the years in which Stalin reigned supreme).

Inflation in the Soviet Union since 1964 has been fairly modest by recent western European standards, but it has been by no means as non-existent as is officially claimed. It is to be detected in disguised increases in the level of official prices, sharp rises in the price of goods on the black market, and in shortages of commodities for which the demand created by increased money incomes greatly exceeds the supply. Khrushchev, dictating the second volume of his memoirs in 1971, observed: 'People I meet often ask me why there are so many disguised price increases nowadays. They describe how the brand name of a certain product changes and the price goes up, while the product itself remains the same.'[14] A prime example of this concealed inflation, as Khrushchev notes, was the raising of the price (together with the relabelling) of vodka in the spring of 1970. Khrushchev regarded the combination of shortages and inflation as a serious political danger for the Soviet leadership and it is likely that his successors (as well as he) were profoundly impressed by the riots in Poland provoked by the rise in the price of basic foodstuffs in December 1970. After discussing how 'the bottom fell out of Gomulka's leadership', Khrushchev goes on to draw the moral: 'What happened in Poland represents a lesson for us. The events on the Baltic coast were a direct result of food shortage and a consumer revolt against rising prices. That's one of the reasons I'm especially concerned about the shortages and disguised price increases in our own economy.'[15]

FOREIGN POLICY

In many respects Soviet foreign policy in the past decade, as David Holloway has pointed out in Chapter 3, has differed in style rather than in essential content from that pursued by Khrushchev. The attempt to make 1964 a turning-point in relations with China was a failure for, notwithstanding the initially conciliatory tone which the new Soviet leadership adopted towards the Chinese Communist Party, relations with China remain roughly as bad as they were. So far as relations with the other East European members of Comecon and the Warsaw Pact are concerned, the turning-point is 1968 rather than 1964. In the period between the XXII Congress of the Soviet Communist Party in 1961 and the beginning of 1968 East Europe does not appear to have been a major preoccupation of the Soviet leadership. They had, after all, more than enough problems on the domestic front to keep them occupied. There were the various hostages offered to fortune by Khrushchev in 1961 with his renewed attack on Stalin at the XXII Congress and the adoption at that same Congress of a new party programme and party rules. The following year was one of sweeping institutional reforms which were followed less than two years later by the ousting of their initiator and by serious attempts on the part of the new leadership to restructure the political institutional framework in a manner less frenetic than the reorganisations of Khrushchev and to put the economy and agriculture on a sounder footing.

In so far as foreign affairs took up the time of members of the Politburo from October 1964 until December 1967, when the crisis within the Czechoslovak Communist Party began to engage Brezhnev's attention, it is fairly evident that it was relations with China, the United States and western Europe, rather than relations with the superficially smoothly-functioning regimes of East Europe which were perceived as the major problems. In 1968 Czechoslovakia became *the* major preoccupation of the Soviet leadership, and in August of that year over half a million Soviet troops (with some token representation of four other Warsaw Pact countries) entered Czechoslovakia in order to change the policies and the leading personnel of the Czechoslovak Communist Party. Since then there have been determined Soviet attempts to achieve a higher level of ideological, cultural, economic and military integration between the USSR and the other East European members of Comecon. The invasion of Czechoslovakia, however, was followed not by a return to the Cold War, but rather (as the chapters of Hanson and Holloway have documented) by a notable improvement in economic and political relations between the Soviet Union and the West from the early 1970s onwards. The existing boundaries in Europe — and the statehood of the GDR — have been recognised, a number of agreements on economic and technical co-operation have been signed, and relations between the German Federal Republic and the Soviet Union in particular, but also between the United States and the Soviet Union have improved quite dramatically in recent years.

INTELLECTUAL FREEDOM AND CENSORSHIP

Developments in the related spheres of intellectual freedom and censorship (its strengthening or weakening) have not been unilinear. In certain areas of scientific activity a greater freedom of discussion has been allowed. The charlatan Lysenko, who continued to wield his baneful influence under Khrushchev as he did under Stalin, was dethroned thanks to the determined efforts of genuine Soviet scientists, among whom Zhores Medvedev played a particularly active part.[16] As Medvedev has written in his most recent book, 'On any question concerning Lysenko and "Michurinist biology" Khrushchev was inexorable; he had personally ordered the oldest centre of learning in the country, the Timiryazev Agricultural Academy in Moscow, to be closed down because he did not agree with the position taken by the scientists there.'[17] Much freer scientific discussion has taken place in a number of disciplines including genetics, biology and agronomy and, among the social sciences, in economics and in some branches of sociology.

In creative literature the position has been very different. Censorship has become much stricter and it is harder for outstanding creative writers to get their works into print. Of the countless instances of a harder literary line, the suppression of such outstanding works as Solzhenitsyn's *The Cancer Ward* and *The First Circle* and the reorganisation of the editorial board of *Novy mir,* including the removal of the journal's editor-in-chief, the late Alexander Tvardovsky, in 1970, are but the most notable. The direction of literature since Khrushchev's departure has, as Zhores Medvedev notes, become 'more consistent and purposeful',[18] and more stringent control has been exercised by party bureaucrats responsible for ideology, by *Glavlit* [the state censorship] and, importantly (as Martin Dewhirst has pointed out in Chapter 8), by the bureau of the secretariat of the Writers' Union. The new line, and its less arbitrary application, has affected even writers whose standing in the eyes of the party leadership is exceptionally high. Zhores Medvedev tells how Mikhail Sholokhov — the Nobel prize winning author, member of the Central Committee, and scourge of the dissidents — was ordered to remove a chapter from his novel, *They Fought for the Motherland,* which referred to some of the methods of investigation employed between 1937-40 and to Soviet prison camps at that time, even though the victim of the torture and the camps in the story (as, not infrequently, in real life) remained true to the party throughout all his tribulations. Sholokhov, as a member of the Central Committee, sought an interview with Brezhnev, in one of his many attempts to preserve the chapter, but was refused on the grounds that Brezhnev could not adjudicate in such an issue as these decisions were no longer within the competence of the general secretary.[19] Eventually, Sholokhov had to reconcile himself to the loss of his chapter and replaced 'the tale of prison-camp tortures with a discussion about fishing techniques'.[20]

THE CHANGING LINE ON STALIN

Though Stalin has not been officially rehabilitated in the post-Khrushchev period, it has become easier to publish articles which mention him in a favourable light than to publish strong criticism of him. Employment of the phrase, 'the period of the cult of personality' (which was in frequent use in Khrushchev's time and referred to the years from 1934 until Stalin's death in 1953) is now absolutely forbidden. Immediately after the October plenum of the Central Committee in 1964 at which Khrushchev was formally deposed, there were some straws in the wind suggesting that Stalin's crimes were going to be played down, though the first year after Khrushchev's fall was one in which no clearly dominant ideological line emerged. Several books critical of Stalin were withdrawn before publication, among them a monograph on collectivisation prepared by the Institute of History of the Academy of Sciences which took a hostile view of Stalin's activities during that period.[21] In 1965, however, a favourable account of the collectivisation process was published in book form[22] by Sergei P. Trapeznikov, who had been rector of the Moldavian party school in the early fifties when Leonid Brezhnev was first secretary of the Moldavian republic's party organisation. Trapeznikov, who in September 1965 obtained the important office of head of the department of the Central Committee responsible for science and educational institutions, was also the author of a significantly neo-Stalinist article that appeared in *Pravda* on 8 October 1965 and which attacked those who, in the author's view, had been too critical of the Stalin period.

The new line on Stalin which was being promoted in influential party circles close to the leadership was in fairly sharp contrast to the line taken by Khrushchev at the XX and XXII Party Congresses when he had forcefully berated his former leader. In retirement, Khrushchev extended his targets for attack (beyond those which he chose to deal with in his famous 'secret speech' of 1956) to include Stalin's method of collectivising agriculture. Shortly before his death in 1971 he was taking issue with those (such as Trapeznikov) who still took a rosy view of the collectivisation process:

> Certain theoreticians and even literary figures in our country have taken a Stalinist position with regard to collectivization; they have chosen to look at collectivization through Stalin's eyes. These people are now saying that collectivization represented a historically inevitable period of transition from capitalist production in the countryside to a socialist economy; they say that this process inevitably required sacrifices — and that the loss of lives was justified as long as it was on the altar of scientific progress.

> What nonsense! What a foolish rationalization of murder and the perversion of Leninist policy. Unfortunately, such rationalizations are to be found in our literature, both in works of history and in works of fiction. Some of the authors I'm talking about are still alive and well — and writing from the same point of view.[23]

The attacks on Stalin which could be published fairly freely in the late Khrushchev years can no longer find a publisher, though there is not so much an exoneration of the purges of the late 1930s as a complete silence on them. There have been a series of compromises on the issue of the rehabilitation of Stalin in which the neo-Stalinist forces have met with some (though only partial) success. Between January and March 1966 Moscow was buzzing with rumours that Stalin was going to be rehabilitated at the XXIII Party Congress in the Spring of that year, and this idea was indeed being aired in party circles. However, counter-pressure from foreign communist leaders as well as from many prominent members of the Soviet intelligentsia helped to prevent such a formal rehabilitation from taking place at that time. By 1969 the neo-Stalinists were in a stronger position and they chose the occasion of the ninetieth anniversary of Stalin's birth which fell on 21 December of that year as an appropriate one for mounting a strong offensive. A two-part article on Stalin, to be accompanied by a portrait, was prepared for publication in the party press of other Communist states as well as that of the Soviet Union. Again the protests of foreign Communist party leaders appear to have been of critical importance and a majority in the Politburo agreed to the replacement of the article already prepared by one of quite different content which 'a majority of the intelligentsia greeted with a certain satisfaction'.[24] (Unfortunately, someone forgot to telephone to Ulan-Bator and, alone among the party newspapers, the Mongolian newspaper, *Unen,* published the original article with acknowledgements to *Pravda.*)[25]

DISSENT: POLITICAL, NATIONAL AND RELIGIOUS

Political and national dissent and religious policy and the activities of religious groups have already been considered in some detail by Peter Reddaway and Michael Bourdeaux in earlier chapters. In all three spheres (political, national and religious), changes have become apparent since 1964. It is in the post-Khrushchev years that *samizdat* emerged as an important socio-political phenomenon and that dissent — especially in the mid-sixties — became increasingly organised. This growth of *samizdat* and the growth (in comparison with the Khrushchev period) of overt political dissent, and even of opposition, were partly a response to the stopping of attacks on Stalin and the Stalin period and the tightening of the literary censorship. While the *private* expression of unorthodox political views by individuals among friends whom they trust continues to this day unabated and, in most cases unpunished (except by damage to career prospects when uttered in the wrong company), many hundreds of Soviet citizens have been severely treated for *publicly* expressing dissident political opinions. Some have been sent to labour camps and others to mental asylums. Some of them were later allowed to emigrate; others were given no alternative to emigration.

The emigration policy has been one of the more dramatic and surprising developments since 1970. It has affected a small but significant group of political dissidents and a very much larger minority within the Jewish community. Over 100,000 Jews have been allowed to emigrate in recent years, though many more still wish to do so. How many more it is difficult to say, for hundreds of thousands of those classified as Jews on their Soviet internal passports are well integrated into Soviet society, and it is most unlikely that a majority of them would consider themselves to be Zionists. A disproportionate element in the exodus has been made up of the Georgian Jews, who are among the least assimilated and who have accounted for 30 per cent of the emigration though they comprise only 3 per cent of all Soviet Jews.[26] Another notable grouping among those who have left or who wish to leave is made up of those Jews who were particularly strongly committed to the process of de-Stalinisation and who have turned to the emigration option as a last resort — one which reflects their pessimism about the political future in the USSR.

The Jews have been treated as a special case in regard to emigration, as in other respects. Already in Stalin's time they were being subjected to special discrimination, and though they have continued to play an important part in cultural life, the discrimination has been marked in areas regarded as politically sensitive. Of all the ethnic minorities within Soviet society, they have (with the help of much external political support) generated the most successful dissident political grouping in terms of achieving a major switch in party and government policy, i.e. the decision to permit emigration. But the nationalism of ethnic groups is a much more widespread problem for the Soviet leadership than the problem of the Jews. It arguably presents the greatest challenge which the leaders of the multinational Soviet state have to face and potentially it is undoubtedly one of the most explosive issues on the Soviet scene. It is an issue, therefore, which will be taken up in a broader context later in this chapter.

Consideration of policy towards the religious groups within Soviet society in the years since the fall of Khrushchev brings us back to our starting-point — the apparently heterogeneous nature of the various trends to be discerned during this period. Still more, it underlines the contradictions and inconsistencies of Khrushchev's own policies. It was Khrushchev, the de-Staliniser, who presided over the most severe attack on the Christian churches since the worst years of Stalin. Whatever the vicissitudes and sufferings of the religious groups since 1964 (and as Bourdeaux makes clear they vary considerably from one such group to another), it is evident that on the whole they have been persecuted very much less than they were in the years when Khrushchev was at the peak of his power.

The summary of political developments and of policy outcomes and orientations which has been presented so far raises a number of important questions, including the following: (1) What underlying consistency or pattern may be detected in this apparently diverse range of policies and political tendencies? (2) How great a change has taken place in the style and in the institutions of political leadership since Khrushchev's time, and to what extent is it possible to discern a clash of departmental interests within the Soviet system, and possibly even the existence of an institutional or bureaucratic pluralism? (3) How far is the party as a whole divided into different political groupings, and what variations over time have taken place in the fortunes of these groupings within the post-Khrushchev period?

A PATTERN TO THE POLICIES?

Taking first the question of whether there is any pattern to, or strategy underlying, the political decisions and policy tendencies of the past decade, it may be said at once that this has not been a period of pure empiricism, if such a thing could ever exist. The party leadership, in spite of differences of emphasis and inevitable personal rivalries among them, appear to have reached broad agreement on a number of political desiderata and policy goals which were only imperfectly realised — if realised at all — under Khrushchev. They have attempted to make a much clearer dividing line than was ever made by Khrushchev between what kind of intellectual activity is essential for the economic progress of the Soviet Union and what is not, and between what is essential for the existing structure of power within the Soviet Union (as well, of course, as for Soviet power in an international context) and what might threaten this. It can be argued, and indeed has been argued by some Soviet dissidents, that intellectual freedom is indivisible. The fact is that the present Soviet leaders have divided it. The division they have made has not only been less haphazard and more consistent than Khrushchev's policy in this sphere: it has put the emphasis on controls, on the one hand, and relative freedom, on the other, in places different from those chosen by Khrushchev and in places which make much better sense from the point of view of the Soviet economy.

It is clear to Khrushchev's successors, just as it became clearer to Khrushchev in retrospect,[27] that there are at least areas of discussion in which to put a stop to the airing of views is liable to be economically harmful. They recognise that the power wielded by Lysenko and his friends over Soviet genetics, biology and agronomy was, among other things, highly detrimental to the development of Soviet agriculture. It is for similar practical reasons that there has been a growth of freedom of discussion among economists, since such discussions are regarded as having at least a potential relevance to the improvement of economic performance, and among those branches of empirical sociology where the results may be of value in economic, political and social management.

The present leadership have, then, supported intellectual activity which they believe may be useful economically and relatively neutral politically. However, they have resolutely rejected the kind of intellectual activity which is, in their view, likely to be politically dangerous and economically irrelevant. It is for this reason that the censorship of creative literature has in recent years been applied much more consistently and rigorously than it was under Khrushchev. There is no doubt that on the whole there is less cultural freedom now in the Soviet Union than there was between, say, 1956 and 1965 (i.e. taking in the 'honeymoon period' of the new leadership). It is, of course, true that the degree of cultural relaxation under Khrushchev varied considerably from time to time, but the very unpredictability and impulsiveness which characterised his approach to cultural questions provided certain opportunities for those of unorthodox political and cultural views.

The same kind of attempt on the part of Khrushchev's successors to measure economic usefulness against possible political danger explains the rejection of a proposal put forward early in 1965 that political science (embracing the study of the structure and activities of the state, political parties, social organisations, mass movements, international organisation and public opinion) be taken up in the Soviet Union as a separate discipline and that political studies be not simply subsumed under Marxism-Leninism, law or history.[28] (There have, however, recently been indications of attempts to have politics — and the methodologies of western political science — studied more seriously than hitherto as a branch of Marxist sociology.)[29]

The various policies and political trends of the past decade can be interpreted partly on the basis of the distinction made by the Soviet political leadership between economically valuable and politically dangerous types of public discussion, and more fundamentally by appreciating that the dominant political tendency within the leadership is defence of the *status quo* — a desire for predictability, stability, and security of tenure, and the avoidance of fundamental political change either in a radical reformist direction or in a Stalinist direction. Thus, the leadership have tried to form a closer alliance with the workers against possibly dangerous heterodox ideas emanating from the intelligentsia and it is in this setting, perhaps, that the more egalitarian incomes policy of the past decade should be seen.

The desire of the leadership to defend the *status quo* governs, above all, their attitude to criticism of Stalin and of the Stalin period. Though there are neo-Stalinists within the party who look back with nostalgia to the discipline and the ideological certainties of the 1940s (when they also had the advantage of being thirty years younger!), the most senior members of the Politburo who had already reached adulthood in the 1930s (see Peter Frank's discussion of political generations in Chapter 5) remember only too well that whatever advantages life under Stalin may have offered them, they did not include those of absolute security of life and tenure or of predictability. There were times, notes Khrushchev, when Kosygin's life 'was hanging by a thread'.[30]

It may appear paradoxical to suggest that the top leadership of the party and government in the Soviet Union today are not neo-Stalinists, while stressing their need and determination to put a stop to criticism of Stalin and of the 'period of the cult of personality'. But the paradox is only apparent, for de-Stalinisation is potentially as dangerous for them as re-Stalinisation. The majority of people in positions of very high political office today took their first steps up the political ladder during the period of Stalin's dictatorship. Some, including such leading Politburo members as Brezhnev, Suslov and Kosygin, had already climbed very far up this ladder (or greasy pole) by the time of Stalin's death. Khrushchev more than once tried to extend the culpability for what went wrong under Stalin behond the absurdly narrow group of Stalin, Beria, Abakumov and a few of their minions to embrace most of the 'anti-party group', but his more cautious colleagues (including some of those who had supported him in the fight against the 'anti-party group' in 1957) restrained him from pressing the charges. Though Khrushchev was far from being without sin, he was prepared to cast the first stone. So far as a majority of his colleagues in the leadership were concerned, however, he had already gone too far. He had pricked the bubble of party infallibility, and in casting aspersions — together with a certain amount of light — on a period of Soviet history during which they had made their political careers, he was putting them on the defensive. How they had made their careers was a potentially dangerous subject for frank discussion. It was much better to concentrate on the achievements of rapid industrialisation and the Great Fatherland War.

Given the premises of the present Soviet political leadership, there is no real contradiction between, on the one hand, the freer scientific-technological discussion which now takes place, improved relations with the West (especially with a view to reducing somewhat the burden of the arms race on the Soviet economy and to importing advanced western technology), the relaxation of some of the restrictions upon emigration (particularly in the case of Soviet Jews) as a means of reducing tensions at home and, more important, obtaining the goodwill of the United States in the tangible form of long-term credits and advanced technology, and, on the other hand, taking a tougher line on internal cultural policy, stressing the importance of ideological rectitude (and at the same time adapting Khrushchev's few ideological innovations to make them less utopian and more instrumental — an instrument of the current needs of the party leadership), suppressing the manifestations of overt political dissent (while taking a more cautious line with religious believers in order to avoid creating new tensions within Soviet society and producing martyrs), and putting an end to the radical reformist trends in Czechoslovakia which threatened to get out of hand and became a dangerous alternative ideological and political model for other East Europeans and even for the Soviet intelligentsia.[31]

CHANGES IN THE STYLE AND INSTITUTIONS OF LEADERSHIP

At the beginning of this chapter some of the institutional changes which have taken place since the fall of Khrushchev were outlined, but so far only limited attention has been devoted to the question of how significant the institutional change has been and how great has been the difference in style of leadership. This involves, first of all, consideration of the thorny problem of individual versus collective leadership, of assessing the powers of the current party general secretary, L. I. Brezhnev, *vis-à-vis* the Politburo, and comparing it with that of his predecessors. The safest answer to the question of the general secretary's power would appear to be that though Brezhnev is more than a first among equals within the Politburo, he is much less than a Khrushchev. There is no doubt that the Politburo collectively is now more powerful than the general secretary individually.

During the greater part of Stalin's rule the situation was, of course, the reverse. The leader was beyond question more powerful than the rest of the Politburo put together. During the peak period of Stalin's powers the Politburo met irregularly — only when Stalin deigned to call it — and its members competed ·with one another to agree more enthusiastically than the next man with his proposals and to ingratiate themselves with the *vozhd'*. Stalin's relations with his Politburo are well captured by Khrushchev in the following passage from his memoirs:

> In 1952 Stalin called us together and suggested that we should convene a Party Congress. He didn't need to persuade us. We all considered it incredible that there hadn't been a Party Congress for thirteen years. Nor had there even been a Central Committee plenum for some time. The Central Committee hadn't met in either its policy-making or its consultative capacity for years. In short, the Party at large and the Central Committee in particular had been taking no part whatever in the collective leadership. Stalin did everything himself, by-passing the Central Committee and using the Politbureau as little more than a rubber stamp. Stalin rarely bothered to ask the opinion of Politbureau members about a given measure. He would just make a decision and issue a decree.[32]

Khrushchev's later power was not of this order and it is highly unlikely that his colleagues ever held him in awe, in sharp contrast with their attitude to Stalin. At all stages of his first secretaryship he met with resistance to some of his policies, and he did not always get his way even in the period between his victory over the anti-party group in 1957 and his fall in October 1964.[33] Nevertheless, his powers in this last period were very great. It is sufficient to note the number of policy and institutional changes which were made within a very short time of his departure by a Politburo that, Khrushchev apart, consisted of virtually the same people as before. The fact that it was possible to conspire successfully against such a leader and succeed in ousting him is illustrative of a great difference between his powers and those of Stalin, but so long as he was there his powers were far greater than those of his colleagues individually or even, in many cases, collectively.

A prime example of a Khrushchevian initiative which proved so unpopular with party and state officials that it was abandoned as early as the plenary session of the Central Committee held in November 1964, was his division in November 1962 of regional and district party, trade union and komsomol organs — as well as soviets at the same levels of the administrative hierarchy — into organs for industry and organs for agriculture. The bifurcation of local party and state organs had been part of Khrushchev's answer to the perennial problem of providing party secretaries with sufficient specialist knowledge to be able to exercise their controlling influence over industrial and agricultural enterprises in an efficient and adequately informed manner. For individual regional party first secretaries, however, Khrushchev's reform meant that they were having to share powers and responsibilities which had previously come under their sole jurisdiction. Many of these *obkom* first secretaries were members of the Central Committee, and the speed with which the reform was reversed after the removal of its author is almost certainly an indication of the strength of their hostility to it.

Khrushchev does not disguise the fact that the 1962 reform abrogated only two years later was his brainchild:

> In my time, we educated a substantial number of agricultural specialists, but we needed to go further than that. We needed to see that our increased specialization was reflected in the management of our agriculture. I wrote a memorandum on specialization, and this memorandum was sent to all regional and district Party committees for discussion. I also made a proposal which was approved at a Central Committee plenum. Now this proposal is considered a mistake, but I am sure the day will come when it will be readopted. Why am I so sure? Because it is intolerable to let Party administrators manage agriculture when they don't have the proper training, yet that's precisely the situation today: as a rule, the people promoted to the posts of secretaries in the district, regional and territorial Party committees have their training in engineering. In other words, they're experts in urban rather than rural affairs. So they are allowed to administer agriculture while the training of many of our agricultural experts goes to waste.[34]

In the view of Khrushchev's critics, he was, on the one hand, adopting an over-simple approach to complex problems by assuming that an institutional reorganisation would effect the necessary changes[35] and on the other hand, he was actually increasing bureaucratic interference and reducing still further the authority of the *real* experts — the economic managers and collective farm chairmen. In the words of the author of a party high school booklet on republican, regional and local party organisations, 'this division was not called for by either political necessity or practical expediency' and 'it generated additional difficulties in economic leadership and agricultural organisation'.[36]

Khrushchev's references in his two volumes of memoirs to his powers in the period when he was both first secretary of the Central Committee and chairman of the Council of Ministers are not without some ambiguity, but their strong tendency is to confirm the view shared both by his Soviet critics and by most western observers that he often acted on his own initiative and at times treated his colleagues in a manner so high-handed that it contributed strongly to his ultimate undoing. The bifurcation of the regional party organs and soviets in 1962 is but one instance of a policy which was very much his own. Khrushchev also claims personal credit, *inter alia,* for the Soviet decision to place missiles in Cuba (in spite of initial resistance to the idea from Castro); for the decision to wreck the Paris summit talks with Eisenhower, Macmillan and de Gaulle, when he set off from Moscow with a conciliatory document and decided in the course of the flight to demand an apology from Eisenhower for the U-2 flight over Soviet territory (so that 'the document had to be turned around 180 degrees'); and naturally he does not attempt to disguise the fact that the enormous campaign to extend the growing of maize in the Soviet Union was his own idea. In a manner somewhat reminiscent of Stalin's hypocritical 'dizzy with success' diatribe in *Pravda* against those who had too ruthlessly implemented his policy of collectivisation, Khrushchev unconvincingly blames the failures of his maize campaign on 'the over-zealousness of some officials'. At the same time, he is realistic enough to note that what others regarded as his maize-mania did much to discredit him.[37]

One strong indication that power within the Soviet leadership is now shared to a much greater extent than it was under Khrushchev, is the fact that the decision taken at the October plenary session of the Central Committee in 1964 to separate the first secretaryship of the party from the chairmanship of the Council of Ministers has so far been upheld. Even Khrushchev himself, reflecting on his remarkable career in the tranquillity and boredom of enforced retirement, came close to admitting that adding the headship of the government to his party first secretaryship reflected an excessive craving for power on his part: 'I've often criticized Stalin for allowing a single person to have two posts, one in the government and one in the Party. Therefore my acceptance of [the premiership] represented a certain weakness on my part — a bug of some sort which was gnawing away at me and undermining my power of resistance.'[38]

Whatever ambitions Brezhnev may have had to emulate the power of Khrushchev, he has had to act within a framework of tighter constraints. There has been no large-scale dismissal of members of the Politburo to compare with the dismissal of a third of the members of the praesidium following the anti-party group crisis. (This action by Khrushchev has sometimes been compared too facilely with Harold Macmillan's dismissal of a third of his Cabinet in 1962. There are two important differences. Firstly, Macmillan was careful to sack his friends, rather than his enemies, and the people who had gone as far as they were likely to go in the leadership stakes, rather than his potential rivals. Five years earlier Khrushchev used the power base he had built up in the secretariat and Central Committee to remove from membership and candidate membership of the praesidium a similar proportion of colleagues, but with the significant distinction that these were people who were opposed to him and who included all his most senior and dangerous rivals. Secondly, Khrushchev's ousting of his leading opponents within the praesidium enabled him to enjoy a further seven years of enhanced power as first secretary. In contrast, Macmillan's difficulties within his party merely increased after his dismissal of so many colleagues, and he was already coming under strong pressure to resign when illness took him out of active politics little more than a year after his drastic Cabinet changes.)[39]

The changes made to the composition of the Politburo in the post-Khrushchev period have been more modest and gradual than those of the previous decade. All eleven members of the Politburo elected at the XXIII Party Congress in 1966 (L. I. Brezhnev, A. P. Kirilenko, A. N. Kosygin, K. T. Mazurov, A. Ya. Pel'she, N. V. Podgorny, D. S. Polyansky, M. A. Suslov, A. N. Shelepin, P. E. Shelest and G. I. Voronov) were re-elected at the 24th Congress in 1971. Though Brezhnev's position within the leadership had become stronger in the meantime, the process of collective co-option worked in such a way that no one could be dismissed, and the composition of the Politburo could be changed only by increasing its membership to fifteen. Of the four new men, V. V. Grishin, D. A. Kunaev, V. V. Shcherbitsky and F. D. Kulakov, the last three are widely regarded as Brezhnev protégés. Further important changes took place in April 1973 when Shelest and Voronov lost their seats in the Politburo and were replaced by three new members representing important institutional interests — Yu. V. Andropov, the head of the KGB; Marshal A. A. Grechko, the minister of defence; and A. A. Gromyko, who has been minister of foreign affairs since February 1957. These newcomers were men of considerable seniority and political standing and representatives of important institutions, and it would almost certainly be wrong to see their promotion solely, or even primarily, in terms of a further strengthening of Brezhnev's position. At a time of *détente,* when the Soviet Union was and is pursuing a very active foreign policy, there were good policy reasons for bringing in the ministers of foreign affairs and defence and, given the possible domestic implications of *détente,* the chairman of the Committee of State Security.

The analogy between the British prime minister's relations with his Cabinet and the Soviet Communist Party leader's relations with the Politburo has always been a very inexact one and, as has already been suggested, it was particularly inappropriate when applied with reference to Khrushchev. Even now the powers of the general secretary are more extensive than those of a British prime minister, but since April 1973 it has become possible to argue that the Politburo is beginning to resemble the Cabinet rather more than it did previously in terms both of size and the spread of departmental interests represented. Since the general secretary's direct control over the secretariat of the Central Committee is likely to be greater than his control over ministers, it is of especial significance that there has been a marked decline in the proportion of Central Committee secretaries enjoying membership of the Politburo. If we take, for example, the membership of the praesidium at the time of the November plenum of the Central Committee in 1958, there were eight Central Committee secretaries (Khrushchev, Aristov, Brezhnev, Ignatov, Kuusinen, Suslov, Furtseva and Mukhitdinov) out of a total membership of fourteen. At the XXII Party Congress in 1961 the size of the praesidium was cut to eleven, of whom four (Khrushchev, Kozlov, Kuusinen and Suslov) were secretaries. Today, in contrast, there are only four secretaries of the Central Committee (Brezhnev, Suslov, Kirilenko and Kulakov) within a Politburo of fifteen full members. Furthermore, three of these four were already members of the Politburo in Khrushchev's time and have not, therefore, been primarily dependent upon Brezhnev's patronage. The period since the fall of Khrushchev is now almost as long as the period from Stalin's death until October 1964. Yet there are six members of the present Politburo who have served throughout that period — indeed, since 1962 or (in most cases) earlier. In contrast, by the summer of 1960 there was only one survivor (apart from Khrushchev) of the praesidium formed immediately after Stalin's death in March 1953 — the arch-survivor, Anastas Mikoyan.

In terms of other offices held by its members, the Politburo is now made up of the heads of four ministries or state committees (in all four cases this representation of specific ministries dates only from 1973, for apart from the promotion of the minister of foreign affairs, the minister of defence, and the chairman of the KGB to Politburo membership in April 1973, two months earlier Polyansky — a Politburo member since 1960 — had become minister of agriculture, while retaining his seat in the Politburo); the chairman of the Council of Ministers and his first deputy; the chairman of the Supreme Soviet; four secretaries of the Central Committee (including the general secretary); two republican party organisation first secretaries; the first secretary of the Moscow city party committee; and the chairman of the Party Control Committee.

In party-state terms, this means eight representatives of

the party machine and seven members of the state machine, and the ratio even became a fifty-fifty one in the period between the Politburo changes of April 1973 and the removal of Shelepin (who was head of the trade union movement) in April 1975. The more significant point, however, concerns the tendency towards broadening the representation of various bureaucratic hierarchies. It is highly probable that actual ministerial membership of the Politburo raises the status of the institution represented and, in comparison with virtual representation by the secretary of the Central Committee responsible for that particular area of policy, enhances the opportunities of the institution in question to present its departmental point of view and to defend its sectional interests. The current trend appears to be in favour of representation of departmental interests and of those people with actual responsibility for the execution of policy in particular important functional areas and away from a system of secretarial overlordship at the highest policy-making level. Just as Whitehall civil servants like to see their minister in the Cabinet, believing that this enhances their status and bargaining power within the governmental network, it is probable that Soviet officials within the Ministry of Agriculture, the Ministry of Foreign Affairs, the Ministry of Defence and the Committee of State Security welcomed the political promotion of their institutional heads in 1973.

The other factor making for a greater degree of bureaucratic or institutional pluralism in comparison with Khrushchev's time is simply that neither Brezhnev nor anyone else in the Politburo has adopted Khrushchev's style of government and while, in many ways, party controls over other institutions are as strong as ever they were, there is less *arbitrary* interference by the leadership with other specialist bodies. The present general secretary, unlike Khrushchev, accepts — or is constrained to accept — that he cannot take decisions in every policy area from foreign policy to family law and from agriculture to literary culture. The four most powerful men in the Politburo would appear to be Brezhnev, the two most senior of the other secretaries of the Central Committee in the Politburo, Suslov and Kirilenko, and the chairman of the Council of Ministers, Kosygin. It is arguable that the power of the secretaries was reduced when Grechko,

Gromyko and Andropov attained full Politburo membership, but Kosygin continues to share overall responsibility for economic policy with Brezhnev, though in day-to-day terms the major economic co-ordinator is N. K. Baybakov, the chairman of Gosplan (State Committee for Planning), who is also one of the deputy chairmen of the Council of Ministers.

Even after the power of some of Brezhnev's senior colleagues and the importance of the Politburo as a whole have been stressed, however, it must be added that the indications are (a) that Brezhnev is more than *primus inter pares* within the collective leadership, and (b) that his power has grown since the early days of his general secretaryship. The ebb and flow of the extent of press publicity which Brezhnev has received may well reflect inner tensions in the leadership, but there is no doubt that he has had far more press publicity and praise than any of his colleagues, and that it is more fulsome in the mid-seventies than it was in the mid-sixties. There have been references to the Politburo 'headed by' Brezhnev,[40] and since April 1973 Brezhnev's name has always headed the list of printed names of Politburo members. Until then the names were published in alphabetical order and, by a fortunate coincidence, Brezhnev's name came first alphabetically. The promotion of Andropov to full Politburo membership meant that this was no longer the case and led to an exception to the alphabetical principle being made in favour of Brezhnev whose name still comes first followed by that of Andropov and his other colleagues in alphabetical order. When illness in late 1974 and early 1975 took Brezhnev out of the headlines, he was prematurely written off by a number of western observers, but from mid-February 1975 he was back in the public eye, taking a leading part in discussions with the British prime minister, Harold Wilson, and holding the centre of the stage in *Pravda* photographs. The following month he received still greater publicity on the occasion of his visit and speech to the XI Congress of the Hungarian Socialist Workers' Party in Budapest.[41]

In terms of policy-making, as a generalisation it may be said that Brezhnev is in overall charge of foreign policy and of agriculture and that he has come to share overall responsibility with Kosygin for the economy. This was not the case in the immediate post-Khrushchev period when Kosygin was more clearly the principal economic spokesman (agriculture apart) and was also diplomat-in-chief. 'Summit talks' with the Soviet leader meant talks with Kosygin; it was Kosygin who, for example, conducted top-level political discussions with President Lyndon Johnson and Prime Minister Harold Wilson in the mid-sixties. By the late sixties the allocation of overall responsibility for foreign policy was changing and in the early seventies Brezhnev emerged quite clearly as the principal Soviet spokesman in the period of *détente*. It was he who took the principal part in talks with Chancellor Willy Brandt, President Richard Nixon and President Georges Pompidou. Brezhnev's evident 'leading role' in foreign affairs has been merely underlined by numerous references in the Soviet press to his personal contribution in this sphere[42] and by the award of the International Lenin Peace Prize to him in July 1973. His prominence in foreign affairs does not, however, mean that he can ignore or override the Politburo in this field. Heads of executive in major powers in the second half of the twentieth century get drawn into top level international talks whether they like it or not. (The indications are that Brezhnev likes it.) It was simply a matter of deciding who was *de facto* head of executive within the Soviet system — Brezhnev or Kosygin — and that particular ambiguity was resolved some years ago in favour of Brezhnev. But the pre-eminence of the Politburo in the last resort is (as Holloway noted in an earlier chapter) suggested (a) by the fact that it met during summit meetings to consider proposals made by the American delegation, and (b) by the promotions of Gromyko, Grechko and Andropov to full Politburo membership in 1973, which confirmed and emphasised the Politburo's role of final arbiter on major foreign policy issues.

It is clear that Brezhnev (in this respect like Khrushchev before him) takes a particular interest in, and assumes special responsibilities for, agriculture. In March 1975 a *Pravda* editorial reminded its readers that the basic lines of the successful agricultural policy that had been pursued in recent years had been laid down a decade earlier at the March plenum of the Central Committee in 1965, when the principal speech was delivered by Brezhnev.[43] Referring to this plenum and to subsequent achievements in Soviet agriculture, the leading article in *Pravda* observed: 'All this is the fruit of the collective work of the party, of its Central Committee, of the Politburo, and of the creative development of Marxist-Leninist agricultural theory, to which the General Secretary of the Central Committee of the CPSU, Comrade L. I. Brezhnev, is making a great contribution.'[44]

Though there is no doubt that Brezhnev is now, and has been for some time, the top man in the Soviet leadership, there have been few, if any, indications that he is trying to push through policies that are against the wishes of a majority of his colleagues. It would appear that he has sought consensus and has tried to operate as far as possible from a safe position in the centre of the Soviet Communist Party political spectrum. While it has not been possible for him to dictate policy, Soviet press comment seems to indicate that he has been the most important individual influence on the direction taken by Soviet foreign and agricultural policy. Yet even in these, as in many other areas of policy, it would appear that Brezhnev has for the most part played what Jerry Hough has called a 'broker-like role'[45] and, so far as foreign affairs are concerned, he has probably leant heavily on the advice of the vastly experienced and highly competent foreign minister, Gromyko.

Though the Politburo collectively wields supreme power, and though the general secretary's voice is the most powerful within that body, the part played by other institutions in political decision-making has developed beyond the point reached under Khrushchev. This has been recognised by Zhores Medvedev who notes both its advantages and disadvantages from his political standpoint:

> The increased independence, responsibility and opportunities available to individual members of the leadership [after the departure of Khrushchev] resulted in a dissociation of power. For the country as a whole this was a very positive phenomenon, because it promoted more cautious and considered solutions to important political and economic problems. It meant that the Minister of Agriculture, for example, was given more opportunity to take independent decisions without fearing

that he would be forced, for instance, to provide for the cultivation of maize in the Leningrad and northern, Archangel, regions, while the Minister of Foreign Affairs was better able to work towards establishing international equilibrium now that he no longer had to worry lest his Head of State [sic] should suddenly arrive at the United Nations, take of his shoe and start banging it on his desk in front of the General Assembly. But at the same time conservative leaders of culture, ideology and science,[46] who during the Khrushchev period had been obliged to adapt to his new line, now had greater autonomy and freedom to make their own decisions.[47]

There appears to exist at the present time a — predominantly conservative — coalition of various institutional interests in which the rules of the game are more clearly laid down than they ever were under Khrushchev. It is a limited institutional or bureaucratic pluralism — in some areas of policy very limited indeed. It is accepted that higher party institutions (the Politburo, the secretariat of the Central Committee and the Central Committee acting through its departments) have the last word if they want it, but other institutions besides these participate in the policy-making process. In the cases of the military and (to a lesser extent) the KGB, it is difficult to avoid the conclusion that their influence and status have increased in the post-Khrushchev era, though in such sensitive areas as these there is no question of actual policy-making power being surrendered to them by the party leadership.

The increase in military influence has been noted by a number of western writers, and the numerous observations on the subject of the former first secretary of the Soviet Communist Party add weight to their conclusions. There is nothing strikingly original in Khrushchev's reflection that soldiers 'always want a bigger and stronger army',[48] but he does provide confirmation of the opposition which he encountered in military circles to his defence cuts[49] and complains about the increased military budgets which followed his departure. He claims quite explicitly that military men have gained a greater influence in policy-making since 1964 and blames the military for giving bad advice in

1967 when they 'had an influential voice in the decision-making which preceded the Six-Day War'.[50]

It is evident from Khrushchev's account that the party leadership are conscious of cross-pressures from the military, calling for increased military spending, and from the mass of people, looking for a higher standard of living. Khrushchev speaks of the dangers of the military 'intimidating' the leadership.[51] Though he acknowledges that most military men are just doing their job in demanding increased expenditure on armaments, he goes on to observe that 'among the military in socialist countries, you can find people who tend to regard the defense establishment as a higher caste. It is important to keep such people in check, to make sure they don't exercise too much influence'.[52] Khrushchev indicates that there were also times when the leadership during his period as first secretary let the military have their way against their better judgement. He recalls a decision to build four cruisers (four 'very expensive show-pieces') and the fact that the leadership had 'second thoughts about whether to build the last two at all' when the second one was almost completed. However: 'We exchanged opinions in the leadership and decided to go ahead as a concession to the military.'[53] Khrushchev was acutely conscious of popular pressures from the other side: 'We recognized that if our people didn't have potatoes we couldn't expect them to shout "hooray" all the time — even if they did shout "hooray", it would be in rather a weak voice. We began to economize on our military expenditures.'[54] He warns his successors 'not to look at the world through the eye-glasses of the military'[55] and suggests that money is now being wasted on unnecessary items and aspects of defence expenditure.[56]

In fact, it must be added, after some substantial increases in defence spending in the second half of the sixties, Soviet expenditure in this field appears to have levelled off, and in 1974 it showed a decrease compared with 1973.[57] It is unlikely that Khrushchev's advice played the slightest part in this, but highly probable that a concern similar to his to forestall popular discontent was a significant factor, though the arms burden on the Soviet economy remains very great.

The part played by the KGB since 1964 is a somewhat

more ambiguous example of an institution whose status and influence have been enhanced than is the case of the military. The state security forces (like the military) have enjoyed much more favourable press publicity in the years since Khrushchev's departure than they did under Khrushchev, and the head of the KGB, who in Khrushchev's time was not even a member of the Central Committee, has in the period since his fall successively enjoyed membership of the Central Committee, candidate membership of the Politburo, and (since 1973) full membership of the Politburo. The fact that Andropov has become the first head of the security forces since Beria to enjoy this privilege does not, of course, mean that the amount of independent authority which he wields is remotely comparable. In this respect there was a greater bureaucratic pluralism under Stalin! Andropov's promotion may rather reflect the fact that the state security service is being called upon by the party to do more than it did under Khrushchev, and it may also be seen as a mark of favour, reflecting the higher status the KGB enjoys in an era when attacks on 'the period of the cult of personality' have been ended, thus allowing the security forces to come out from under the shadow of the tortures and killings perpetrated by the NKVD and to bask in the reflected glory of newspaper tales about glorious 'Chekists'.

It is important to note that when we are discussing the military and the KGB, we are discussing very large and (because of the coercive powers they employ) potentially dangerous institutions. For that very reason, notwithstanding the high status which the defence and security forces currently enjoy, they are closely supervised by the appropriate departments of the Central Committee of the party. They are not, therefore, likely to prove to be the clearest examples of an institutional or bureaucratic pluralism within the Soviet system, even though they manifest some such tendencies. Bureaucratic pluralism is a phenomenon quite widely discernible within the Soviet Union and one clearly recognised by many Soviet observers of the political scene within the USSR. There is nothing particularly new about departmental or local organs putting the interests of their own institution or locality above the 'general' interest, but as the number and size of institutions and departments has grown, the problem has become more intractable. M. I. Piskotin, writing in 1973, notes that the number of ministries in the USSR has grown from thirty-six in 1939 to fifty-two in 1956 and fifty-nine in 1972 and that in recent years the growth in the number of state committees has been even faster.[58] The more differentiated the ministerial and departmental system becomes, suggests Piskotin, the more difficult it is to plan, co-ordinate and control on a state-wide basis. Interdepartmental problems are becoming all the more difficult to solve because of an increasing tendency towards 'lack of co-ordination between departments' or 'departmental disconnection' (*vedomstvennaya razobshchennost'*). This departmental lack of co-ordination or separatism impedes the process of concentration, specialisation and co-operation in industrial production and the finding of the optimal type of production association.[59] It means that ministries working within overlapping areas will sometimes adopt different and conflicting approaches to the same technical problem. Such a situation of departmental disconnection appears to exist, for example, between the Ministry of Foreign Trade under N. S. Patolichev and the State Committee for Science and Technology under V. A. Kirillin and D. M. Gvishiani — if the accounts of some foreign businessmen are to be believed.

'Departmental disconnection', 'narrow departmentalism', and even (more colloquially) 'departmental ideology' are common objects of criticism in the Soviet Union. Party organs are constantly being enjoined to fight against such manifestations of bueaucratic pluralism[60] and it was partly with this struggle in mind that a change was made to the party rules at the XXIV Congress in 1971 which gave primary party organisations in ministries the right to check up on the work of the ministerial apparatus, thus, in the words of a *Pravda* editorial of late 1974, significantly enlarging 'the opportunity of Communists to exert influence upon the improvement of the style of administrative work and on the strengthening of state discipline'.[61] Party organisations are required to deal uncompromisingly with manifestations of a 'narrow departmental approach, bureaucratism and formalism'.[62]

Bureaucratic pluralism manifests itself at least as clearly at the local level as at the all-Union or Union-republican levels. It is argued, for example, by William Taubman that 'the politics of Soviet urban development *is* a species of bureaucratic politics whose primary features are well-known in non-Soviet settings'.[63] The surprising fact is that the civic authorities in the USSR frequently have less control over the local environment and local services than, say, their British counterparts. The problem arises in the Soviet Union — as elsewhere — because of the existence of conflicts of interest. As Taubman notes, an industrial enterprise does not earn the esteem of its ministerial overlord, nor any prizes and bonuses, by contributing to civic welfare within its urban setting but through increasing output and productivity. If the enterprise controls housing and other services, this strengthens its attraction for potential employees and its bargaining power *vis-à-vis* the local Soviet. Thus, the odd phenomenon of the Soviet style 'company town' persists. That is to say, there are towns in which major industrial enterprises resist attempts by the local Soviets — backed by pleas from party organs — to persuade them to give up services such as housing (and sometimes even water supply and sewage) which they administer and to allow these services, and the personnel employed in them, to come under the jurisdiction of the town Soviet. As Taubman puts it: 'We have not yet plumbed the full significance of the fact that the Soviet governmental system . . . is riven up and down by bureaucratic politics; that Soviet policies and lack of policies . . . mirror the clashes and compromises, antagonisms and alliances, of powerful bureaucratic agencies and their representatives; that governmental behaviour reflects not only the Politburo's deliberate political purpose . . . but also the mode of operation of complex large-scale organizations that even a powerful leadership cannot always and everywhere control.'[64]

THE CHANGING FORTUNES OF POLITICAL GROUPINGS

The third of the three questions posed on page 230 raised the issue of the extent to which the party as a whole might be divided into different political groupings and of the changing fortunes of these various groupings and political tendencies within the post-Khrushchev period. Roy Medvedev has identified three groupings or tendencies which, he argues, have emerged since the October plenum of 1964. The first of these he calls the 'neo-Stalinists' and he suggests that neo-Stalinism is the predominant ideology of a 'large part of the party and state apparatus, especially in its middle ranks, in the regional and city party committees and among the ideological bureaucrats'.[65] This is consistent with the findings of an anonymous *samizdat* writer quoted by Medvedev who claims that neo-Stalinist views are most frequently to be found among party workers in the age group forty-five to fifty-five, a generation which did not experience the repression on a massive scale of the 1930s.[66] Many of the party members of an older generation than this remember too well how the party apparatus was terrorised as much as any other institution from 1934-8.

The second major grouping or tendency to be discerned within the party since 1964 is, according to Medvedev, that of the 'moderates or conservatives'.[67] This is a broad categorisation and, of course, it contains many different shades of opinion. It is a spectrum which comes close to the neo-Stalinists at one end and to the reformists at the other. The third tendency which Medvedev sees as existing within the party is that which he calls the 'party-democratic' tendency.[68] He admits that this third broad grouping has been the least effective of the three, and that is, if anything, an understatement. In the immediate post-Khrushchev period, the 'party-democrats' or radical reformists could, in a suitably guarded manner, publish their views, but by late 1965 they were already on the defensive and the invasion of Czechoslovakia in 1968 was a devastating blow for them. The events in Czechoslovakia, so horrific from the point of view of the neo-Stalinists and alarming too for the party conservatives, could be regarded by those who wished to preserve the *status quo* or to return to a still sterner line as the logical outcome of the policies being advocated by the 'democratic' or 'liberal-reformist' wing of the party. (In fact, there is no reason to suppose that if party and police controls and censorship were removed, and debate and group political activity permitted to the extent to which all these things manifested themselves in the 'Prague Spring', anything like the orderly and peaceful transition to some form of democratic socialism — which was under way in Czechoslovakia — would occur in the Soviet Union.) At least since 1968, if not earlier, the 'party democrats' have only been able to remain *party* democrats by keeping their views to themselves, for those who have spoken out, including Roy Medvedev himself, have been expelled from the party. Medvedev acknowledges that the conservative leadership, subjected to pressure from different sides, have given way much more readily to 'pressure from the right, from the side of the neo-Stalinists' than to 'pressure from the left, from the side of the various progressive groupings'.[69] He adds, quite rightly, that the former type of pressure within the party has been considerably stronger than the latter, and there is no doubt that the former grouping have found it much easier to publish and propagate their views than have those party members whose views are close to the outlook to be found in the Italian, Spanish and Australian Communist parties.[70]

In spite of the setbacks suffered by the more radical reformist elements within the Soviet Communist Party, it must be noted that the hard-liners have not had things all their own way. On several occasions the conservative centre has asserted itself against those who have been calling for a harder line involving more discipline within Soviet society (including a stricter labour discipline but possibly also some curtailment of the material privileges of the elite) and harsher measures against dissident intellectuals. Alexander Shelepin was the focal point of this movement and he appears to have made a bid for power in 1965, backed by influential supporters within the *apparaty* of the party, the komsomol and the KGB. Shelepin's offensive and the existence of a Shelepin group have very recently been confirmed by Alexander Solzhenitsyn in a book published in Paris in 1975.[71] Solzhenitsyn writes that it is possible with near certainly to say that in August-September 1965 'an abrupt return to Stalinism was being prepared under the leadership of "Iron Shurik" Shelepin'.[72] Among the views pressed by the group headed by Shelepin, notes Solzhenitsyn, were the need to take a Stalin-like grip of the economy and management (on which Shelepin came into conflict with Kosygin), the need to take a tighter grip on ideology (on which no one in the leadership was in disagreement with Shelepin), the desirability of coming to terms with Mao-Tse-tung and recognising the basic correctness of his line, the necessity of recognising that Stalin was guilty only of the abrogation of collective leadership and the illegal repression of party and Soviet cadres, the view that it was time to revive the useful concept of 'enemy of the people', and the need to look closely at the journal, *Novy mir,* to see why it was so much praised by the bourgeoisie.[73] From the close colleagues of the head of the KGB, V. E. Semichastny, there was a demand for the arrest of a thousand intellectuals in and around Moscow, but in fact the party leadership responded at this time with the arrest of only two — Sinyavsky and Daniel (in the first half of September 1965).[74]

Shelepin and his group suffered a series of setbacks between late 1965 and 1968. Shelepin himself lost his chairmanship of the Committee of Party-State Control before the end of 1965 and, much more seriously, his position in the secretariat of the party in 1967 when he was moved to the less powerful position of head of the trade union movement. His demotion was rapidly followed by the removal from positions of power of many of his supporters, among whom the most notable casualities were the head of the KGB, Semichastny (who was replaced by Yuri Andropov in May 1967), and the Komsomol head, S. P. Pavlov (who was moved to the substantially less important post of chairman of the Sports Council in 1968 and replaced as Komsomol first secretary by E. M. Tyazhel'nikov). Writing in 1967 (but in an essay only just published), Solzhenitsyn mentions 'the defeat of the Shelepinist enterprise' as one of the few pieces of good political news to come his way at that time, adding: 'The power of Shelepin would have meant my immediate end.'[75]

The party leadership a few years later again showed their ability to deal with any strong and relatively independent voices within the party (and with 'dogmatists' as well as 'revisionists') when in 1970 they removed V. S. Tolstikov, an ambitious man in his own right and not part of the Shelepin group, from his powerful position as first secretary of the Leningrad regional party organisation and sent him to China as Soviet ambassador. Finally, the undercurrents of conflict with Shelepin came to the surface again in 1975 and at the April plenary session of the Central Committee he was at last dropped from the Politburo. Given that his career had begun to take a downward turn ten years earlier, it is an indication of the strength of his support in sections of the party and state apparatus (notwithstanding the severe setbacks which his supporters had previously suffered) that the members of the Politburo took so long to rid themselves of a colleague whose ambitions and hard-line postures they perceived as a threat.

Some of the most important political arguments are, of course, those which take place within the broad spectrum of the 'conservative' or 'moderate' centre. While it would be a contradiction in terms to say that this grouping included radical reformists who desired fundamental change in the political system or dogmatic neo-Stalinists, it does embrace those of a more technocratic disposition and those for whom party controls must always take precedence over technocratic norms. Within the Politburo Kosygin has been the most important representative of the former tendency and Suslov a powerful spokesman for the latter. At a level just below that of the Politburo and secretariat, the 'technocratic' tendency is represented by such people as the chairman of the State Committee for Science and Technology, V. A. Kirillin, and the deputy chairman of that state committee, D. M. Gvishiani[76] (Kosygin's son-in-law); and the 'partocratic'[77] emphasis is to be found, *par excellence,* among officials of the Department of Propaganda of the Central Committee and those who are professionally concerned with ideological questions. On page 231 we suggested that the present Soviet leadership have supported intellectual activity which they believe may be useful economically and relatively neutral politically, while rejecting activities which are politically dangerous and economically irrelevant. Within these parameters, however, serious political discussion may still take place, for there are many issues which do not fall into such clear-cut categories as those just mentioned. There is a wide range of policies which may be of economic benefit but which carry political risks. Moves in the direction of a socialist market economy — which would threaten the functions and powers of sections of the party and state *apparaty* — come into this category and, as a result, the Kosygin economic reform of 1965 (which was by no means as far-reaching as the Hungarian or

Czechoslovak economic reforms) has never been fully implemented. At this level of the party hierarchy, it is clear that no one wants to challenge the fundamentals of the political system; the distinction is between those who are prepared to take some political risks for the sake of serious economic reform and those who believe that political security and economic progress can for the most part be achieved by methods tried in the past, though they may be supplemented by such short cuts as are offered, for instance, by the import of western technology on a larger scale than hitherto.[78]

A detailed chronology of Soviet political change since the fall of Khrushchev cannot be undertaken here, for it would need to take account of the differences between one policy area and another. In many ways, however, the years which can be seen as the crucial ones in the determination of the direction to be followed are 1965 and 1968. The period between October 1964 and the autumn of 1965 was not exactly a time when a hundred flowers bloomed, but several schools of thought did indeed (relatively openly) contend. Initially the party leadership were doubtless concerned to reduce anxiety at home and abroad and to reassure people that the dismissal of Khrushchev, the exposer of Stalin, did not mean a return to Stalinism. The turning-point came in the autumn of 1965 when the Shelepin offensive took place. Though this enterprise was unsuccessful in terms of the career advancement of its proponents, the months of September-October 1965 produced many signs that the honeymoon period of the new leadership was over. The relatively liberal editor of *Pravda,* Alexei Rumyantsev, was dismissed; shortly thereafter, Trapeznikov published his *Pravda* article denouncing excessive criticism of the Stalin era; and Sinyavsky and Daniel were arrested.

The consolidation of the supremacy of the conservative centre (accompanied, however, by a much more comprehensive routing of the 'party-democratic' or liberal-reformist wing of the party than of the neo-Stalinist wing) was confirmed between the autumn of 1965 and the end of 1968. In 1966, shortly before the XXIII Party Congress, Sinyavsky and Daniel were sentenced to seven and five years hard labour, and Mikhail Sholokhov, in his speech to the congress, managed to imply that they ought to have been shot. In general, a hard line on ideological and cultural questions emerged from the congress and this tendency was enormously strengthened in 1968 when events in Czechoslovakia gravely alarmed the party conservatives and gave the neo-Stalinists a chance to exert greater influence. One manifestation of the tougher line was the vigorous suppression of a form of spontaneous political activity which had developed in the post-Khrushchev years — the collection of signatures for letters of protest addressed to the party leadership. This had reached the height of its impact and effectiveness just before the XXIII Congress when such diverse figures as the publicist Ernst Genry, former Ambassador Ivan Maisky and Academician Pyotr Kapitsa were among the group of Soviet notables who signed a letter exhorting the congress not to rehabilitate Stalin. Fear of the power of heterodox political ideas, of the kind which had proved so influential within the Communist Party of Czechoslovakia, was greatly intensified in 1968 and the repercussions of the leadership's alarm were immediately felt by the Soviet intelligentsia. Even the idea of economic reform (i.e. technocratic as well as liberal or democratic reform) suffered a setback as a result of the Czech developments and the Soviet armed intervention in Czechoslovakia in August 1968. The Czechoslovak experience appeared to illustrate the links between economic and political reform, and the reformist political activity of the leading spokesman of the Czechoslovak economic reformers, Ota Šik (who became a deputy prime minister of Czechoslovakia in 1968), only added to the difficulties of Soviet advocates of moves towards a socialist market economy. As Kaser has pointed out in the previous chapter, even the projected devolution of material supply was delayed after the invasion of Czechoslovakia, and it has not been implemented yet.

While departmentalism, localism, and conflict among various political groupings and tendencies can create tensions within the polity, they do not necessarily represent a threat to the long-term stability of the political and social system. Such threats do, however, exist within Soviet society — if only in an embryonic form. There are sources of tension and potential sources of tension which are capable, in due course, of producing fundamental political change. It is to these that we shall now devote some attention — albeit briefly, for a full exploration of each would be a large undertaking in itself.

THE NATIONALITIES PROBLEM

Quite apart from the overt national dissidence which has become more apparent in the post-Khrushchev period and which has been discussed by Reddaway in Chapter 6, there is the larger potential problem for the Soviet leadership of the persistence of a strong sense of national consciousness among many of the 130 or so ethnic groups in the Soviet Union and the possibility that nationalist ideology may grow stronger among certain ethnic groups in whom it is now weak. For some of the more culturally developed nationalities, various forms of nationalism have become relatively more attractive in the post-Khrushchev period as optimism about what can be achieved through political reformism has receded. Thus after the hard line which was adopted on political and ideological questions with particular force and clarity during 1968, many Soviet Jews turned for the first time to Zionism as a serious alternative ideology to liberalisation or 'revisionism' within a Soviet context. During the same period, a variety of forms of Russian nationalism gained increasing support in the ranks of the Russian intelligentsia. Among people for whom being in disagreement with the party and state authorities is one of the essential attributes of an *intelligent*, Russian nationalism increased its drawing power since it was, on the one hand, a less severely repressed variety of political deviation than most others and, on the other, an alternative to the official ideology which appeared to offer more hope of success than, say, Hungarian-style 'liberalisation' or Czechoslovak-style 'democratisation'.

While, initially, Russian nationalism might appear from the standpoint of the party leadership to be a fairly harmless (even useful) deviation, in the longer term, if its influence continues to spread throughout the Russian intelligentsia, it could seriously undermine the already shaky Marxist-Leninist theoretical foundation of the Soviet system. Since it is partly that ideological cement which holds the Soviet Union together, Russian nationalism, in conjunction with the opposed nationalisms of other major ethnic groups, could represent a long-term threat to the political and social system. So far it has been the nationalism of non-Russians which is perceived as the serious danger. In 1967 the Estonian party organisation came under attack from the all-Union party authorities for not taking a firm enough line with Estonian nationalism; in 1971 a group of Latvian Communists, most of whom were party members of long standing, wrote a letter to the leadership of a number of western Communist parties drawing attention to a policy of 'eradication of everything national' in Latvia; and in 1972 there were riots in the Lithuanian city of Kaunas in which the demonstrators demanded an extension of national and religious freedom in their republic. Nationalism is also a powerful factor in the Caucasian republics of Georgia and Armenia. During the 'Georgian scandal' of 1972 when many party officials in the Georgian republic lost their posts (including the first secretary of the republican party organisation, V. P. Mzhavanadze), not only was widespread corruption in Georgia exposed, but attention was also drawn to the existence of an excessive degree of Georgian nationalism, especially among intellectuals and young people.[79] Nationalism within the western Ukraine remains very strong and an important feature of the manifestations of Ukrainian nationalism within the past decade is that many of the spokesmen for national rights have been people who considered themselves to be Marxists and even Leninists. In contrast, the Soviet central Asian republics have shown far fewer signs of strong national consciousness, but it will be a considerable achievement on the part of the Soviet leadership if they can prevent nationalism developing among the Asian nationalities as their material and cultural standards continue to rise. These republics are only now, for the first time, producing a sizable native intelligentsia and it is the intellectuals, not the peasantry, who are likely to articulate nationalist views.

It is possible that such nationalism can be safely contained within the system and that a majority of Soviet citizens will, as is probably the case with most now, have a dual 'national' loyalty — to their own ethnic group and to the Soviet people as a whole. At the moment those national groups which have the political resources of a Union republic at their disposal are those who tend to fare best in terms of concessions to their national, cultural and economic interests. One conceivable way of ensuring that national pressures remain no more than demands for a better deal for particular national groups within the system, rather than turning into separatist or 'anti-Soviet' movements, would be to strengthen the institutional framework within which such demands can be articulated. The example of Yugoslavia — where national pressures have become a still more serious problem for the federal authorities in Belgrade as the federal rights of the republics have been extended — suggests, however, that the answer to this problem in a multinational state is not such a simple one. On the one hand, the repression of national rights and cultures and the restriction of the existing degree of political autonomy in the Union republics may provoke a more intense and (from the standpoint of the system) a more dangerous nationalism. On the other hand, devolution of power to the republics and to other numerically significant minority nationalities who do not at present possess such institutional supports as a union republic provides could stimulate demands for further devolution and exacerbate the problems of planning on a state-wide basis (as appears to have happened now in Yugoslavia).

It is clear that the Soviet leadership see the nationalities question as potentially a highly dangerous one and they are very sensitive to what they interpret as excessive concessions made to nationalist sentiment. Thus, Pyotr Shelest, who on most counts would not qualify as one of nature's liberals, was removed from the first secretaryship of the Ukrainian party organisation in 1972 and from the Politburo in 1973, accused of being too soft on Ukrainian nationalism.[80] It is also highly probable that one of the difficulties which has held up the publication of the new draft Soviet constitution for fourteen years (the announcement that one was to be prepared came from Khrushchev in 1961 and the latest revision of its publication target date is that it will be ready in time for the XXV Party Congress in 1976) is the difficulty of formulating the constitutional line on the nationalities question. It is likely that the hypothetical 'right of secession' will be removed on the grounds that it is historically outmoded, but the dilemma remains of risking increased national discontent by taking away existing national and republican rights or, alternatively, of stimulating national self-assertion by leaving intact rights which might be taken more seriously in a constitution published in the mid-seventies than ever they could be in relation to a constitution which appeared in 1936 just as the physical purges were reaching their height.

SOCIO-ECONOMIC GROUPS

A second major potential threat to the present distribution of power within the Soviet polity is the possibility of large and important social groups acquiring a strong sense of group (or class) consciousness. As a result of a variety of preventive measures, ranging from material incentives to institutional controls, group political activity in the Soviet Union has emerged only in a very limited way and at a 'micro' rather than a 'macro' level. That is to say, the two social strata which at the present stage of social development could, by collective action, undermine the existing political and social system — the working class and the intelligentsia — have been depoliticised and internally disunited.

At the moment it seems almost inconceivable that either the workers or the intelligentsia in the Soviet Union could act as a social class in the sense of interacting politically and articulating collective demands. Yet however remote such an eventuality may appear, it is probable that these are two spectres which haunt the Soviet leadership. Within the past decade they have been provided with the clearest examples of such action — in Czechoslovakia in 1968 and in Poland in 1970. In the former case, a highly politicised intelligentsia took the leading part in the preparation of the reform movement and in producing the fundamental changes which were underway within the Czechoslovak political system. It is true (as many public opinion polls demonstrated) that there was also widespread working class support in 1968 for the political changes (though unskilled workers were suspicious of the economic reform), but the breakthrough was made by the intellectuals while the workers initially remained passively on the sidelines.[81] In Poland the reverse was the case. The intelligentsia, having been thoroughly intimidated in 1968, stood aside in December 1970 while the workers' demonstrations which brought about the fall of Gomulka took place.[82]

It can be argued that a working class revolt is the most dangerous for the Communist Party leadership, in view of the theoretical links between the party and the workers. The cases of the Prague Spring and the Polish December do not necessarily substantiate that view. The conservative forces within the Czechoslovak Communist Party were so much on the defensive in their attempts to prevent fundamental changes from taking place that they required reinforcement from over half a million foreign troops and the maximum political support of the Soviet Union before they could reverse the radical reformist trends. In Poland the workers achieved important personnel changes and significant material concessions, but their demands for fundamental political changes ('democratisation of relations at factory level, changing the nature of elections in certain organisations, including that of the party, true autonomy and a new approach in the trades unions, publicising information without distortion, an effective fight against bureaucracy, the abolition of privilege of position',[83] etc.) appear almost five years later to have made comparatively little headway.

The hypothetical possibility of a degree of class unity and of determination to assert themselves politically being achieved *either* by the intelligentsia *or* the working class is, however, calculated to fill the defenders of the Soviet *status quo* with alarm. When serious political conflict or unrest breaks out in Czechoslovakia, Poland or Hungary, in the last resort there is the threat and possibility of Soviet intervention to 'normalise' the situation. However remote such a contingency may be, the Soviet leaders must occasionally gloomily wonder: if Soviet intellectuals were to behave like Czech intellectuals in 1968 or Soviet workers were to act like Polish workers in 1970, from where would foreign intervention come to defend their 'socialist gains'?

DEMOGRAPHIC AND GENERATIONAL FACTORS

A third potential source of tension within the Soviet polity and society which could in time lead to significant political change may be found in the demographic and generational factors elucidated in earlier chapters by J. A. Newth and Peter Frank. Newth brings out clearly the demographic dimension of the nationalities question. Potentially the most important aspect of this politically is that which he summarises as the 'territorial redistribution away from the Slav core towards the periphery'. One reason why the nationalism of minority national groups has been more easily contained within the Soviet Union than within, say, Yugoslavia is simply the fact that in the Soviet Union there have been more Russians than all other nationalities put together. That is still the case — but only just. In the near future Russians are going to lose their overall majority, though the three Slav nationalities (Russians, Ukrainians and Belorussians) will still form the overwhelmingly predominant ethnic grouping for some considerable time. In the long run, however, the doubts which Newth suggests must exist about the ability of the western parts of the USSR to sustain their existing numbers, coupled with the fact that the eastern republics (following a great reduction in mortality, and especially infant mortality, during the Soviet period) 'are in the classical phase of population explosion',[84] are of great political relevance. National consciousness remains very strong within the Soviet Union. Though the problems created by the official Soviet classification of social groups make the data difficult to interpret, Newth's observation that the most recent Soviet census showed more than twice as many marriages 'across the class line' as there were 'across the national line' would appear to lend support to such a view. Given the changing proportional relationship between Slavs and non-Slavs, the form which this national consciousness may take becomes one of the great questions of the Soviet political future.

As Frank has pointed out in Chapter 5, the demography of the party is also a pointer to possible political change. It would appear that substantial personnel changes in the top leadership cannot be far away, and the most likely occasion for them will be the XXV Party Congress. The three 'young men' left in the Politburo after the removal of Alexander Shelepin on 16 April 1975 were Kulakov, Polyansky and

Shcherbitsky (all of them fifty-seven), and five members were over seventy (Pel'she, Suslov, Podgorny, Kosygin and Grechko). Of the remainder, the two most powerful among them (Brezhnev and Kirilenko) were sixty-eight, and with Shelepin's departure the average age of the fifteen-man Politburo rose to over sixty-five.

Personnel changes do not by themselves necessarily lead to fundamental political changes, and in the short term it is highly unlikely that such change will take place. What does seem clear, however, is that in the course of the next two decades the party leadership (the Politburo and secretariat of the Central Committee) is going to be gradually taken over by people who reached the age of political consciousness (see Chapter 5) in the post-1939 period, i.e. after the mass terror had ended. It is possible that such people will be more prepared to accept the risks entailed in political reform than has the political generation who were the beneficiaries of the terror (but who must often have been terrified — if, by happy chance, not terrorised — themselves). At the very least the generational change is likely to bring to a head the argument between those who favour a more technocratic approach to Soviet economic problems (and who are prepared to pay the price of a slackening of certain ideological and institutional controls) and those for whom *partiynost'* (Party spirit) and the 'leading role of the party' (as manifested for example in its detailed control over cadres) must at all times take precedence.

INSTITUTIONAL CONTROLS

If the nationalities question, the politicisation of major social groups, and certain features of the demography of Soviet society and the party may be seen as actual or potential sources of tension which could in time help to promote basic political change, it is important to recognise that there are also a number of powerful forces militating against this.

An examination of the possible sources of basic change within the Soviet political system directs attention to broad social forces which may in time affect the ethos and the policies of those who hold positions of institutional power or which, alternatively, may radically alter the existing structures of power. The emphasis has to be on broad social forces because the system of institutional controls works so effectively that it is not possible for an organised group consciously to set out on a path of political reform and to seek support for its views. The nature of the party (and other institutional) controls has been described often enough and need not detain us here.[85] The general point is that political action can seldom be effective without organisation and, with rare exceptions, organised political activity in the Soviet Union is under such close supervision from higher party organs that even party members working within the various institutions and organisations are given little opportunity to indulge in serious political heterodoxy. (In several other East European Communist states, in contrast, party members have been and, in some cases, still are allowed a greater 'political space' within which to operate, so that different organisations and institutions indulge not only in 'narrow departmentalism' but at times pursue divergent political goals.)

Complementary to all the other institutional controls there is the enormously important control over careers and appointments which party organs possess. This is especially so in the case of the so-called *nomenklatura* posts. These are positions at various levels of the administrative hierarchy from the all-Union to the district level which are considered to be of political or economic importance and appointments to which must be approved by the party committee at that particular level.[86] The choice is limited to people who are on the *nomenklatura* list and who have already, therefore, received the party's attestation of political fitness. A place on the *nomenklatura* is also intended to be a guarantee of a certain level of ability, but complaints are often heard that when people are removed from a responsible position because of shortcomings in their work, this fact is glossed over in their reference and they are enabled to move to another *nomenklatura* post.[87] So far as mere inefficiency is concerned, the degree of mutual tolerance is sufficient to provoke criticism from party theoreticians[88] and, more scathingly, from dissident intellectuals. A. D. Sakharov, for example, has put it thus:

... there is the traditional attitude toward Party cadres that is expressed in what is called *nomenklatura*. This means that even if a person fails in some kind of work, as long as he is a leading Party worker he will be transferred to some other job not very different in material advantages from the one he gives up.

The whole manner of getting a job and advancement is very strongly connected with the interrelationships within the system. Each important administrator has attached to him personally certain people who move with him from place to place as he is transferred. There is something irresistible about this and it seems to be a kind of law of our state structure.[89]

While the *nomenklatura* system in this sense encourages individual and group relationships, advancement within it naturally depends upon an acceptance of the basic norms of the system. There is, therefore, a very strong incentive indeed for people on the *nomenklatura* not to deviate from the path of political orthodoxy, for to do so is to run the serious risk of ruining their career. This may appear a mild deterrent in comparison with the prospect of physical annihilation offered in Stalin's time, but on the whole it is a very effective one.

SOCIO-ECONOMIC FACTORS

Nothing would be more likely to stimulate social discontent in the Soviet Union (as elsewhere) than economic failure. Though the Soviet economy faces many problems, they do not appear to be any more severe than (though in a number of respects they are different from) those which the western economies are currently encountering. While Soviet citizens doubtless still have a sense of relative deprivation when they reflect upon the quality and quantity of western consumer goods, the mass media in the USSR make them well aware of the crisis of contemporary capitalism and of rising un-employment in western Europe and North America. The energy crisis and the rise in the price of primary products has been as beneficial for the Soviet Union as it has been damaging for most western economies, and the reduction in the relative attractiveness of the western economic example is in itself a source of stability of the Soviet political system, given the fact that the official definition of 'socialism' closely links the existing political structure with the pertaining property relations and economic policies.

Soviet citizens are far from being as shut off from the outside world now as they were under Stalin, but they are still in a better position to make economic comparisons over time than between countries. This former comparison, too, is likely to be to the advantage of the present leaders and (by extension) the system they represent. The gains made by agricultural workers, industrial workers, the more poorly paid sections of the intelligentsia, and pensioners have already been discussed in the chapters by Nove and Kaser and in an earlier part of this concluding chapter. The levelling-up was actually initiated by Khrushchev, but it is probably his successors who have reaped most of the credit, for not only have real incomes risen faster and income differentials been further reduced since 1965 than under Khrushchev, but a number of egalitarian initiatives on Khrushchev's part reached the point of actual implementation only after his departure. Thus, for example, it was Khrushchev who announced that collective farm workers were to receive old-age pensions for the first time, but this policy was not put into effect until after he had left the political scene.

One reason why the present Soviet leadership have not had to face the kind of crisis which occurred in Poland in December 1970 is that they have been much more careful than their Polish counterparts not to stretch the tolerance of the Soviet consumer — and, in particular, working class consumers — to danger point. Far from introducing a sharp rise in the price of basic foodstuffs as the Gomulka leadership did, they have operated what Alec Nove has (earlier in this book)[90] called 'the most gigantic agricultural subsidy known in human history'. The size of the subsidy paid to keep food prices stable is a cost borne for the sake of political stability and is a powerful indication of the ability of industrial and agricultural workers to influence certain areas of policy even in the absence of autonomous working class pressure groups. It is primarily the opinions of manual workers which are being anticipated or taken note of in the maintenance of the enormous food subsidies, for higher-paid Soviet citizens would prefer higher prices and shorter queues. Members of the party elite have the best of both worlds, since those on the upper reaches of the *nomenklatura* have access to special shops where they can buy goods which are much less easily available in shops open to the masses. Given the economic arguments against the enormous rise from year to year in the agricultural subsidy, its continuation at ever-increasing levels indicates a degree of caution and political responsiveness on the part of the present leadership which must contribute strongly to the system's political stability.

POLITICAL CULTURE

Finally, in addition to the institutional and socio-economic supports of the present political system, there are also political cultural supports which should not be ignored. The concept of an historically conditioned political culture has little in common with the idea of 'national character', for whereas the latter is usually regarded as something innate and unchanging, a political culture can be briefly described as the fundamental beliefs and values, political knowledge and expectations, and foci of identification and loyalty which are the product of the specific historical experience of a people.[91] As such, a political culture is by no means immutable, though it tends to change more slowly than do institutional structures or patterns of overt political behaviour. Important analytical distinctions may be made both between the official political culture and the dominant political culture, and between the dominant political culture and the various sub-cultures. How far the official and the dominant political cultures coincide is a matter for empirical investigation. In the case of the Soviet political culture, such empirical work is still in its early stages, but there does appear to be a fairly substantial area of overlap between the official political culture, into which great pains are taken to socialise the citizens, and the political values and beliefs which are actually widely held. This is not to deny that there are numerous political sub-cultures with significant differences among them, often based upon different national and social groups. A comprehensive study of Soviet political culture would thus have to take account not only of sub-cultures within the Russian political culture but of the very different cultures of the Baltic republics, Georgia,

Armenia, the Ukraine, and the Central Asian republics. This is not the place to argue the point in detail, but it seems reasonable to suggest that the dominant Russian political culture is also the dominant Soviet one.

In the Soviet Union the lack, for the most part, of first-hand knowledge of alternative political arrangements (other than authoritarian alternatives) is a cultural support for the present political structure. Though there are indeed many exceedingly important discontinuities as well as continuities between tsarist and Soviet Russia, some of the continuities in values and practices deserve emphasis, however briefly. They include the strong tendency to place faith in people (and especially in a strong leader) rather than in political structures or legal norms and constraints, the absence of institutionalised opposition, the fear of chaos and high premium put upon loyalty and unity (values strengthened in the twentieth century by the breakdown of order in the First World War, the chaos of the Civil War, and the suffering and heroism of the people during the Second World War), the gulf between state and society, the mutual distrust between the intelligentsia and people (*narod*), as well as the propensity to regard as 'normal' such phenomena common to both tsarist and Soviet Russia as strictly hierarchical political organisation, political police surveillance, administrative exile, literary censorship, and internal passports.

If there has been no equivalent of the Polish December in the Soviet Union in recent years, this is mainly because the present Soviet leaders have carried out a much more conciliatory and politically responsive economic policy than the Gomulka leadership. But in the immediate post-war period Russian workers and peasants did not revolt in conditions of deprivation infinitely worse than those suffered by the Poles in 1970. This may no doubt be strongly associated with the power of the political police under Stalin and with support for some of the basic features of the Soviet order on the part of industrial workers. But Nadezhda Mandelstam — in the second volume of her remarkable memoirs[92] — sees this political passivity as a reflection of 'an excruciating capacity for endurance' on the part of the ordinary Russian, 'a patience . . . born not of religious faith but of the traditional treatment of the ordinary people as a race apart'.[93]

In the past thirty years the material conditions of the mass of the Soviet people have improved beyond recognition, but a fear of chaos and disorder (which Nadezhda Mandelstam, in her earlier volume of memoirs, described as 'perhaps the most permanent of our feelings')[94] still persists. This fear, a product of both Soviet and pre-revolutionary Russian experience, affects the intelligentsia at least as much as it does other social groups. It is this factor and the very different political experience and first-hand political knowledge of Soviet and of Czech intellectuals, for instance, which partly accounts for the great differences between the strength of political reformism within Soviet and Czechoslovak intellectual circles during the period of overt de-Stalinisation, and it is part of the explanation why the Soviet leaders have been spared a Russian version of the Prague Spring (as well as a Soviet equivalent of the Polish December). Even among critical Soviet intellectuals who know what they are against, only a minority know what they want. Some simply want to replace what they see as an unenlightened elite with an enlightened elite, but have no idea how to institutionalise this change in which they place so much hope. This is partly because they distrust the mass of the people — the *chern'*, as they often pejoratively refer to them.

The fear of chaos (which, like distrust of the Germans, is one of the ideas that permeates all social groups from the party elite to the peasantry) is probably not entirely misplaced. Given the national and social tensions which the present political structure keeps under rigorous control, it is not unlikely that a radical loosening of that structure would lead to violence and an anarchic situation within the state. In view of the enormous progress which has been made in material terms, and the possibilities of living a peaceful and moderately comfortable life[95] which are now open to a majority of Soviet citizens — always provided they do not engage in unofficial political activity — it is not surprising that they, as well as the party leadership, should be unwilling to embrace the risks involved in attempting to introduce radical change.

NOTES

1 The points are numbered simply to separate one important policy area from another and with no intention of suggesting that the outcomes and achievements of Soviet policy are being ranked in any order of importance.

2 At the XXIII Party Congress in 1966 the First Secretary was renamed General Secretary (Stalin's title until 1934) and, at the same time, in another reversion to pre-Khrushchev nomenclature, the Praesidium of the Central Committee became the Politburo.

3 Riy Medvedev, *Kniga o sotsialisticheskoy demokratii* (Amsterdam and Paris, 1972) p. 25.

4 On the Committee of Party-State Control, see Grey Hodnett, 'Khrushchev and Party-State Control', in Alexander Dallin and Alan F. Westin (eds), *Politics in the Soviet Union: 7 Cases* (New York, 1966) pp. 113-64; and Jerry F. Hough, 'Reforms in Government and Administration', in Alexander Dallin and Thomas B. Larson, *Soviet Politics since Khrushchev* (Englewood Cliffs, N. J., 1968) pp. 23-40, esp. 27-8.

5 B. N. Moralev, *Respublikanskie, kraevye, oblastnye, okruzhnye, gorodskie i rayonnye organizatsii partii* (Moscow, 1967) p. 9.

6 *Ustav kommunisticheskoy partii sovetskogo soyuza: utverzhden XXII s'ezdom, chastichnye izmeneniya vneseny XXIII i XXIV s'ezdami KPSS* (Moscow, 1972) p. 24.

7 See L. G. Churchward, *Contemporary Soviet Government* (London, 1968) esp. pp. 126-9.

8 William Taubman, *Governing Soviet Cities: Bureaucratic Politics and Urban Development in the USSR* (London, 1973) p. 34.

9 Ibid., p. 33.

10 For a discussion of the persistence of material, educational and cultural deprivation in the countryside, see Viktor Perevedentsev, 'Izmerenie peremen: zametki sotsiologa', in *Nash sovremennik*, no. 3 (1974) pp. 135-51; summarised in ABSEES, vol. 5, no. 3 (July 1974) pp. 3-4.

11 Roy Medvedev, *Kniga o sotsialisticheskoy demokratii*, p. 13. Against the 16.7 per cent of Medvedev's claim, the Peterson Report put 1971 labour productivity in Soviet agriculture at 11 per cent of that of the United States. *US Soviet Commercial Relationships in a New Era*, Dept. of Commerce, Washington, DC (Aug 1972) p. 32.

12 L. A. Kostin, 'Partiynoe rukovodstvo osushchestvleniem pro-grammy sotsial'nykh meropriyatiy', in V. A. Kadeykin (ed.), *Voprosy vnutripartiynoy zhizni i rukovodyashchey deyatel'nosti KPSS na sovremennom etape* (Moscow, 1974) pp. 231-2.

13 Ibid., p. 231.

14 *Khrushchev Remembers: The Last Testament*, vol. 2 (London, 1974) p. 145. The tape recordings on which the two volumes of Khrushchev memoirs are based are in the Oral History Collection of Columbia University. They have been subjected to spectrographic analysis and their authenticity is now beyond doubt. I have

discussed this unique source for the student of Soviet politics in greater detail in my review of volume 2 of the memoirs, 'A Voice from the Kremlin', *Times Literary Supplement*, 31 Jan 1975.

15 *Khrushchev Remembers: The Last Testament*, p. 146.
16 On the debunking of Lysenko, see Zhores A. Medvedev, *The Rise and Fall of T. D. Lysenko* (London, 1969) and David Joravsky, *The Lysenko Affair* (Cambridge, Mass., 1970).
17 Zhores A. Medvedev, *10 Years After Ivan Denisovich* (London, 1973) p. 5. The complete closure of the Timiryazev Academy did not in fact take place. Some of Khrushchev's more impulsive and 'hare-brained' decisions were not fully implemented.
18 *Ibid.*, p. 120.
19 *Ibid.*
20 *Ibid.*
21 *Ibid.*, p. 40. One book, critical of Stalin's lack of preparation for war and of his mistakes during the early period of the war — A. M. Nekrich, *1941. 22 Iyunya* (Moscow, 1965) — was withdrawn from sale *after* it had been published in 50,000 copies.
22 S. P. Trapeznikov, *Istoricheskiy opyt KPSS v osushchestvlenii leninskogo kooperativnogo plana* (Moscow, 1965).
23 *Khrushchev Remembers: The Last Testament*, p. 109.
24 Roy Medvedev, *Kniga o sotsialisticheskoy demokratii*, p. 61.
25 *Ibid.*
26 Teresa Rakowska-Harmstone, 'The Dialectics of Nationalism in the USSR', in *Problems of Communism* (May-June 1974) p. 16.
27 Though Khrushchev in his time supported the agricultural short-cuts and panaceas first of Vil'yams (Williams) and then of Lysenko, at least in the first instance he was able to recognise retrospectively that the political decision in favour of Vil'yams and against his major opponent, Academician Pryanishnikov, in the 1930s was economically harmful. The reason why Stalin (and so, inevitably, given the period, Khrushchev) came out in favour of Vil'yams had, Khrushchev notes, 'nothing to do with an objective analysis of the relative merits of the two theories . . . Pryanishnikov's theory of mineral fertilisers would have required enormous capital invest-ments in order to build fertiliser plants and new machinery. We were short of capital at the time and so Williams's theory was more attractive'. Unfortunately, as Khrushchev goes on to observe, 'Williams's system didn't work'; great harm was inflicted upon Soviet agriculture; and so, 'having belatedly acknowledged that Pryanishnikov was closer to the truth than Williams, we dug Academician Pryanishnikov's notes out of the archives and adopted his theory'. *Khrushchev Remembers: The Last Testament*, pp. 110-11.
28 See the proposal of F. Burlatsky, 'Politika i nauka', *Pravda*, 10 Jan 1965, and for its rebuttal the article of E. V. Tadevosyan, 'Diskussiya o politicheskoy nauke', in *Voprosy filosofii*, no. 10 (1965) pp. 164-6. For interesting accounts of the debates which have taken place among Soviet scholars concerning the study of

political science, see the articles by David E. Powell and Paul Shoup, 'The Emergence of Political Science in Communist Countries', in the *American Political Science Review*, vol. LXIV, no. 2 (June 1970) pp. 572-88; and Rolf H. W. Theen, 'Political Science in the USSR: "To be or not to be" ', *World Politics*, vol. XXIII, no. 4 (July 1971) pp. 684-703.

29 See A. A. Fedoseev, *Politika kak ob'ekt sotsiologicheskogo issledovaniya: kritika metodologicheskikh osnov sovremennoy burzhuaznoy politologii* (Leningrad, 1974) esp. pp. 121-2. Fedoseev (p. 122) concludes his work by suggesting various ways of expanding and institutionalising the critical study of 'bourgeois political science' in the Soviet Union and suggests that if his proposals are taken up they will 'not only be conducive to the perfecting of criticism of bourgeois political science, but will also exert a definite influence on the further development of Marxist political thought as a whole'.

30 *Khrushchev Remembers*, vol. 1 (Sphere paperback ed., London, 1971) p. 225. Kosgin's closest call came at the time of the Leningrad Affair, following the death of Zhdanov in August 1948. A number of leading officials were executed at this time, among them a secretary of the Central Committee, A. A. Kuznetsov. Khrushchev recalls: Men who had been arrested and condemned in Leningrad made ridiculous accusations against [Kosygin] in their testimonies. They wrote all kinds of rot about him. Kosygin was on shaky ground from beginning because he was related by marriage to Kuznetsov. Even though he'd been very close to Stalin, Kosygin was suddenly released from all his posts and assigned to work in some ministry. The accusations against him cast such a dark shadow over him that I simply can't explain how he was saved from being eliminated along with the others. Kosygin, as they say, must have drawn a lucky lottery ticket, and this cup passed from him.

Michael Kaser in his article, 'Le débat sur la loi de valeur en URSS' *Annuaire de l' URSS* (Paris, 1966) pp. 555-69, relates the demotion of Kosygin to the dismissal (and eventual execution) of Voznesensky a few months later.

31 Confirmation that, given their premises, the Soviet leaders were right to be concerned about developments in Czechoslovakia, even from the point of view of their influence within the Soviet Union itself, comes from Zhores Medvedev: 'Prior to August 1968 the abolition of censorship in Czechoslovakia and the general democratisation of society under Dubček had served as an attractive model for many intellectuals in the USSR, and had stimulated many speeches in favour of reform.' After the invasion 'all those reforms took on the appearance of a Utopian dream, a thing of the distant future, so that many liberal-minded people in the Soviet Union switched to a cautious wait-and-see position'. *10 Years After Ivan Denisovich*, p. 108.

32 *Khrushchev Remembers*, vol. 1, pp. 243-4.

33 For a detailed analysis of the conflicts during this period, see Carl A. Linden, *Khrushchev and the Soviet Leadership 1957-1964* (Baltimore, 1966).

34 *Khrushchev Remembers: The Last Testament* vol. 2, p. 137.

35 See, e.g., *Economicheskaya gazeta*, 11 Nov 1964, pp. 2-3.

36 Moralev, *Respublikanskie, kraevye, oblastnye, okruzhnye, gorodskie i rayonnye organizatsii partii*, p. 7.

37 See *Khrushchev Remembers*, vol. 1, pp. 449-63; vol. 2, pp. 511, 450-2, and 132-9.

38 Ibid., vol. 2, pp. 17-18.

39 I have discussed this and other aspects of the power of the British Prime Minister in my article, 'Prime Ministerial Power', *Public Law* part I (Spring 1968) pp. 28-51, esp. 38-41; part II (Summer 1968) pp. 96-118. For a different view, see John P. Mackintosh, *The Government and Politics of Britain* (London, 1970) esp. Chapter 8, 'Political Leadership – Can the Prime Minister be Sacked?'; Jerome M. Gilison, *British and Soviet Politics: Legitimacy and Convergence* (Baltimore, 1972) esp. Chapter V, 'Legitimacy, Leadership and Policy-Making'.

40 See, e.g., *Pravda*, 16 May 1973; 18 Apr 1975.

41 See *Pravda*, 17-22 Mar 1975.

42 See, e.g., *Pravda*, 28 Apr 1973; 14 July 1973.

43 The most salient points of this speech by Brezhnev have been summarised and discussed by Alec Nove in Chapter 1 above.

44 'Agrarnaya politika partii', *Pravda*, 24 Mar 1975, p. 1.

45 Jerry F. Hough, 'The Soviet System: Petrification or Pluralism', in *Problems of Communism* (Mar-Apr 1972) pp. 25-45, esp. p. 43.

46 The Russian word for 'science' and 'scholarship' is the same and it is likely that Medvedev had in mind such areas of scholarship as history rather than the natural sciences.

47 Zhores A. Medvedev, *10 Years After Ivan Denisovich*, pp. 57-8.

48 *Khrushchev Remembers: The Last Testament*, vol. 2, p. 540.

49 Ibid., p. 230.

50 Ibid., pp. 345-6.

51 Ibid., pp. 535-6, 540-1.

52 Ibid., p. 541.

53 Ibid., p. 33.

54 Ibid., p. 535.

55 Ibid., p. 540.

56 Ibid., p. 535.

57 Cf. Chapter 3 above (Table 3.2, p. 65).

58 M. I. Piskotin, 'Funktsii sotsialisticheskogo gosudarstva i apparat upravleniya', in *Sovetskoe gosudarstvo i pravo*, no. 10 (1973) pp. 3-11, esp. p. 10.

59 Ibid.

60 See, for example, Kadeykin (ed.), *Voprosy vnutripartiynoy zhizni i rukovodyashchey deyatel'nosti KPSS na sovremennom etape*, esp. p. 184.

61 'Partiynyy komitet ministerstva', *Pravda*, 28 Nov 1974, p. 1.

62 Ibid.
63 Taubman, *Governing Soviet Cities*, p. 17.
64 Ibid. See also pp. 61 and 95.
65 Roy Medvedev, *Kniga o sotsialisticheskoy demokratii*, p. 58.
66 Ibid., pp. 58-9.
67 Ibid., p. 60.
68 Ibid., p. 63.
69 Ibid., p. 62.
70 Medvedev draws attention to the closeness between the ideas prevalent among the third ('party-democratic') grouping within the CPSU and 'certain tendencies in the world communist movement', having in view 'in the first instance the position of such Communist parties as, for example, the Italian, Spanish, Australian and some others'. Ibid., p. 66.
71 A. Solzhenitsyn, *Bodalsya telenok s dubom: ocherki literaturnoy zhizni* (Paris, 1975).
72 Ibid., p. 112.
73 Ibid.
74 Ibid.
75 Ibid., p. 127.
76 Gvishiani is the author of an important book, *Organizatsiya i upravlenie*, 2nd ed. (Moscow, 1972), which exemplifies the technocratic tendency in that it subjects western writing on the theory of organisation and management to detailed analysis and finds much of value as well as much to criticise. The book exists in English translation as *Organisation and Management: A Sociological Analysis of Western Theories* (Moscow, 1972).
77 The term 'partocracy' is a coinage of Abdurakhman Avtorkhanov. See his *The Communist Party Apparatus* (Chicago, 1966).
78 It is perhaps worth stressing that technocratic reformists are by no means necessarily liberal reformists by intent. And while it is possible to make an analytical distinction between the neo-Stalinist and the technocratic *tendencies* within the party, one encounters in the Soviet Union *individuals* who come close to embodying both these positions. There exist party members in their thirties who are at one and the same time attracted to western 'management science' and to the 'discipline' which they associate with the Stalin era. Not having been touched personally by the terror (they were still children when Stalin died), they are prepared already to take the long view of history and to see Stalin as a heroic figure, in the mould of Peter the Great, who propelled a recalcitrant Russian people (by whatever means necessary) a century forward.
79 See, for example, the report, 'V tsentral'nom komitete KPSS: Ob organizatorskoy i politicheskoy rabote Tbilisskogo gorkoma Kompartii Gruzii po vypolneniyu resheniy XXIV s'ezda KPSS', *Pravda*, 6 Mar 1972, pp. 1-2. Those involved in the corruption included many prominent Georgian party and state officials and party intellectuals. Some of the more highly-placed of those who had participated in corrupt practices lost their jobs, but in a significant

number of cases they had enough friends in the relevant party control committees to protect them from expulsion from the party. As a result, Soviet-style 'benefit of clergy' operated, and no criminal charges could be brought. Party members are protected from prosecution unless the Committee of Party Control delivers them into the hands of the state prosecuting authorities by removing the protection provided by the malfeasants' party card.

80 See, e.g., Rakowska-Harmstone, 'The Dialectics of Nationalism in the USSR', esp. p. 13.

81 On this, see, e.g., Vladimir V. Kusin, *The Intellectual Origins of the Prague Spring* (Cambridge, 1971); Vladimir V. Kusin, *Political Grouping in the Czechoslovak Reform Movement* (London, 1972); Galia Golan, *The Czechoslovak Reform Movement* (Cambridge, 1971); Alex Pravda, 'Some Aspects of the Czechoslovak Economic Reform and the Working Class in 1968', in *Soviet Studies*, vol. XXV, no. 1 (July 1973) pp. 102-24; A. H. Brown, 'Political Change in Czechoslovakia', in Leonard Schapiro (ed.), *Political Opposition in One-Party States* (London, 1972) pp. 110-37.

82 On the position of the intelligentsia and the workers in Poland in 1968 and 1970, see the interesting essay by Włodzimierz Brus, 'Contradictions and ways to resolve them', in his *The Economics and Politics of Socialism* (London, 1973) pp. 103-14. See also David Lane and George Kolankiewicz (eds), *Social Groups in Polish Society* (London, 1973); *Canadian Slavonic Papers*, vol. XV, nos 1-2 (1973) (special issue devoted to Poland).

83 Brus, *The Economics and Politics of Socialism*, p. 111.

84 See Chapter 4 above, p. 83.

85 See, most notably, Leonard Schapiro, *The Communist Party of the Soviet Union*, 2nd ed. (London, 1970); Merle Fainsod, *How Russia is Ruled*, 2nd ed. (Cambridge, Mass., 1963); Abdurakhman Avtorkhanov, *The Communist Party Apparatus.*

86 For a recent interesting Soviet account of cadres policy generally and the *nomenklatura* in particular, see E. Z. Razumov, 'Problemy kadrovoy politiki partii', in Kadeykin (ed.), *Voprosy vnutri-partiynoy zhizni i rukovodyashchey deyatel'nosti KPSS na sov-remennom etape*, pp. 180-214, esp. 196-202.

87 Ibid., p. 197.

88 Ibid.

89 Andrei D. Sakharov, *Sakharov Speaks* (London, 1974) pp. 169-70.

90 Cf. Chapter 1, p. 10

91 I have discussed the case for, and some of the problems involved in, studying Soviet political culture in my *Soviet Politics and Political Science* (London, 1974) Chapter 4, pp. 89-104, and have drawn upon some passages in that earlier discussion in the final section of the present chapter.

92 Nadezhda Mandelstam, *Hope Abandoned* (London, 1974).

93 Ibid., pp. 269, 271. Mandelstam notes, however, that Stalin's famous toast to the Russian people of May 1945 in which he praised their 'patience' was not well received by the particular

group of manual workers with whom she came in contact. They did not show patience in their everyday social lives. Their 'patience' was more of a fatalistic attitude towards the political process, a belief that Soviet policy, like the winds and the waves, was not subject to the control of ordinary mortals. This fatalism became less marked after Stalin's death than it was in the thirties and forties, for as Khrushchev noted: 'Once Stalin was dead, people's mouths were unlocked . . . it wasn't a matter of the demand for food increasing so much as it was the increase in freedom to speak about the demand.' *Khrushchev Remembers: The Last Testament*, pp. 118-19.

In the post-Stalin period one can begin to speak meaningfully about 'public opinion' in the Soviet Union, even though the measure of repoliticisation remains limited.

94 Nadezhda Mandelstam, *Hope Against Hope* (London, 1971) p. 96.
95 There are still, however, substantial variations in the degree of material comfort or hardship from one region and locality to another, and the availability of goods in rural communities is vastly different from that in the major cities.

Calendar of Political Events: October 1964 – April 1975

1964

14 October. Plenary session of the Central Committee of the CPSU. N. S. Khrushchev removed from the first secretaryship of the Central Committee and replaced by L. I. Brezhnev.

15 October. A. N. Kosygin appointed chairman of the Council of Ministers in succession to Khrushchev.

6 November. Extension of social security benefits to collective farmers authorised by the Council of Ministers.

16 November. Plenary session of the Central Committee. The plenum adopted a resolution on the unification of industrial and agricultural regional party and Soviet organs. F. R. Kozlov was released from membership of the praesidium of the Central Committee in view of his severe illness (of which he died in 1965). P. E. Shelest and A. N. Shelepin became members of the praesidium and P. N. Demichev a candidate member. V. I. Polyakov was removed from his post as a secretary of the Central Committee.

1965

24-6 March. Plenary session of the Central Committee. Agricultural reform outlined by Brezhnev in his report 'On urgent measures for the further development of agriculture in the USSR'. Report by M. A. Suslov 'On the results of the consultative meeting of representatives of the Communist and Workers' Parties 1-5 March 1965'. K. T. Mazurov was transferred from candidate to full membership of the praesidium. D. F. Ustinov became a candidate member of the praesidium and a secretary of the Central Committee. L. F. Il'ichev was removed from the secretariat of the Central Committee.

8 and 12 September. Arrest of writers Sinyavsky and Daniel in Moscow.

27-9 September. Plenary session of the Central Committee. Economic reform outlined by Kosygin in his report 'On the improvement of industrial management, the perfecting of planning and the strengthening of economic stimuli of industrial production'. Kosygin announced the forthcoming abolition of the Supreme Economic Council of the USSR and of the *sovnarkhozy* (regional economic councils) and the creation of new and revived ministries. F. D. Kulakov was elected a secretary of the Central Committee and V. N. Titov was removed from the secretariat.

6 December. Plenary session of the Central Committee. Following a report on the work of the Committee of Party-State Control by Brezhnev, the replacement of this committee by a Committee of People's Control was agreed. The draft state economic plan and state budget for 1966 were approved. V. V. Shcherbitsky became a candidate member of the Politburo and I. V. Kapitonov a secretary of the Central Committee.

9 December. N. I. Podgorny lost his position as a secretary of the Central Committee and succeeded A. I. Mikoyan as chairman of the praesidium of the Supreme Soviet of the USSR.

1966

22 January. Council of Ministers of the USSR passed resolutions on the transfer of the first group of industrial enterprises to the new system of planning and economic incentives and on the introduction of new wholesale prices for the production of light industry enterprises.

10-14 February. Trial of Sinyavsky and Daniel (sentences: seven and five years, respectively).

19 February. Plenary session of the Central Committee. The draft directives for the XXIII Party Congress on the five-year economic plan were approved.

26 March. Plenary session of the Central Committee approved the Central Committee Report prepared for the XXIII Party Congress.

29 March-8 April. The XXIII Party Congress was held in Moscow. The Bureau of the Central Committee for the RSFSR was abolished. The party rules were amended to end the compulsorily high percentage turnover in membership of party organs. The titles of 'first secretary' and 'praesidium' were changed to 'general secretary' and 'Politburo'.

8 April. Announcement of composition of leading party organs following the first meeting of the Central Committee newly elected by the Congress. *Full members of the Politburo:* L. I. Brezhnev, G. I. Voronov, A. P. Kirilenko, A. N. Kosygin, K. T. Mazurov, A. Ya. Pel'she, N. V. Podgorny, D. S. Polyansky, M. A. Suslov, A. N. Shelepin and P. E. Shelest. (A. I. Mikoyan and N. M. Shvernik were not re-elected.) *Candidate members of the Politburo:* V. V. Grishin, P. N. Demichev, D. A. Kunaev, P. M. Masherov, V. P. Mzhavanadze, Sh. R. Rashidov, D. F. Ustinov and V. V. Shcherbitsky. *Secretariat:* L. I. Brezhnev (general secretary), Yu. V. Andropov, P. N. Demichev, I. V. Kapitonov, A. P. Kirilenko, F. D. Kulakov, B. N. Ponomarev, A. P. Rudakov, M. A. Suslov, D. F. Ustinov and A. N. Shelepin.

25 May. Plenary session of the Central Committee discussed problems of land irrigation and agriculture.

16 September. Introduction into the RSFSR Criminal Code of Articles 190-1 and 190-3 to help combat dissent.

12-13 December. Plenary session of the Central Committee discussed foreign policy and the struggle for unity of the international Communist movement, and approved the draft economic plan and state budget for 1967. M. S. Solomentsev was elected a secretary of the Central Committee.

1967

12 April. Marshal A. A. Grechko became minister of defence following the death of Marshal R. Ya. Malinovsky.

23 April. Special session of the Comecon Council attended by first party secretaries and chairmen of councils of ministers on socialist economic integration.

16 May. Solzhenitsyn's letter to the IV Congress of the Writers' Union denouncing censorship.

18 May. V. E. Semichastny removed from the chairmanship of the KGB and succeeded by Yu. V. Andropov.

20-1 June. Plenary session of the Central Committee discussed Soviet policy in the Middle East, and approved the 'Theses of the Central Committee of the CPSU for the 50th anniversary of the Great October Socialist Revolution'. Andropov became a candidate member of the Politburo and (following his appointment to head the KGB) ceased to be a secretary of the Central Committee.

June. N. G. Yegorychev replaced by V. V. Grishin as first secretary of the Moscow city party organisation.

July. A. N. Shelepin appointed to the chairmanship of the trade union movement in succession to V. V. Grishin.

5 September. Decree published rehabilitating the Crimean Tartars but without permission to return to the Crimea.

26 September. Plenary session of the Central Committee discussed ways of improving the standard of living, and approved the state economic plan and state budget for 1968. A. N. Shelepin removed from the secretariat 'in connection with his election' as chairman of the trade union movement.

7 November. Fiftieth anniversary of the Bolshevik Revolution.

1968

9-10 April. Plenary session of the Central Committee. Report by Brezhnev on foreign affairs and problems of achieving unity in the world Communist movement, with special reference to Czechoslovakia. K. F. Katushev elected a secretary of the Central Committee.

30 April. Appearance of issue no. 1 of the *Chronicle of Current Events.*

1 July. Signing of agreement in Moscow on the non-proliferation of nuclear weapons.

15 July. Formal letter of rebuke and warning sent to Czechoslovakia following discussions on the Czechoslovak question by the Soviet, GDR, Polish, Hungarian and Bulgarian leaders in Warsaw.

17 July. Plenary session of the Central Committee at which Brezhnev reported on the results of the Warsaw discussions on Czechoslovakia.

29 July-1 August. Meeting of the Soviet Politburo with the Czechoslovak praesidium at Čierna nad Tisou in Slovakia.

20-1 August. Invasion of Czechoslovakia.

23 August. Demonstration on Red Square against the invasion of Czechoslovakia.

9-11 October. Trial of Red Square demonstrators (sentences: from three years' exile to three years in camps).

30-1 October. Plenary session of the Central Committee at which agriculture and foreign affairs were discussed.

9 December. Plenary session of the Central Committee at which the draft state economic plan and the state budget for 1969 were approved.

1969

March. Clashes between Soviet border guards and Chinese forces on the Ussuri river.

6 June. Crimean Tartar demonstration in Moscow.

26 June. Plenary session of the Central Committee on the problems of achieving unity in the international Communist movement.

11 September. Meeting between Kosygin and Chou En-lai in Peking.

15 December. Plenary session of the Central Committee heard and approved a report by Brezhnev 'On the practical activity of the

Politburo in the spheres of foreign and domestic policy', and approved the state economic plan and state budget for 1970.

1970

11 February. Removal of A. Tvardovsky and colleagues from the editorial board of *Novy mir* announced.

2-3 July. Plenary session of the Central Committee devoted to discussion of agriculture.

13 July. Plenary session of the Central Committee. It was agreed to hold the XXIV Party Congress in March 1971.

12 August. Following talks in the Soviet Union between Brezhnev and the chancellor of the Federal Republic of Germany, W. Brandt, an Agreement was signed recognising the present frontiers of the two Germanies and of Poland.

18 September. V. S. Tolstikov removed from the first secretaryship of the Leningrad party organisation and made Soviet Ambassador to China.

4 November. Formation of the Human Rights Committee in Moscow.

7 December. Plenary session of the Central Committee approved the state economic plan and state budget for 1971.

14 December. Visit to Moscow of Polish Foreign Minister and Politburo member Jędrychowski for talks following riots in Poland which led on 19 December to the removal of Władysław Gomułka.

1971

5, 14 and 19 March. Series of measures announced by the Council of Ministers, the Central Committee of the Party, and the praesidium of the Supreme Soviet on the strengthening of the powers of the soviets and the codification of their existing rights.

22 March. Plenary session of the Central Committee approved the draft Central Committee report prepared for the XXIV Party Congress and the draft five-year plan for the period 1971-5.

30 March-9 April. The XXIV Party Congress was held in Moscow. Emphasis on foreign policy goal of seeking a new European security settlement based on the territorial division reached at the end of the Second World War. It was agreed that party congresses should in future be held once in five years. (Previously — in principle — they met every four years.) Party rules were changed to strengthen the supervisory role of primary party organisations.

9 April. Announcement of composition of leading party organs following the first meeting of the Central Committee newly elected by the Congress. *Politburo:* L. I. Brezhnev, G. I. Voronov, V. V. Grishin, A. P. Kirilenko, A. N. Kosygin, F. D. Kulakov, D. A. Kunaev, K. T. Mazurov, A. Ya. Pel'she, N. V. Podgorny, D. S. Polyansky, M. A. Suslov, A. N. Shelepin, P. E. Shelest and V. V. Shcherbitsky. *Candidate members:* Yu. V. Andropov, P. N. Demichev, P. M. Masherov, V. P. Mzhavanadze, Sh. R. Rashidov and D. F. Ustinov. *Secretariat:* L. I. Brezhnev (general secretary), P. N. Demichev, I. V. Kapitonov, K. F. Katushev, A. P. Kirilenko, F. D. Kulakov, B. N. Ponomarev, M. S. Solomentsev, M. A. Suslov and D. F. Ustinov.

27-9 July. Adoption of comprehensive programme for further economic integration with Comecon.

11 September. Death of N. S. Khrushchev (aged 77).

22-3 November. Plenary session of the Central Committee discussed foreign policy and international activity since the XXIV Congress. M. S. Solomentsev was elected to candidate membership of the Politburo and relinquished his position in the secretariat.

1972

11-15 January. Widespread arrests and flat-searches in the Ukraine and Moscow designed to suppress the *samizdat* journals, the *Ukrainian Herald* and the *Chronicle of Current Events*.

6 March. Publication in *Pravda* of severe censure of the party organisation of the Georgian capital of Tbilisi.

18-19 May. Riots in Kaunas following the self-immolation of Romas Kalanta in support of greater political and religious freedom for Lithuania.

19 May. Plenary session of the Central Committee approved a report by Brezhnev on the international situation. I. V. Kapitonov reported on the forthcoming exchange of party cards. B. N. Ponomarev became a candidate member of the Politburo.

May. P. E. Shelest replaced as first secretary of the Ukrainian party Central Committee by V. V. Shcherbitsky.

22-30 May. Visit of United States President Richard Nixon to the Soviet Union. Signing of Anti-Ballistic Missile Treaty, the Interim Agreement on Offensive Missiles, and the Agreement on the Establishment of the Joint US-USSR Commercial Commission.

29 September. V. P. Mzhavanadze replaced by E. A. Shevardnadze as first secretary of the Georgian party Central Committee.

18 October. Signing of Soviet-United States Trade Agreement in Washington.

18 December. Plenary session of the Central Committee approved the state economic plan and state budget for 1973. V. I. Dolgikh was elected a secretary of the Central Committee, and V. P. Mzhavanadze was removed from candidate membership of the Politburo following his forced retirement from the first secretaryship of the Georgian Party.

1973

2 February. D. S. Polyansky appointed minister of agriculture (in succession to V. V. Matskevich) while retaining his seat on the Politburo.

26-7 April. Plenary session of the Central Committee devoted to foreign affairs. P. E. Shelest and G. I. Voronov were removed from the Politburo and Yu. V. Andropov, A. A. Gromyko and A. A. Grechko became Politburo members. G. V. Romanov was elected to candidate membership of the Politburo.

18-22 May. Visit by Brezhnev to the Federal Republic of Germany for talks with Brandt. Relations between the USSR and the FRG reached a 'new, normal for peacetime' level, and a number of economic and cultural agreements were signed.

18-25 June. Visit by Brezhnev to the United States for talks with Nixon. Signed Agreement on the Prevention of Nuclear War and agreements to promote trade between the USSR and the United States.

11 July. Presentation in Moscow of International Lenin Peace Prize to Brezhnev.

10-11 December. Plenary session of the Central Committee approved Brezhnev's report on the activities of the Politburo in domestic and foreign policy and approved the state economic plan and state budget for 1974.

1974

11 and 17 February. Demonstrations in Moscow and Tallin by Germans demanding to emigrate to West Germany.

12-13 February. Arrest and deportation from the USSR of Solzhenitsyn.

18-21 June. Twenty-fifth anniversary Session of the Comecon Council: co-ordination of the 1976-80 plans as part of a fifteen-year programme.

3 July. Brezhnev and Nixon signed agreements on nuclear arms control at end of Nixon's visit to the Soviet Union.

24 July. Plenary session of the Central Committee addressed by Brezhnev.

18 October. Jackson-Kissinger letters claim agreement on the part of the Soviet leaders to ease emigration restrictions.

23-4 November. Talks between Brezhnev and President Ford in Vladivostok.

16 December. Plenary session of the Central Committee approved the state economic plan and state budget for 1975. P. N. Demichev was removed from the secretariat of the Central Committee following his appointment as minister of culture on 14 November in succession to Ekaterina Furtseva, who died on 25 October.

24 December. New regulation on internal passports under which such passports were to be extended to all Soviet citizens, i.e. including the peasantry.

1975

14 January. Soviet decision to abrogate the USSR-USA Trade Agreement of 1972.

22 February. Significant improvement in Anglo-Soviet relations announced in *Pravda* following talks in Moscow between a British delegation headed by Prime Minister Harold Wilson and a Soviet delegation led by Brezhnev.

16 April. Plenary session of the Central Committee. Report by Gromyko 'On the international situation and the foreign policy of the Soviet Union'. Date of the start of the XXV Party Congress fixed for 24 February 1976. A. N. Shelepin was removed from membership of the Politburo 'at his own request' (*Pravda*, 17 Apr 1975).

Note: Unless otherwise stated in the Calendar, any comments within quotation marks are from the *Ezhegodnik Bol'shoy Sovetskoy Entsiklopedii [Yearbook of the Great Soviet Encyclopaedia]* of the year following the event in question. The editors are grateful to Peter Reddaway for providing dates of events involving dissidents. For reasons of space the calendar is necessarily brief and selective, but an attempt has been made, *inter alia*, to record all plenary sessions of the Central Committee and all movement into and out of the Politburo and secretariat of the Central Committee from the fall of Khrushchev to the end of April 1975.

Index